Elmer Kelton Country

Elmer Kelton Country

The Short
Nonfiction of a
Texas Novelist

Texas Christian University Press
Fort Worth

Library of Congress Cataloging-in-Publication Data

Kelton, Elmer.
    Elmer Kelton country : the short nonfiction of a Texas novelist /
by Elmer Kelton.
      p. cm.
    ISBN 0-87565-118-6.—ISBN 0-87565-119-4 (pbk.)
    1. Kelton, Elmer—Homes and haunts—Texas, West. 2. Texas, West,
in literature. 3. Texas, West—Civilization. I. Title.
PS3563.A2932Z465 1993
814'.54—dc20
                                                  92-40639
                                                         CIP

Design by Barbara Whitehead

Acknowledgements

"The Big Dry" was originally published in Volume 4, Issue 3 (1973) of *Persimmon Hill*, the official publication of the National Cowboy Hall of Fame.

"Fiction Writers are Liars and Thieves" is reprinted with permission from *The Bounty of Texas*, Publications of the Texas Folklore Society, Number XLIX, University of North Texas Press, 1990.

"When the Well Runs Dry" is reprinted with permission from *Texas Monthly*, October 1985.

"The Time It Always Rained" is reprinted with permission from *Texas Monthly*, August 1987.

"Earth, Wind, Rain, Fire," is reprinted with permission from *Texas Monthly*, May 1988.

Most other articles were originally published in *Livestock Weekly*, San Angelo, Texas, and are reprinted with permission of Stanley Frank, publisher.

Contents

Foreword

"The ranching profession considers Kelton one among them," said John Merrill, director of the ranch management program at Texas Christian University. "This is his profession"—he waved a copy of the Livestock Weekly—*"and the literary work is his hobby."*

CLEARLY, Elmer Kelton has two distinct audiences. One is ranch people who know him, as Merrill does, for his work for the *San Angelo Standard-Times, Sheep and Goat Raiser Magazine,* and, most importantly, *Livestock Weekly,* from which he retired in 1990.

Other readers know Elmer Kelton as a novelist. Since his first book, *Hot Iron,* was published in 1955, he has written about thirty-five novels.

In 1971, he made the break from paperback novels with a story called *The Day the Cowboys Quit.* Since then, he has published seven major novels—*The Time It Never Rained, The Good Old Boys, The Wolf and the Buffalo, Stand Proud, The Man Who Rode Midnight, Honor at Daybreak,* and *Slaughter*—while continuing to write traditional westerns under his own name and under the pseudonyms of Lee McElroy and Tom Early.

He has won five Spur Awards from Western Writers of America for the best novel of the year, four Western Heritage (Wrangler) Awards from the National Cowboy Hall of Fame, and has been honored for lifetime achievement in literature by WWA, the Texas Institute of Letters, and the Western Literature Association. His novel about the Texas drouth of the '50s, *The Time It Never Rained,* has been called one of the dozen best American novels of the twentieth century.

As a novelist, Kelton sets his characters in the land he knows best—primarily West Texas—and writes of a world with which he is thoroughly familiar. By the accident of his birth, he was gifted with a deep sense of the feelings and knowledge of West Texas; by the achievement of a writing career of more than forty years and thirty-plus novels, he developed his art from the powder burner to the true regional novel.

John Merrill is quick to point out that many major western writers were westerners only by adoption and some lived in the West only for short periods of time. The classic example, of course, is Zane Grey, a dentist from Illinois who visited the West only periodically and tended to hide in hotels when there. "By living among them and working with them, Elmer Kelton has learned and recorded far beyond the others. In terms of birth, upbringing, everyday involvement, he is the real thing and has been all his life," Merrill says.

To those who know Kelton as a novelist, it is disconcerting to think of his fiction as a hobby. But there is that whole other world out there where his novels are little known and he is admired and respected as an authority on livestock and range conditions. This nonfiction collection was assembled, with Kelton's enthusiastic cooperation, to show the connections between his separate careers.

Several audiences are anticipated. Those who know Kelton as a livestock journalist will find here articles about people they know or knew, a land they understand, a way of life and a system of values they share with Kelton.

Those who know him as a fiction writer will find in these selections not only the seeds of the novels but also a wider picture of the author as a man. The causes that engage his interest are clearly delineated—environmental problems, agricultural developments, the history of West Texas and the ranching lands, the reminiscences of old-timers, the sport of rodeo, the craft of writing.

But the best enjoyment of this collection is reserved for those who know and appreciate Kelton as both journalist and novelist. The article "Where Have All the Cowboys Gone?" mentions an old-time cow puncher, footloose, homeless and often hungry, who died of a heart attack, apparently while opening a gate to cross a pasture. Readers will recognize a figure and an incident from *The Good Old Boys*. Themes from *The Time It Never Rained* are delineated and repeated in "When the Well Runs Dry" and even "The Time It Always Rained." The account of Gregorio Cortez, first published in *Livestock Weekly*, provided the story line for *Manhunters*, and the incident of the buffalo soldiers lost in the desert of West Texas became central to *The Wolf and the Buffalo*.

In an odd way, readers should be grateful that Kelton's fiction was not successful enough to allow him to retire early because his nonfiction added a depth and texture to his novels that sets them dramatically apart from those of many western writers.

And that, finally, is the importance of this collection. It goes beyond showing Kelton as the outstanding livestock journalist to demonstrating how integral his nonfiction work is to the body of his fiction. Readers and students of western literature must be forever grateful.

Judy Alter
Fort Worth, Texas

Introduction

MY forty-two-year career in agricultural and livestock journalism was a happy accident. My strongest ambition from the time I was eight or nine years old had been to become a fiction writer . . . a rich and famous one, of course. I grew up on the McElroy Ranch near Crane, where my father, Buck Kelton, was a working cowboy, then foreman and eventually general manager. Despite the long cowboy tradition in my family, going back to my great-grandfather, I was never very good as a cowhand or a horseman. It became clear very early that I would have to find an occupation more compatible with whatever abilities I did have.

My mother, Bea Kelton, had been a teacher before she married, and she taught me to read when I was five. At seven I was given a test and placed in the third grade, which made me the runt of my classes and kept me sadly outmatched at any kind of sports. I retreated into books as a refuge from my shortcomings both as a cowboy and as an athlete. I devoured any book or magazine that came to hand, regardless of its subject matter. But always I kept coming back to those writings that touched upon my own family heritage . . . Texas, the West, cowboys and cattle.

When I was a senior in high school my father cornered me on the front porch one day and declared that it was time I decide what I was to do for a living. It was clear enough that I lacked the proficiency to earn my wages as a cowboy. I had known for a long time what I wanted to do, but I had never mentioned it to him. I did not think he would understand. Now I had to give him an answer. I said I wanted to go to the University of Texas, study journalism and become a writer.

To my father, *work* was something you did ahorseback or with a pick and shovel, not at a desk. I had been right all along. He did *not* understand. He gave me a look that would kill Johnson grass and said, "That's the way with you kids nowadays; you all want to make a living without having to work for it."

He relented, however, and I entered the university in the fall of 1942 at age sixteen. My choice of journalism as an entree to professional writing grew out of my taking a high-school journalism course under Paul Patterson, who became something of a mentor and has remained one of my best friends. Today he is widely known as a Texas folklorist.

After a stint as an infantryman in Europe, I came back to finish at the university and graduated at midterm in January 1948. Midterm is an awkward time, but it proved lucky for me. The *San Angelo Standard-Times* needed someone to write farm and ranch news. I was evidently the only member of the small journalism graduating class who had a country background, so I got the job.

Late in my senior year I had finally sold a fictional short story to a western pulp magazine, *Ranch Romances*, after having tried to break into the market since my return from World War II service. It appeared that I was on my way at last to fame and fortune, and that my stay in newspaper work would be brief.

I had grown up reading the *Fort Worth Star-Telegram* and knew the work of its venerable Frank Reeves, dean of the Texas livestock journalists. Even so, I was only dimly aware that a career existed in agricultural journalism. I gave no thought to it as a possibility for myself until the unanticipated call to San Angelo. For a long time I continued to think of the newspaper job as temporary. I went on writing pulp-magazine fiction nights and weekends and in the mid 1950s moved into full-length novels.

Reality eventually set in. I began to accept the brutal fact that fiction writing's economic rewards are limited. Only a relative handful of fiction writers make a good living at it; most support themselves with some other occupation and write as a sideline.

Fortunately for me I quickly came to enjoy my career as an ag journalist. I had always regretted my shortcomings as a cowboy and wished I could have fallen a little closer to the tree. This career kept me in constant contact with ranchers and farmers. If I could not do it myself, at least I could write about others doing it. I was like a would-be ball player who cannot throw, catch or hit but finds himself a niche as a sports writer.

For fifteen years on the *Standard-Times* I traveled about West Texas, attending stock shows and field days, writing feature articles about ranchmen, cowboys, old-timers, range and livestock researchers and the like. In 1963 I became editor of *Sheep and Goat Raiser Magazine,* owned by the Texas Sheep and Goat Raisers Association. Though I enjoyed the ranch people I was working for and with, I found myself out of my natural element in one important respect. Most of my time for nearly five years was spent trying to sell enough advertising to make the payroll and pay the printing bill. It was a task that went to bed with me at night and sometimes awakened me in a cold sweat. Writing took a distant back seat to the business end of the operation. In 1968 I joined *West Texas Livestock Weekly* and returned to what fitted me best, interviewing and writing.

A majority of the articles in this collection are from *Livestock Weekly.* The *West Texas* part of the name was eventually dropped because the circulation had spread far beyond West Texas. We had at least a token readership in almost every state in the union and several foreign countries, though the majority of it was in Texas and the adjoining states. Stanley Frank had founded the paper in 1948 and had built it up through hard work, determination and a keen sense of what his livestock-producing readers wanted. He had worked on the *Standard-Times* before I did, and had also written for livestock publications that catered to producers of registered cattle. He came to deplore the hype that so often attended that kind of trade and was determined to have none of it in his newspaper. He made his newspaper into what has been described as a cowboy's *Wall Street Journal,* centering it around solid market news that readers could depend upon, augmented by feature articles and Ace Reid "Cowpokes" cartoons to provide entertainment value. He also wrote a highly readable weekly opinion column which he called "Unregistered Bull in a Hotel Lobby."

Working for *Livestock Weekly* let me do the kinds of things I had enjoyed most on the daily newspaper, though I traveled in a far wider circle, stretching on occasion into New Mexico, Oklahoma, Kansas and Colorado. Much of my writing was on economic and political issues affecting the livestock industry, but I was also able to meet and write about a lot of interesting people. A large part of this collection falls into that vein, for while market news and economic analyses are vital, they date quickly. Stories of personal experiences are timeless.

Unfortunately, a great many of the people I wrote about are no longer living. I feel blessed to have been able to know them and document their stories. Sometimes things they told me found their way into my fiction, which I continued to write at night and on weekends. The people I wrote about in my daily newspaper work could have been the sons and daughters, grandsons and granddaughters of characters in my historical fiction. Some actually became characters, at least in part, in my more contemporary works such as *The Time It Never Rained* and *The Man Who Rode Midnight*.

Circumstances altered my ambitious plan to stay in newspaper work only briefly, then become a fulltime fiction writer. Forty-two years later I retired, in 1990. But I have always felt that the two parallel careers complemented each other in many ways. My fiction taught me how to write straight news stories and feature articles with more life and vitality. By the same token, the discipline of newspaper writing taught me how to shape my fiction concisely and to make a point. It also taught me that the writer cannot wait around for the muse to strike him. You write every day whether you feel like it or not, and you meet your deadlines. Inspiration is nice, when you can find it, but perspiration is what gets the job done.

In a sense, I always felt that I wore two hats: one as an ag journalist, the other as a fiction writer. Many readers who followed me in one field were unaware of my work in the other. A couple of times when I was gathering newspaper stories, I was asked if I knew that somebody with the same name was writing westerns.

My reply was *yes*, I knew, and I hoped the guy was getting rich. Or at least famous.

Elmer Kelton
San Angelo, Texas

THIS BOOK is dedicated to my many colleagues in the livestock and agricultural journalism field, who never get considered for the Pulitzer, and seldom even a raise; to the dedicated county agents and vocational agriculture teachers with whom I have shivered many a freezing day at junior livestock shows and sales; to the unsung researchers whose patience and perseverence have brought so many good things to the people who live on and from the land; and, finally, to the thousands of ranchers, farmers, cowboys and sheepherders whose trails have crossed mine over the years.

Land and Water

Tom Farr Says Killing Prairie Dog
Gave Mesquite Freedom to Spread

Livestock Weekly, April 15, 1971

THAT MESQUITE brush has spread tremendously in Texas during recent generations is beyond dispute. My father said when he was a boy on ranches north of Midland, it was sometimes a challenge to find firewood. Untold millions have been spent in that region in recent years in a vain effort to control mesquite. The invasion has been blamed on many factors: overgrazing, the suppression of fire and the introduction of livestock from brushy regions into those which previously did not have it. More than a few oldtimers have cited another possible factor: the elimination of the prairie dog. Tom Farr was one who believed in this theory.

≈

SEYMOUR, TEXAS   Tom Farr says when he moved to his present ranch more than fifty years ago, he used to take his wagon out of its way to avoid running over a mesquite sapling, hoping it would grow up big enough to cut for a fence post.

He believes one of the industry's big mistakes of forty or fifty years ago was eradication of the prairie dog, which not only carried off most of the beans from the scattered few mesquite trees but also nibbled off the seedlings. When the prairie dog was killed out, the mesquite spread.

3

Farr has no idea how much money he has spent in recent years fighting back against mesquite encroachment.

That, of course, is just one of the lesser changes he has seen in his time. Farr will be eighty June 6. He was born and brought up in Baylor County, not far from the ranch where he lives. For about thirty years, beginning in the mid-1930s, he was a large-scale buyer of cattle in a wide area of Texas, Oklahoma, and sometimes in other states. In the last five or six years he has largely curtailed his buying activity, though he still buys calves to run on his own country.

His father, J. B. "Buck" Farr, settled on a ranch west of Seymour in 1888, raising horses and mules, cattle and wheat, hauling his wheat all the way to Henrietta for milling, a four- to-five day round trip by wagon. The Farrs had a regular frame house, the lumber probably hauled from Henrietta, but many of the neighbors lived in half dugouts.

Tom Farr grew up working cattle and following a team of mules. His father always said he left Waco to get away from cotton, and he planted mostly wheat. The elder Farr was a staunch Hereford cattle man. Farr recalls, "My father said if he had to go down in the cattle business, he had rather go down holding a good one by the tail than a sorry one."

When Tom Farr became old enough to go on his own, he followed his father's general example except that he had not been burned out on cotton, so he raised some of that too. To this day he still plants a fifteen-acre cotton allotment to stay legal with the government. He really doesn't want it, but he plants to keep the allotment tied to the land.

"I'm only glad that the government never did take over the cattle business the way it did cotton and grain," he says.

He started trading in cattle at fifteen, though he can't specifically remember his first deal. For many years he ran cows and calves, but he switched over to a calf and yearling operation after the drouth of 1933 forced him to liquidate most of his cows. Since then he has kept only a small cow herd "just for expenses."

Starting out buying calves and yearlings for his own use, he would sell if someone offered him an interesting profit, then buy some more. Before long he was buying and trading on a considerable scale, not only in Texas and Oklahoma but sometimes as far north as the Dakotas. During the World War II years when Safeway was feeding cattle, he was a Texas and Oklahoma order buyer for that firm, buying feeder calves, yearlings and bulls to ship—sometimes by the trainload—to the chain's feedlots at Bakersfield, California.

He doesn't know how many cattle he bought but says, "There'd be a train of them reaching across the United States if they were all put together."

His worst experience financially was the big drop in cattle prices in 1952. "Somebody asked my son how much money I had lost. He said I didn't lose any money—I just lost 500 head of steers." That was about what it amounted to when the final tally was run up.

One of the biggest changes he has seen in the last few years has been the margin between fat and feeder or stocker cattle.

"We used to buy calves at the market price, winter them, put the gain on them and sell them for $3 to $5 cwt. more than we paid for them. The margin is still there, only they've turned it the other way. Now we're buying some light calves as high as fifty cents and hoping that after we keep them a year we may get thirty-five cents."

He farms about 1,200 acres, of which about 800 goes into wheat, the rest largely oats and maize, all dryland. He usually harvests 600 to 800 acres of wheat and oats, grazing out the rest. This program is flexible, however; if the yields do not look promising, he may graze out more of it.

He lets his cattle graze off most of the milo land. "We turn them in when the maize is in the dough and just let them hog it out," he says. "It puts a lot of pounds on the cattle and saves a lot of labor. Anyway, sometimes you can buy milo cheaper than you can raise it."

Farr partners a lot with his son Gerald, of Fort Sumner, New Mexico. In the last few years the son has done most of the buying, getting steer calves principally out of Mexico. Farr likes the Mexican calves; the weight is right and sickness problems are slight. The Farr cattle usually move off grain fields in May and go to grass west of Vaughn, New Mexico. In recent years, most have gone off grass in the fall and into commercial feedlots.

Farr usually supplements his grain-field calves with cake, a little ground maize, oats or barley. "Baled or shelled oats are the best feed you can give a calf on a grain field," he declares.

During most of Farr's trading days, a majority of the calves he bought were either straight Hereford or straight Angus. He has watched the growth of crossbreeding with much interest. He believes it will prove a long-range benefit to the industry. "Most ranchers know enough not to run their cattle down on crossbreeding," he says. "They'll keep a good beef type."

He particularly likes a black bald-face calf. His preference is to mate a Hereford bull to an Angus cow; he believes the Angus cow gives more milk and the Hereford bull is more active, producing a little better percentage calf crop.

He says he always enjoyed trading cattle. "It is a kind of disease. If you ever catch it, there's no cure for it." But he finds a majority of his old trading friends are gone, and traveling isn't as easy or as much fun as it used to be.

The Big Dry

Persimmon Hill, 1974 (Volume IV, Number 3)

THE TWO most traumatic periods of my life have been World War II and the seven-year drouth of the 1950s—in which order, I am not sure. I was an agricultural reporter for the *San Angelo Standard-Times* during the 1950s, and the drouth became my steady, running story for that entire period. I watched what was happening to my friends as well as to ranching members of my own family. Out of that eventually came the novel whose title will probably be placed on my tombstone, *The Time It Never Rained*. Most of the things which happened to characters in that book happened to real-life people I knew or knew about. This article, written on request for the National Cowboy Hall of Fame's magazine, is a factual account of that terrible period.

≈

IN THE fall of 1953 a Kansas farmer buying lambs in West Texas told me it had been a bad year for him. "We had three drouths this summer," he said.

I told him not to feel too put-upon, for West Texas had already had three summers in one drouth. I didn't know the "big dry" still had four hard years to go.

The great drouth which parched the Southwest during the 1950s was not the same for everybody. Some people in the semi-desert range country of the Trans-Pecos were feeling it by the late 1940s, as was some of northern Mexico. For the rest of West Texas and eastern New Mexico it began in 1950 or 1951. Neighboring states such as Oklahoma, Kansas and even Arkansas and Missouri felt it later, but the eventual effect was the same for everyone it touched: extreme financial hardship and sometimes the loss of farms and ranches that had weathered many lesser drouths.

7

I was a farm and ranch reporter for the San Angelo, Texas, *Standard-Times* during those unhappy years. I had grown up on the McElroy Ranch in Crane and Upton counties, where my father, Buck Kelton, spent thirty-six years—first as a cowboy, than as foreman and finally as general manager. Dad knew he was in a drouth before 1950 ever rolled around. Average rainfall on the McElroy, affectionately known to cowboys as the Jigger Y, was only a shade over twelve inches a year at best, and the late '40s hadn't even come up to the average. It was the kind of country a real estate agent once described to me this way: "Sorry as hell, but pretty good."

At first people weren't particulary alarmed. If a ranchman started to complain, some old-timer would tell him to quit belly- aching; this was nothing compared to 1933, or even worse, to 1918. Now those, they said, were *drouths*.

Gradually, though, as the "dry spell" stretched into its third and then its fourth and fifth years, the "this-ain't-nothin'" people quit talking. I often remember the late Arch Benge, a wiry, wizened, rawhide-tough old rancher who had been a sheriff in the rough oil-boom and prohibition days. He was as inclined as any of them to talk about the mean drouths he had seen in other times. But one day he told me sternly, "Anybody who says he's seen a worse one than this is either a bald-faced liar or a damn sight older than me." And hardly anyone was older than Arch.

Drouth in the Southwest does not necessarily mean a total absence of rain; it is instead a long period when rains are too light and too scattered to sustain a consistent growth of grass or crops. The result is a gradual deterioration rather than a sudden and dramatic calamity.

False hopes led stockmen into deep trouble. The onset of the drouth found most ranchers well-stocked. In the beginning it was easy to cull out some old cows or some broken-mouthed ewes in hopes this would lighten the load enough until rain came. But it was much harder for a stockman to sell off his better and younger stock. In most cases he had spent years breeding up a type of cow he liked, or a ewe that would produce a good lamb and still shear eight or nine pounds of grease wool that would grade "fine." As dry months turned into dry years, most people tended to hold back too long on culling. In the hard dry winter they felt in their bones that they would soon go into a wet spring. When dry spring turned into dry summer, they felt that surely they were due for a turn-around at the autumnal equinox.

The result was that the average ranch stayed overstocked for the amount of grass it had at any given time, no matter how deeply the ranchman thought he had already cut.

Supplemental feeding has become a way of life for the average southwestern ranchman during the last two generations. Even in a wet year most will feed some protein supplement in the form of cubes or cottonseed cake to help keep up the animals' strength through the worst of the winter months, typically January into early March.

But as the drouth bit deeper and deeper, this feeding period started earlier and ended later. It became the rule rather than the exception for West Texas ranchers to feed into May and to start again by September or at least October. I remember some ranches that never completely quit for two to three years straight.

The economic consequences were disastrous. Many ranchers built up feed bills of twenty to twenty-five dollars per head on ewes they couldn't have sold for ten dollars. Always the hope of a rain just around the corner kept them holding on, and borrowing to buy more feed. Eventually many reached the point that they couldn't afford to sell out, and a bank couldn't afford to close them out. Rancher and banker were forced to "hang and rattle" together.

Fortunately most country banks were inclined to stay with the farmers and ranchmen. They were initially caught up in the same false hopes, and like the stockmen eventually found themselves in too deep to quit. In contrast to some previous drouths, foreclosures were the exception. Unlike the one of 1933, for example, which struck in the midst of a general economic depression, this drouth came when other parts of the economy were strong and when banks in general had a broad base of other income including oil to fall back upon.

Nevertheless, some good friends of mine went under. Hardest hit were those who leased their land rather than owned it. Many land-owners received oil lease payments or royalties, sometimes lavish, often modest, but this helped them hold their places together. Even

9

if they had no oil prospects, they could borrow against the land. But the leaseholder usually had little equity beyond his livestock. When that was borrowed up, unless the bank elected to stand behind him, he had no choice except to fold. Some went out voluntarily, even though their bankers were willing to stay, for they did not want to keep compounding a debt which might haunt them the rest of their lives.

Financial burdens were made worse by an exceedingly poor livestock market through the roughest years. As the new decade began, cattle and sheep prices had risen to their highest levels in history—levels they were not to reach again for twenty years—cow-calf pairs selling for $400, steer calves for forty cents a pound, lambs for thirty-five cents or better.

But the Korean War brought price controls, and some of Washington's bureaucratic brains decided beef was too high. A price rollback was ordered. To do such a thing to a large, powerful, highly organized group such as labor would be unthinkable, but bureaucrats have never minded knifing the rancher in the ribs. The result was an imposed price debacle just as the drouth was taking a firm hold. From forty cents one fall, calves dropped to slightly more than twenty the next and into the teens the third, at a time when ranchmen were desperately in need of money and least able to stand to the jolt. The price drop was not all caused by the rollback, of course, but that was the first and most brutal blow in that it was man-made and malicious. The politicians got the cheaper beef they wanted, but cattle weren't the only thing which went to the slaughterhouse.

At first the better cows and ewes found a market from stockmen in areas not yet touched by dry weather. But as drouth inexorably reached out in all directions from its Texas and Mexico starting place, these markets dried up. It was heart-breaking to see a set of fine young heifers go through an auction ring and find no bidders except the packers, especially to a man who had raised those heifers, and their mothers and great-grandmothers before them. Strong men would sometimes climb to the topmost row of an auction where they could sit alone, unseen, while they blinked away tears watching a cherished set of cattle or sheep go under the hammer.

Many attempts were made to circumvent the drouth by moving away from it. I remember a friend east of San Angelo who had a good stock farm. After the drouth had been on for two or three years, he sold out, took what equity he had left and bought a farm in Arkansas. The drouth followed him there and ruined him. The last I knew for certain he was working for wages on a ranch, and I heard later that he died broke, unable ever to get a new start.

Twice Dad tried unsuccessfully to save a good set of young replacement heifers for the McElroy Ranch. One time the area around Van Horn, out in far West Texas, received some rain and appeared likely to have a good season. Dad heard of a grass lease and took it, hauling out some of these heifers he wanted to keep for cows. But the rain was only a reprieve, not a pardon. Before long Van Horn was back in the same dry condition as everybody else.

Another time Dad sent some heifers up to the Flint Hills of Kansas, hoping it would rain on the McElroy before the grazing season was out. It didn't, and the heifers eventually had to be sold at a loss a long way from home. Needless to say, the drouth went to the Flint Hills with the cattle.

Stockmen tried an infinite variety of new things to try to beat the drouth. Many took outside jobs wherever they could find them, some in the oilfields, some in industrial plants, some for the very feed companies whose products were keeping them broke. Many ranch wives went back to college to get their certificates so they could help out by teaching school. A brother of mine installed a caged-hen operation, as did a number of other ranchers and farmers around the country. Bill Tullos, who had started ranching west of San Angelo as a young World War II veteran fresh out of service, saved his ranch by feeding out hogs, contracting garbage from an Air Force base and offal from a chicken processing plant.

It was a wide-open field for range conservationists. At their behest, ranchmen experimented on many new ideas. Some of these worked and some didn't. Ranchmen who formerly wouldn't have a plow on the place began disking, chiseling and pitting rangeland, trying to make it absorb the scanty rains which did manage to fall. They began

11

an earnest fight against brush, which was sapping moisture away from the struggling grass plants. Rootplowing, later a major weapon against brush encroachment, got its start as a desperation measure during the 1950s drouth.

Range reseeding also received its impetus during this period. Before the drouth it was widely regarded as a far-out and unnecessary idea; people thought nature provided plenty of seed, and the only thing needed was rain. A great many grass varieties tried during this period were a failure, but a few worked well, opening the way for great improvements in later years.

Wherever there was prickly pear, ranchmen learned to use it for feed. It was a lesson passed down from the old-time Mexican ox-cart freighters of a century and more ago, who used to burn the thorns off over a campfire. In the 1950s, ranchmen in West Texas were using butane-powered burners in their fight against the drouth.

It was always amazing to a newcomer to see how cattle and sheep learned to listen for the roar of the pear-burner and to come running. Cows would wade eagerly into pear still so hot that it singed the hair from around their mouths.

Farmers were going through the same dismal experiences as the stockmen, of course. It would not be true to say that everybody's crops failed for the whole seven years. But usually the crop yields would be so poor that the farmer barely made living expenses, and many years he would not even get his seed back.

I have always wished the newspaper had not discarded the negatives of some pictures I made on a late-September afternoon on a cotton farm just north of San Angelo. The farmer had raised a crop of what he called "bumble-bee" cotton, the stalks stunted, most of them maturing only three or four bolls. In those days before mechanical pickers took over, transient crews of Mexican-Americans would work through the cotton country. This farmer had carried a crew out to his place, but they took one look and left, knowing they couldn't make beans trying to pick that poor crop.

On this particular afternoon the farmer had tied an old wooden ladder behind his pickup so that it would drag lengthwise at the end of a chain. His wife and children sat on the ladder. He drove the pickup up and down the rows as slowly as it would run, and his family reached out and picked those scattered bolls as they rode by.

Someone asked me awhile back what pictures come to my mind when I think back on the drouth. I think of the dark brown dusters that used to come rolling in out of the north and west, turning the afternoon sun into a glowing copper ball. I think of the old milk-bucket rack by the back door of our house on the McElroy, and of the buckets bumping and clattering across the yard as the wind lifted them off of the pegs and sent them sailing. I think of cattle and sheep standing in pasture corners by the gate where the feed truck or pickup normally came in; they had nothing else to do, because it was a waste of energy to roam around over bare pastures.

Most of all, I remember my many friends who met this long ordeal with courage and determination, and with a humor that never quite failed them even in the worst of times. In a way, that humor was the most remarkable thing of all. It has often been said that a good sense of humor helped the pioneers survive, and I believe it, because they passed it on to their sons and grandsons, daughters and granddaughters. Every time I thought I had heard the final new drouth joke, another would spring up.

The one told most frequently, until it had a beard three feet long, was to the effect that when Noah built his ark and it rained for forty days and nights, West Texas got only a quarter of an inch.

They told of the farmers sitting around the gin yard waiting for their pitifully small cotton crop to be baled. Somebody began passing a jug around. As the whisky got lower and the men got higher, they began to talk of all the things they were going to buy with the money from their crop. One was going to get a sewing machine for his wife, another a playroom for the kids, a third a new car. Said the fourth farmer: "Pass me that jug again, boys, I ain't quite out of debt yet."

They told of the northerner who hated snow and came to West Texas to buy a ranch where he never need trudge in snow again. Over and over he questioned the prospective seller but never quite trusted his assurances that snow was unknown. Finally he got a chance to talk to old Juan, the Mexican-American foreman who had been on the place for forty years. "Tell me, Juan, have you ever seen it snow here?" Juan replied, "No, señor, but twice I have seen it rain."

And there was the Englishman who was looking over a ranch an eager real estate dealer was trying to sell him in the dry Trans-Pecos. As they were driving over a pasture, a roadrunner darted out of the greasewood and went trotting along in front of the car. "My word," exclaimed the Englishman, "what is that?" The agent, a quick thinker, said, "That is a bird of paradise." The Englishman snorted in disgust, "He's a beastly long way from home!"

The government had drouth-aid programs. Some of these helped; some of them actually hindered. On balance I have a feeling that the feed programs probably hurt the stockman more than they helped him.

Most helpful probably were the federal loan programs, under which a farmer or ranchman who had reached the end of his string with a bank or production credit association could turn to the Farmers Home Administration for further aid. There were instances, probably, when the FHA only abetted a man in getting in even deeper when all best judgment would have indicated he should get out. But in the long run, farmer and rancher defaulting of FHA debts was negligible. Given any chance at all, virtually every one of them eventually paid out.

The federal feed program, at least in the beginning, was a delusion and a snare. The basic problem was that it started without much planning or overall control, a crash program to get feed out to the farmers and ranchmen who needed it. The aim was commendable, but politics got in the way. A group of Congressmen came through Texas on a drouth tour just as the first stirrings began. Their message to the county committees was: "Get the feed out, forget the red tape. We'll stand behind you."

The trouble was, they went back to Washington and never showed up again. Dozens of county committees, made up mostly of farmers and ranchmen who always thought the shortest distance between two points was a straight line, began distributing feed the way they thought it should be done. It was months before the U.S. Department of Agriculture finally put any detailed rules on paper. In the meantime, queries from county offices were usually answered with a noncommital: "Use your own best judgment."

All this came back to haunt county officers, the stockmen and the feed dealers later when federal auditors arrived and began applying the USDA regulations retroactively. Ranchmen were billed for feed which had been offered and accepted in good faith but not in compliance with rules which a plodding bureaucracy had not even formulated at the time. Feed dealers were charged with violations, blacklisted and assessed huge penalties. A number of county committeemen were thrown to the wolves to appease the auditors.

There were some true cases of fraud—there always are—but they were the exception.

One eastern senator who had a reputation as a muckraker—but never raked any of it at home where he might touch his own voters—made headlines with charges of fraud against certain Texas ranchers. These usually hit the front pages across the country. Almost without exception they were proven to be false, but if the truth made any of the major newspapers it was always somewhere just before the classified ads, under a small ten-point head.

Eventually justice was done and the USDA relented on these cases, but not before a great deal of unnecessary anguish, expense and embarrassment to many innocent people.

In fairness I would have to say the USDA handled the feed programs with more expertise in the latter part of the drouth, although it was never able to contend with its own built-in inflationary tendencies.

There were always those ranchmen whose pride and personal codes of ethics would not let them accept government aid. For these, the federal programs had a devastating effect because they tended to inflate the prices of feed beyond whatever levels they would otherwise have reached.

One instance I vividly remember was a Friday-afternoon announcement from the USDA that it was going to give stockmen ten dollars a ton subsidy to help them bring in hay from distant points. The following Monday hay was up fifteen dollars a ton. The government had lost its ten dollars and the stockman another five. Imagine the effect on the rancher who wasn't even taking federal aid!

The drouth finally broke in 1957, shortly after President Dwight David "Ike" Eisenhower made an inspection trip to the disaster areas. Jubilant ranchmen called them "Republican rains." The rains began in the spring and were the most general the Southwest had seen in years. It was a long time, however, before some stockmen would concede that the long ordeal was over. They had been fooled too many times by scattered rains that were never followed up. Most wanted to see the green grass grow to their boottops before they were ready to consider the war was over.

The drouth—like war—was not without its positive side. It taught stern lessons about soil conservation and range management which have become holy writ to the present ranching and farming generation. It taught that overstocking for any extended period will take away far more than any temporary benefit the stockman might gain. It taught rotation grazing and periodic resting of pastures, which today are the rule rather than the exception in the Southwest.

Because of the drouth's bitter lessons, ranchmen today are generally better caretakers than they were twenty-five years ago. It is not that they didn't always intend to be, but because they know so much more now. They learned it the hard way and are unlikely ever to forget it.

And the drouth—like a war—made a man test his will and endurance. Those who fought through it and survived were unlikely to be intimidated by small things, ever again.

Henry Turney An Environmentalist
In Old-Fashioned Sense Of Word

Livestock Weekly, December 8, 1977

HENRY TURNEY became an ecologist in the best sense of the word before the term came into common and often mis-applied usage. He was both a professional conservationist and a rancher. Though some of today's so-called ecologists regard that as a contradiction in terms, the fact is that most ranchers and farmers today *are* conservationists at heart. They have to be, for their future and that of their descendants depend upon the continued productivity of the land.

≈

DUBLIN, TEXAS   Rancher Henry Turney finds himself agreeing occasionally with people who make him very nervous. He was an environmentalist back when the word hadn't even been invented. He is still one, though his conservative ideas differ sharply with many people who use the word "environment" like a banner.

Turney, long a member of the Texas State Soil Conservation Board, has looked at the range management situation from both sides of the fence. He joined the Soil Conservation Service on a Monday in June, 1935, after having been graduated from Texas A&M the previous Saturday. The SCS was a brand new agency then.

He was one of the first SCS men in Texas to become known as a range specialist. He spent sixteen years in the agency, counting his World War II service years. Driving home one evening in 1951 after spending a day with old-time rancher Carrie Owens at Goldthwaite, he gave himself a stern lecture.

"If you're smart enough to advise these old boys who have been fighting the battle for years, why don't you go out and try it for yourself?" Shortly afterward he resigned from SCS to devote his attention to a stockfarm he had bought in 1940 near the Purves community of Erath County where he had grown up.

"It turned out to be the worst time to wean myself from a regular paycheck," he recalls ruefully. "It didn't rain for the next seven years."

A laying hen operation helped pull him and his family through as a supplement to cattle, Angora goats and cash crops such as peanuts.

After the drouth he managed to buy adjoining land in 1959 and 1963, bringing him to about 1,225 acres. That might look small in places farther west, but at the edge of the Cross Timbers it is considered a good-sized place.

He has been able to try out for himself many of the ideas he had as a professional conservationist. One of his present pastures still belonged to someone else when he, as an SCS range man, assisted in one of the state's first experimental plantings of little bluestem on it in 1948. The seed was so scarce that it was planted in three-foot rows. That planting thrived, and today the grass is so dense that mesquite seedlings can rarely be found in it, though mesquite tends to be a pest on adjacent areas.

It pains Turney to hear a professional conservationist claim that grass can choke out existing mesquites; he doesn't believe it. But he does believe it can inhibit or starve out new seedlings and thus halt further spread.

Little bluestem was probably the dominant native species in this immediate area when the white man first challenged the Indian for ownership. It retreated severely over several generations of concentrated grazing. Turney credits the success of his planting to the fact that it was a native.

Though he believes introduced and "improved" grasses often have a valid place, he is a strong proponent for the use of native grasses whenever possible. This point sometimes gets him into friendly arguments with former colleagues.

"I remember when Rhodesgrass was going to solve all our problems. Scale wiped it out," he says. "Weeping lovegrass was the new wonder grass in the late 1930s. It didn't solve all the problems either. Then King Ranch bluestem was going to be the solution, no doubt about it. In the late 1960s, coastal bermuda became the big hope for Central Texas, and it did a good job as long as cattle prices were high and fertilizer was low.

"Now everybody's excited about Kleingrass. It shows a good bit of promise, but to me it's still experimental. I guess I've seen so many grasses come and go that I drag my feet."

He points out that most cattle in Central and West Texas today still graze principally the native grasses that nature selected to fit each soil type and moisture situation. He doubts that man can improve much on nature without making extensive and expensive extra inputs.

He acknowledges that introduced grasses and grazing crops can get more production out of a piece of land under many circumstances than the native grass, but the extra production is never free. The operator must constantly assess whether the extra cost is justified. Sometimes it is, Turney says, and sometimes it isn't.

For many years his 110 acres of coastal bermuda more than justified what he put into them. Today, since cattle and fertilizer prices met each other moving in opposite directions, his native grass comes considerably closer to showing a profit than the coastal, even though he has cut fertilizer use in half.

"We're always looking for wonder cattle the same way we look for wonder grasses," he declares. "But we don't get something for nothing."

His eighty-four cows include many half-Swiss as well as Herefords and Angus, most bred to an Angus-Brahman cross bull to produce the fattest calves he ever had. His half-Swiss cows give a lot of milk, but he finds them harder to winter. The same milk production which holds out the hope of heavier calves makes the cows require more nutrition than the area's grass can give them in the winter months. Consequently, though he would prefer fall calves, he has to breed for spring calves so he can carry dry cows through the winter.

Some so-called environmentalists criticize the farmer and rancher for what they term misuse of the land and favor putting them under control by wise government agencies that will always know the proper thing to do. An old government conservationist from way back, Turney runs a fever every time he hears this.

He contends that most land today is in better condition than it was forty to fifty years ago, environmentalist claims to the contrary notwithstanding.

"We have not had a dust bowl in forty years," he declares. "The gullies of the Piedmont have pretty well healed, and most of the steep slopes of the Texas blacklands are now in grass."

Another point: "This country has plenty of cheap food. In fact, we ship a lot of it to nations that have many plans and regulations."

Experience has perhaps tempered some of his early hopes for spectacular results from conservation practices. As a practical matter he has found that much conservation work is done more to protect an existing investment and situation than to bring large new improvements or profits. Many new activist converts to the environmental cause still expect the spectacular.

He finds that environmentalist goals sometimes even clash with one another. Angora goats have long been part of his own range improvement program, highly important in controlling brush regrowth. This worthy end has come into conflict with environmentalist pressure to protect predatory animals, in his case coyotes. Up to about three years ago he hadn't heard a coyote howl since he was a boy. He hears them aplenty now. In the last three years he has not sold off a single goat; he has made a strong effort to keep all his kids. In spite of that, and of penning or shedding at night, his total goat numbers have dropped more than fifty percent.

Texas had no grass or range management courses when he finished Texas A&M University in 1935. The emphasis was on animals, not on what they grazed. The new SCS had to import a Utah man, Liter E. Spence, as state range specialist for Texas. He took Turney and twenty or twenty-five other new employees on a long field trip over the western part of the state, giving them a crash course in grass identification. These men were then considered the agency's grass experts for Texas. They had to learn mostly from personal observation and experience.

Turney believes educational institutions today still are not giving enough emphasis to range as compared to livestock and crops. He commutes to Stephenville one day a week during part of the school year to conduct a course in what he terms "aristology" at Tarleton State University.

He has reason to have reservations about some formal training on livestock. While at A&M he was a member of the livestock judging team which won at Chicago's International Livestock Show. "We were taught to put up the blocky, low-set, compact cattle," he recalls. "We did, and we won.

"That kind of cattle almost ruined the business."

Western Ranges Said Better Than
At Any Time This Century

Livestock Weekly, June 21, 1979

SELF-APPOINTED, self-anointed environmentalists in recent years have painted the rancher in a black hat and have exerted tremendous pressure to remove livestock from public lands in the West. They have laid waste to forests, producing paper to carry their message of exploitation and ruin of the range by cattle and sheep. In some quarters a cry has arisen to get rid of the livestock and bring back the buffalo, ignoring the fact that the buffalo's grazing habits are very nearly the same as those of cattle. The late Edward Abbey once declared that the entire West stinks of cattle. That is nonsense. A tourist can drive across hundreds of miles of the West at times and not see enough cattle to fill a gooseneck trailer. I was glad to hear a bonafide range scientist like Thad Box make the statements in this article. But while people like *Beyond Beef* author Jeremy Rifkin who follow Abbey have a large forum and gullible audience, Box and his peers are mostly heard by the converted.

≈

LOGAN, UTAH   The rancher, especially the sheepman, has been getting a bum rap for many range and wildlife problems of Utah and other western range states. That, at least, is the opinion of Dr. Thad Box, dean of the college of natural resources at Utah State University.

In one particular, the encroachment of people and houses onto foothill ranges is directly responsible for a constant decline in Utah's mule deer. Some of these houses are occupied by environmentalists who blame livestock owners for the problem.

Box contends that because of better livestock management by ranchers, the overall range condition across Utah and other western states is actually better today than at any time in this century.

He concedes that this opinion is not shared by many who label themselves conservationists. They continue to call for reductions or elimination of livestock on the public ranges in the belief that this will enhance wildlife and other land uses.

Box, a native Texan, finds the public-lands states much different from Texas, where most lands are privately owned.

"In Texas, range management is a biological science," he says. "Here it is a social science. We have more people problems than actual range problems."

About two-thirds of Utah's land is owned either by the federal or the state government.

Box believes it has been adequately demonstrated that the proper handling of livestock can actually enhance the range for wildlife. Utah has recognized this by opening up some state lands that had long been closed to domestic animals. In some cases the state arranges with stockmen to put on large numbers of animals for relatively short periods to flash-graze an area and reduce grass and weeds, favoring shrubs browsed by deer.

For mule deer, which ordinarily range over relatively large areas, the real problem is winter feed. Except for an isolated deer herd, the state has no shortage of summer range for its mule deer. But as the animals drift down into the foothills for the winter, they find themselves shut off more each year by the encroachment of housing. It's the houses that are the problem, not livestock, Box declares.

Last winter he saw considerable numbers of mule deer on the USU campus, which sits in the northeastern part of Logan on foothills of the broad Cache Valley. Deer frequently come down and forage for winter feed among the residential areas of Logan and other cities and towns.

While mule deer have suffered, better grazing management has considerably improved forage conditions for cattle and sheep. Box says elk have also increased, moving counter to the trend for deer. Because elk are grazers more than browsers, they have benefited from the same improving grass conditions that have favored livestock.

Box is concerned about the steady decline in sheep numbers over recent years. He believes cattle range is enhanced by well-managed sheep grazing. Without sheep to keep it under control, weedy growth often outpaces grass to the detriment of cattle, elk and many other wildlife species. "Sheep are badly needed throughout the West to maintain a balance," he declares.

Most sheep in Utah are kept under herd because of the open-range situation, and labor availability is a bigger problem every year. The average age of the state's sheep operators keeps going up. As the older generation retires or dies, the younger generation tends to cut down or eliminate sheep in favor of cattle.

Box says one of the more positive steps taken in Utah toward range improvement the last few years is a loan fund established for that purpose by the state legislature. Ranchmen can borrow money interest-free to improve privately owned ranges. Traditionally it has been very difficult to obtain loans for this purpose through normal lending institutions, Box says, because the highly variable rainfall pattern often makes repayment slow.

Brush control and grass reseeding are among practices most often done under this program. Because most ranchers conduct their operations partly on their own privately owned land and partly on state and/or federal land, some coordination with the state and federal authorities is usually necessary under terms of the loan program.

Often the nature of the range improvement work will mean the livestock must go to and from the public range earlier or later than normal, and therefore the agencies must be brought into discussions for the range plans to be put into effect.

Box says this often works to mutual advantage. If a rancher plants an improved grass such as crested wheatgrass, he may be able to hold his flock back from the summer range several weeks longer than usual and allow certain range improvement work to be done on the public lands too.

Typically, in northern Utah, sheepmen breed their ewes on Bureau of Land Management desert during the winter. They lamb out in spring under confinement on their privately owned lands. Then they move the sheep up onto Forest Service land in the mountains for summer grazing, bringing down milk-fat or heavy feeder lambs in the early fall.

The major push in range improvement during recent years has been for improvement of the critical spring range. Pastures have been seeded with introduced species such as crested wheatgrass or Russian wildrye, as well as with natives. Brush control, particularly sagebrush removal, often has to go hand-in-hand with range seeding.

Sagebrush is controlled principally by mechanical methods these days. Actually, the plant was relatively easy to control with 2,4-D; it didn't even have to have 2,4,5-T. But these herbicides have been almost totally removed from public lands, and water quality controls have made them difficult to use even on private lands.

Sagebrush is not hard to kill. Plowing it or dragging rails behind a tractor are effective. It is also a good candidate for fire control; fire gives a good percentage rootkill. However, sage is a prolific seeder, reproducing itself quickly from seed already in or on the ground.

Most ranchers who use the fire technique will reseed grass behind the fire. Otherwise grass recovery is likely to be scattered and sparse, and sagebrush reinfestation will probably be faster for lack of competition.

Some grass-breeding work has been done in the state, trying to upgrade quality of the natives by concentrating on strains that favor good points and breeding out or at least reducing bad points such as noxious qualities. There has even been an active program for shrub improvement, selecting strains of sagebrush and bitterbrush that are browsed by livestock and wildlife.

It has been known for years that animals ate some kinds of sagebrush but not others. Box says he envisions both isolated and wholesale plantings of the better sagebrush strains. The thought is that because sagebrush is going to grow anyway, it is to everybody's advantage to push those strains that are useful.

Unspoiled Tract Saves Piece
of Original Tallgrass Prairie

Livestock Weekly, October 22, 1981

VERY little of Texas looks quite the same today as it did a hundred or so years ago. Urban development, highways and various land uses such as farming and grazing have changed the vegetation and ofttimes to some degree even the topography. A small piece of East Texas tallgrass prairie has been preserved in basically its virgin state. It can serve not only as a benchmark for assessing the gains and losses of the land around it but as a potential seed source for grasses and forbs which have virtually disappeared elsewhere. The Nature Conservancy near Paris is not without controversy, but in my judgment this is a worthy project.

≈

PARIS, TEXAS   When the white man first came to Northeast Texas he found it part of a massive tallgrass prairie that stretched northward and northeastward all the way into the foothills of Alberta, Canada.

He marveled, then proceeded to plow it up. Today, so little of the tallgrass prairie remains intact that even a 100-acre block in virgin condition is considered unique and remarkable, and draws visitors from a wide area.

Such a block is the Tridens Prairie, a ninety-seven-acre tract eight miles west of Paris. It has never felt the sting of a plow. For decades it was preserved as a source of natural prairie hay, never treated with fertilizer or sprayed with herbicides. Since 1972 it has belonged to the Texas Nature Conservancy, a privately financed organization devoted to preserving scattered unspoiled tracts as benchmarks.

The site was named for its abundance of a native grass species known as longspike tridens.

A field day on the prairie last week drew a sizeable crowd, largely conservationists, despite its falling into one of the wettest weeks of recent years.

Robert W. Dyas of Iowa State University has been visiting the site ever since he was stationed at nearby Camp Maxey during World War II. He said it is a splendid example of the original but now vanished prairie upon which he grew up in Iowa.

"The Tridens Prairie represents what the tallgrass prairie once was, all the way into Canada," he declared. "I hope we can let it serve as a museum, a reference library to show future generations what the great prairie really was." He finds in it many plant species considered rare, including blue wild indigo, white prairie rose, button snake-root. It abounds in Indiangrass and big and little bluestem, not rare but no longer plentiful in many areas.

Mrs. Cameron Pratt, property stewardship chairman for the Conservancy, said one practical function of such preserved areas is to serve as plant gene pools. This will allow plant breeders to go back to original strains for specific genes needed in upgrading improved varieties. Such availability may prove of great value in feeding growing populations around the world, especially as many original plants disappear under modern cultural practices. Such preserved areas also may serve as a benchmark to measure progress or regression in the condition of lands around them.

Though much of the shortgrass country on the plains remains in more or less original condition, the tallgrass prairie to the east of it has almost disappeared, Mrs. Pratt said. In the Midwest it is restricted mostly to roadsides and cemetery plots. Even in Northeast Texas, which probably has more of it than any other area, most of the native range has been altered by fertilization, herbicides, planting of improved species, and so on.

The Conservancy is trying to handle the site in a manner that more or less duplicates the way it was used in nature, except that no practical method has been found for grazing it. The tract has never been fenced, and it is considered impractical to fence it for relatively short periods of use. Grazing is approximated by mowing it for hay at irregular intervals. The site is also subjected to occasional prescribed burning to duplicate the natural wildfires that used to sweep the prairies and keep down the large woody growth.

Tridens Prairie is a mile or so north of the small Brookston community, once regarded as the prairie grass hay capital of the country. The noted Smiley Meadows was just one of the large hay operations which thrived for decades. The Texas & Pacific Railroad built a line from Fort Worth to Brookston to accommodate the prairie hay trade. Smiley Meadows was once a contractor to the royal stables in England as well as to the U. S. Army's cavalry units.

That is all in the past. Most of the hay meadows have gone to wheat, cotton and corn. Where haying continues on scattered tracts it is devoted mainly to cultivated forages rather than original prairie hay, or the native grass is periodically treated with herbicides to keep it free of brush and weeds. The grass community therefore is no longer in its original mixtures.

Tridens Prairie was never in the Smiley operation. It was part of the Zachariah Westfall survey conducted during the empresario colonization period before Texas' revolution from Mexico. Westfall owned but never saw 1,280 acres, which he sold for $100.

Fred Guthery, wildlife professor of Texas Tech University, Lubbock, said man's changes in land use have not always been detrimental to all forms of wildlife. "In a large sense we have tradeoffs rather than straight losses," he commented.

For example, though the wolf and the buffalo symbolized the original prairie and disappeared when the white man settled on it, patchwork agriculture benefited certain other wildlife forms such as the prairie chicken. Guthery said bobwhites and mourning doves are probably more plentiful today than they were originally. He asserted that the Midwest today probably has more waterfowl than it had in early times. The ringnecked pheasant, fairly plentiful in many areas today, was introduced.

Guthery also added that less than one percent of the original tallgrass prairie remains today in anything like its original condition.

Dwight Chaney, dean of academic instruction at Paris Junior College, summarized the history of white settlement in Northeast

Texas and the general tallgrass prairie country. He said it took nature twenty-five million years to form the prairie and man just a few decades to change it almost entirely.

The early settlers, largely family farmers directly or indirectly from the Middle Atlantic region, were interested in plowing rather than grazing the prairie. "Soon the wind which had fanned the wildfires of the prairie were fanning dust behind the plows," Chaney commented.

The high prairie had always been treeless except near water, kept clean by fire. The settler dreaded fire and fought to control it. Without this natural agent the prairie community changed even where it was not plowed. In time nearly all of it fell under the plow, however, grass being traded for cotton and corn.

Fred Smeins, Texas A&M University professor, said such natural areas are needed in strategically distributed areas to preserve various original plant communities. He reiterated Mrs. Pratt's comments about the growing need for plant gene pools as many of the native plants become rare and endangered.

Such tracts also provide an opportunity to gauge the changes undergone by nearby soils under the influence of long cropping with cotton and other cultivated plants, he added.

When the Well Runs Dry

Texas Monthly, October 1985

THIS article, written at a time when Texans were about to go to the polls in a referendum on a Texas water plan submitted by the state legislature, was intended to provide background on the state's precarious water supply situation. Voters approved the plan, though at this writing the state does not seem to have done a great deal about it. We still face a formidable long-range problem, and conflict over the Edwards Aquifer seems to portend an epic struggle between rural and urban interests for a limited water supply.

≈

SOME of my earliest recollections are of the West Texas boomtown of Crane in the first years after oil was discovered there. It was a motley mixture of small frame houses, side-boarded tents, and tin shacks. A fixture beside most back doors was a large water barrel, its top covered by boards or a piece of sheet metal weighted down by a rock. Townspeople bought their water for a dollar a barrel from the back of a wagon or truck that had hauled it for miles over treacherous roads where wheels sometimes sank to the hubs in dry sand. Workhorses, mules, and milk cows roamed the townsite, and it was a minor tragedy when one worried the cover off a water barrel and drank its fill, spoiling what it left behind.

Water was scarcer than oil for Cranites in those times, and to waste it was unthinkable. Families often bathed in shifts on Saturday night without ever emptying the washtub. When the last body was reasonably clean, often the water was poured on a small flower bed or vegetable garden, as was dishwater and the leavings from Monday's scrub board.

After a time, Crane built a towering water tank—ever afterward

a challenge to high school seniors—and installed a spiderwebbing of
service lines. Suddenly, water was available at the turning of a tap,
in plentiful supply and right in the house. Flower beds thrived all over
town, and many of my schoolmates were less fragrant in Thursday
and Friday classes. One can only guess the quantum leaps by which
water use multiplied.

What happened in the Crane that I remember from the early '30s
has happened all over Texas, magnified not only by the state's huge
increase in population but by a more than tripled per capita usage
of water. Looming in the not-distant future like a dust storm on the
South Plains horizon is a dark specter that almost every Texan is
aware of but prefers to ignore: a shortage of water.

We out here in West Texas are resigned to having our destiny
controlled by those who live east of Interstate 35. That's where the
votes are. But they are the votes of people who haven't lived with
water shortages day in and day out, as we have. To those who have
not felt the pinch, water remains an abstract issue. They haven't been
raised from childhood to wash dishes by turning the faucet on and
off, on and off, rather than letting the water run. They criticize West
Texas farmers for irrigating upstream but never ask whether it makes
sense to save that water for rice farmers downstream. They don't
believe us when we say that water is a statewide problem. And it is
scant comfort to know that time will prove us right.

The state's problem is elemental. Its water supply is limited, but
its population is not. Texas grew from 5.8 million people in 1930 to
9.6 million in 1960 and to more than 15 million in 1983. Water use
increased from 2 million acre-feet (an acre-foot of water will cover
one acre one foot deep) in 1930 to nearly 18 million in 1980. Some
parts of Texas are already straining to meet the immediate needs of
an existing population, yet almost every local chamber of commerce
is promoting more growth on the traditional theory that bigger is
better for business.

My own city, San Angelo, seeks growth like the rest, but at least
it had the good judgment a few years ago to drop its long-time booster
slogan, "The Wool and Water Wonderland." That water wonder-

land claim went a little sour in the face of enforced water rationing and ridicule in national news media because our lakes were so dry they kept catching fire.

The painful fact is that nature limits Texas' water supplies. As much as we might like our towns to be as green as the English countryside, it just doesn't rain enough. An old but exaggerated rule of thumb says, if you start in East Texas and move west, you lose an inch of rainfall a year for every fifty miles. By the time you reach El Paso, you're running on the rim. Out here, drouth is a steady boarder who may stray for a little while but always comes home for supper. Prosperity is a flirtatious stranger who occasionally waves but never pauses long enough for a first-name acquaintanceship.

Rainfall patterns do not change for the convenience of the chamber of commerce. It will not rain more in the foreseeable future than it has rained in the historic past. We are stuck with what we've got. There seems to be a booster assumption that if we can bring enough industry and new people to an area, we can somehow become immune to the economic punishment of recurring drouth and heavy reliance on agriculture. But the larger the city, the greater its water needs. New industrial plants bring more people; they do not bring more rain.

Texas gets its water from two sources, underground and surface, and both are running short. About two thirds of the state is underlain by twenty-three aquifers, only seven of which can be classified as major. Groundwater furnished sixty-one per cent of the total water used in 1980, amounting to 10.8 million acre-feet. But groundwater's recharge rate from rainfall is less than half the withdrawal rate, so the difference—5.5 million acre-feet—is being depleted. "Overdrawn" is the term my banker uses. At some point in the future, that supply will no longer exist. The people, however, will still be there. Thirsty.

The surface water budget is also running at a deficit. Texas already has 184 major reservoirs with a capacity of at least 5,000 acre-feet each. Their total storage capacity is more than 32 million acre-feet. As promising as that might appear at first blush, the dependable surface water supply (the amount that can be withdrawn during extended drouth) is only about 11 million acre-feet a year—half of what the water experts tell us we will need by the year 2000. Some people wonder why we should build more dams when so many of our lakes are below capacity. The answer is that in wet years they will be too full, and flood waters that we could otherwise capture will escape into the Gulf of Mexico. Even if we assume that all the workable reservoir sites on the dam builders' wish list are developed by then, the total dependable water supply will be barely the minimum needed. And there isn't time, money, or political support to build all those dams by the end of the century.

But the gloomy reports do not deter the boosters. At this writing, San Angelo restricts watering lawns and gardens. Nevertheless, like every other city, it seeks new industry, new growth. And Corpus Christi, just months ago parching in its worst water crisis, is rejoicing over the boom promised by the Navy's decision to berth the battleship Wisconsin and several other vessels there. A hundred battleships wouldn't make more rain fall upon the limestone hills of Real County, the upper Nueces River watershed so vital to Corpus Christi's water supply, and a 1983 report by the U.S. Bureau of Reclamation declared that essentially no economically developable water supplies remain in the Nueces River basin.

The same Hill Country area that sends surface water trickling leisurely toward Corpus Christi feeds the Edwards Aquifer, upon which San Antonio depends. An Edwards Underground Water District spokesman has commented that pumping in San Antonio affects water levels as far west as Sabinal, sixty miles away. By 1980 pumping from the Edwards was already 75,000 acre-feet past the recommended annual level and still increasing. Meanwhile, builders keep putting new subdivisions on top of the recharge zone.

San Antonio and Corpus Christi, at least, are using renewable water supplies, limited though they may be. But much of West Texas is mining underground water supplies that have been built up over untold thousands of years. The recharge rate is minimal or even unmeasurable, but the withdrawal rate during the last three decades would scare the britches off the early pioneers who fetched water by the bucket. The West Texas agricultural economy is built upon these nonrenewable water resources, which will inevitably be exhausted or drawn down to depths no longer economically feasible to pump.

No more sobering example of a dried-out agricultural economy can be found than at Pecos. Thirty years ago as a farm and ranch reporter I visited Pecos regularly to write about the waist-high irrigated cotton stretching mile upon mile. I recently drove across that once-lush farming district. It was like a visit to a graveyard, and a poorly kept one at that. Hardly one field in ten remains in production. You can drive along some of the section-line farm roads that border abandoned fields and see nothing green except Russian thistle and other invader plants.

Pecos and neighboring Fort Stockton had their big farming boom in the late '40s, when drought made irrigation seem like the royal road to plenty. Old-timers warned that the water was limited, and some at Fort Stockton sued in vain when nearby high-powered pumps drew down historic Comanche Springs to a trickle, ruining traditional ditch-irrigation operations that for generations had lived from its flow.

Year by year, water tables dropped as engines sucked water at a thousand gallons a minute or more. At the same time, costs climbed for irrigation farmers as hungry insects pioneered their way to the new feeding grounds and as the residual fertility of virgin soil was sapped. By the early '60s the region was in financial trouble. Some still blame the 1962 Billie Sol Estes scandal for wrecking the local economy, but that was only a symptom. Too much of the vein had been mined out. The withered debris of the farming area southwest of Pecos bears an uncomfortable resemblance to abandoned mining regions of the far West.

On the plains, not only agriculture but also most towns and cities depend upon the gradually depleting Ogallala Aquifer. The high cost of energy for pumping water has already taken thousands of acres out of irrigation, causing a reversion to dryland farming. But plains farmers at least have that option. Their average rainfall of eighteen inches, though far below what they wish it were, gives them a running chance for a dryland crop. Pecos' twelve inches makes that chance too remote to risk the seed and fuel.

The reversion to dryland, whether already a fact or a long-range probability, has had a devastating effect upon Panhandle land values, compounding the deflation that all of agriculture has experienced in the last two or three years of poor commodity prices. That effect has also been felt by plains towns and cities heavily dependent upon the farmer. I was told of an irrigated farm that sold originally on the South Plains for $1100 an acre and resold recently for $700 an acre. Many an unfortunate farmer has planned, scrimped, and sweated for years to build a comfortable equity in his land, only to find that he has lost most or all of it to a water pinch the rest of Texas must acknowledge sooner or later.

The Ogallala Aquifer lies under about forty Texas plains counties and reaches into several other states, extending as far north as Nebraska. Texans have sought answers for years, of course, but by and large each region, each city, and each town has seen after its own interests and paid little attention to broader needs. The last session of the state legislature approached the water problem with some degree of unified purpose, which has to be taken as a hopeful sign that we are begining to see the bigger picture. When Pecos went sour, the economic repercussions reached far beyond Reeves County, to banks in Dallas and Houston, to suppliers all over the state and beyond, and to the tax base at the state level. If the High Plains suffers, Texas suffers. When San Antonio, Corpus Christi, and Austin ration water, citizens of other towns must nervously ask how much longer they can escape similar curtailments.

We are all in the same boat. If there is better use of water upstream, those downstream will benefit. Senator Bill Sims of San Angelo, a rancher and longtime lobbyist for the sheep and goat industry, managed to include in the Texas water plan a provision for research on brush control as a way to increase groundwater recharge. He cites Texas A&M University estimates that mesquite seriously infests 56 million acres of the state and that each tree uses on average three hundred gallons a year. That is more per tree than some people of my acquaintance used in the days when they carried water in a bucket.

Sims has a precedent for his argument that an ambitious brush control program would yield substantial amounts of water downstream. Northwest of San Angelo is small, clear Rocky Creek, which flowed year-round in Fort Concho's frontier days. Uncle Bob Mims, an early-day wagon boss, told me that in his youth he could spot a cow two miles away across Rocky's open valley. By the '20s, the 74,000-acre watershed had grown up in brush so thick that he could ride almost within spitting distance of a cow and not see her.

After the lengthy drouth in the '30s, Rocky ceased to flow except for short periods after a rain. It was regarded as a dead stream, like so many west of the 98th meridian. Younger men accepted the change, but Mims would not. Though far along in years, he became an ardent advocate of conservation, persuading younger men to the cause. One of his converts was George Skeete, who ranched near the head of the twenty-mile-long creek. Skeete began removing brush, not with any thought of reviving Rocky but simply to grow more grass. After some time a half-forgotten old spring began to flow. As other ranchers along the creek cleared brushy pastures, more springs and seeps became active. Cleaning up the watershed turned into a mission for conservationists and local ranchmen. By the late '60s—too late for Bob Mims to see it—Rocky was flowing year-round, providing a significant amount of water to San Angelo's municipal supply downstream. It has flowed ever since, slowing but not quitting during extended dry weather. For twenty years soil conservationists have been taking visitors to Rocky Creek, urging its lesson upon them.

I can almost hear the East Texas skeptics now. Despite the millions of dollars spent annually for control, mesquite continues to gain ground, they will say. And much of the water gained from brush control will remain in the soil profile, promoting growth of more productive vegetation that will benefit the landowner. Why should we provide the money? they will ask. Brush control is the landowner's problem; let him take care of it.

To be sure, the landowner will benefit from better grass cover. But curtailing water waste by clearing brush is of more importance to the public at large than to the rancher, who usually needs little more water than just enough for his livestock. When Lake Corpus Christi's level went down last year, city officials were disconcerted to see how much the holding capacity had been compromised by heavy siltation. A good vegetative cover on the watershed is the best protection against erosion. The Soil Conservation Service has estimated that mesquite takes as much as 63 million acre-feet a year out of the ground, three and a half times the total human water use in the state. We won't have to save much of that to make it worth everybody's while.

It is obvious that no one is going to pull a rabbit out of a hat and solve Texas' water problems with any one grand gesture like the importing of water. The hard fact is that we'll almost certainly have to learn to make do with what we've got. Solutions are likely to be painful, costly, and controversial. Building more dams is only part of the answer, not the answer. Getting more recharge into the aquifers is a major challenge that must be addressed, and yet it too will be only a partial answer. Recycling wastewater, as Lubbock has started doing, holds promise for stretching available supplies.

Not only do we use tremendous amounts of water but we also pollute additional quantities through loose industrial practices, oilfield misuse, and inadequate municipal waste treatment. A symposium speaker recently declared that on any given day, probably half of the sewage treatment systems in Texas would fail to pass inspection. Texas cities are notoriously cavalier about the welfare of their downstream neighbors. San Angeloans used to display a cruel bumper sticker: "Flush often—Paint Rock needs the water." Citizens of tiny Paint Rock, thirty miles downstream, did not laugh.

Probably the biggest and most difficult challenge will be in learning how to make better use of less water, admitting to ourselves that water can no longer be squandered in the often profligate manner to which we have been accustomed. The most effective method of control, and also the most painful, is through price. When I was a boy, those Crane folks did not save water because some local ordinance said they must; they saved it because at a dollar a barrel it was too expensive to waste. Like it or not, we will pay much more for water in the future than we paid in the past. We may finally have to concede that St. Augustine grass is not for everybody. (I have been trying for forty years to convince my wife that if she will water the lawn less often, the grass roots will grow deeper and be hardier. She remains unconvinced.)

It is too much to expect that those transitions will come peacefully and without rancor. The politically strong will present a severe challenge for the weak. Rural interests have lost their historic dominance in the legislature. Agriculture has been by far the major user of Texas water and will be vulnerable to stronger political forces. In 1980 it used 13 million acre-feet; municipal and domestic purposes used only 2.8 million and manufacturing 1.5 million. As supplies tighten, pressure will grow for agriculture to give up a substantial part of its share. Agricultural organizations are gearing up for that fight and admitting among themselves that the deck is stacked against them.

Bigger cities will claim priority over smaller ones simply by virtue of their greater population, and cities will seek to exert authority over water far beyond their boundries. San Antonio already regulates development over the Edwards Aquifer, miles past its city limits. It is conceivable that in the foreseeable future San Antonio will try to dictate to goat ranchers out in Uvalde County.

It will be tempting to try to set up far-reaching regulation out of Austin to cover all contingencies, especially if we fool ourselves into thinking we can find somebody else to pay the bill. But Austin is hardly the repository of all knowledge and light, as some of its downstream neighbors will testify when they watch its raw sewage float by. For every story about farmers' waste of water there are stories about urban golf greens and lush lawns in well-to-do neighborhoods. There is waste in all regions; none of us is innocent. What the less populated areas fear most about statewide or federal control is the thought that their water will be carried away to urban areas, where the votes are. Each watershed, each aquifer, is unique, and the administration of each must be unique. State and federal agencies tend to look for answers that are like stretch socks; one size fits all. Years of experience with distant bureaucrats should have taught us by now that the nearer to home we can retain control, in this case probably through local or regional water districts, the more influence we can exert.

But whatever we do, it is time to begin. We have accorded the old averted gaze to our water problems too long already. We are all in this boat together, like it or not, and the boat shows a strong likelihood of being beached on a mudbank. Crane's dollar-a-barrel water, now a footnote in our history, could become a chapter in our future.

The Time It Always Rained

Texas Monthly, August 1987

THE YEAR 1987 was unusually wet for Texas, especially West Texas, where a drouth is much more to be expected than excess rainfall. Because I had written a novel called *The Time It Never Rained*, set during the seven-year drouth of the 1950s, *Texas Monthly* asked me to write an article about 1987 and call it "The Time It Always Rained." In it, I mentioned that one dark side of the year's prosperity was likely to be large range fires later as the grass dried and cured. This proved true, several damaging blazes being capped by the spectacular Shackelford County wildfire of March 1988. Some people thought I owned a crystal ball, but there was no special prescience on my part. Many ranchers were saying the same thing. We had seen it before. Not often, of course, but a few times.

≈

THE ENTIRE state enjoyed an unusually wet spring this year that broke rainfall records in many areas and brought flood misery to some unfortunates. But the phenomenon of abundant rainfall was probably the most dramatic in West Texas, which historically has known much about cactus and little about mushrooms.

My city, San Angelo, had already registered nearly twenty-three inches of rain by the end of June, more than five inches beyond the official average for the whole year. At the northern approach to the city stands a chamber of commerce sign welcoming the traveler to San Angelo. The metal surface has begun to rust. A New York editor who had never seen West Texas came to visit us in early June, expecting saguaro cactus and cow skulls. Flying out to San Angelo in a commuter plane, she looked down in disbelief upon thousands of shimmering lakes and stock tanks. She said she was half afraid she had boarded the wrong flight and was over Minnesota.

There are always among us those garrulous old-timers who have seen something bigger or smaller, longer or shorter, better or worse, than whatever the subject under discussion happens to be. Most of them have quit talking about the wetter years they can remember from some distant past. Ask them now, and they'll tell you this is the wettest they have ever seen West Texas.

The contrast to the norm is drastic. In his prize-winning historical study, *The Great Plains*, Walter Prescott Webb explains how the arid land west of the 98th meridian—which runs just west of Austin—has always tested the mettle of the people who have tried to eke out a living from it. Webb illustrates how the recurring struggle for survival has had a long-term effect upon the individualistic character and culture of those generations who have stuck it out, especially those who have lived close to the land and depended upon grass or crops for their livelihood.

Once I asked my father—who at the time had lived for some seventy-five years west of that decisive meridian—how many truly wet years he could remember. He came up with just four: 1906, a year when large acreages of West Texas rangeland were sold to unlucky prospective farmers blinded by the deceptively rich, green grass; 1919, a year that broke one of the meaner drouths of this century; 1941, when we spent part of the summer recutting the next winter's supply of firewood because the huge rick we had just finished went floating off down the draw; and 1957, which broke the grand-daddy of all West Texas drouths.

Dad, if he were still living, would have to red-flag 1987 as the wettest one of all. It has filled long-dry playa lakes all over the plains. One of these lakes, swollen like a boil on a cowboy's backside, forced the closing of heavily traveled U.S. Highway 87 for weeks between Lamesa and Lubbock. From the Edwards Plateau and Cross Timbers all the way out to the Trans-Pecos, long-dry seeps and springs have begun to yield clear water in places few of this generation have ever seen it. A ranchman who has an old dam on little Kickapoo Creek near the Tom Green-Concho county line had never seen so much water backed up and spilling over. He became concerned that another dam might have broken somewhere upstream, threatening his own. Upon inspection he found all upstream dams intact; the water was simply a result of increased spring flows from the unprecedented rains.

A motorist driving westward from Austin in normal times usually finds a great deal less green color by the time he reaches San Angelo. From San Angelo west toward El Paso the land becomes drier and more desolate-looking with each mile, its semi-desert nature inescapable. This year that situation was reversed. For months the grass was greener toward Fort Stockton than at San Angelo, and greener at San Angelo than at Austin.

Farmers and ranchers, unprepared for such abundance, are discovering that rain can be a mixed blessing, though any West Texan would rather wipe mud from his boots than sand from his eyes. This spring many farmers whose winter wheat had somehow survived a severe late-season freeze found their fields too muddy to harvest at the proper time. They had to watch the quality—and therefore the price—of their grain decline while the matured crop stood exposed to the rigors of the elements. Others lost early plantings of cotton and other summer crops to washing and drowning, or they never could plant in the first place because they could not drive their tractors into boggy fields. Some who finally managed to plant cotton did so dangerously late.

Rain has its downside for livestock producers too. Diseases thrive on wet weather, and a plague of insects and parasites usually follows good rains. Horn flies and face flies can torment cattle to a point that they lose weight even in green grass that tickles their bellies. As a rule, however, ranchers are more than willing to accept the risk, since cattle, sheep, and goat prices move up with the rain gauge. The old cattleman declares, "I'll take a rain and a calf any time."

The vegetation creates special problems for sheep and goat operators by lodging burs, seeds, and other impurities in wool and mohair. Contaminated fleeces sell at a discount. The sheep is a dry-weather animal, provided ranges do not get too dry. It likes short grass better than tall grass. By early summer West Texas sheepmen who had not yet sold this year's lamb crop were beginning to sense that the "washy" feed, full of water and short of nutrients, was exacting a toll on lambs that earlier had shown great promise. Internal parasites, particularly stomach worms, are much more potent in sheep and goats than in cattle during such times.

The rank growth of grass and weeds will pose a fire hazard later in the year as it turns dry. Ranchers use controlled burning as a cheap, nonchemical way to retard unwanted invader brush, and they won't have the usual West Texas problem of growing enough grass to fuel a hot fire. We can expect headlines about spectacular range fires blazing out of control. Deer hunters next fall will be receiving stern lectures about their smoking habits before landowners turn them loose to prey upon the whitetail herds.

Perhaps the greatest detriment is psychological. West Texas ranchers and farmers are so accustomed to adversity that they seem unable to enjoy prosperity to its fullest, because of a feeling—historically well justified—that it cannot last.

The pessimistic mind-set is well illustrated by a story that came from the breakup of the seven-year '50s drouth: It had rained for days in the Fort Stockton country. The sun had not been seen in more than a week. One afternoon as a group of coffee drinkers left the Taylor Cafe, a tiny rift appeared in the dark clouds, and a small ray of bright sunshine touched tentatively upon a rain-soaked land.

"I sure hate to see that," groaned a rancher. "I saw a real bad drouth start just this way."

That is the rub. Our pleasure in the generous rains is tempered by the certainty that they will stop and that West Texas will gradually revert to its normal drouthy self.

Earth, Rain, Wind, Fire

Texas Monthly, May 1988

IT IS ironic that West Texas' rare wet years can create major problems of their own. Much as a rancher loves to see a good stand of grass, he has to live with the possibility that it will become a severe fire hazard when it dries and cures. Early spring of 1988 followed the unusual rains of 1987. On March 10, one of the biggest range fires in Texas history began near the Callahan County community of Clyde and swept northwestward into Shackelford County. This is the story of that fire and its immediate aftermath. It would be too much to say that the story had a happy ending, though it did have a few positive effects, despite its tremendous emotional and financial costs. The outpouring of generosity to the fire's victims was heartwarming. Rains brought grass back sooner than expected. The fire devastated prickly pear, a scourge to that area, and set back invading mesquite seedlings for several years.

≈

EVEN while West Texas ranchmen were enjoying near-record rainfall last spring and summer and growing more grass than many had ever seen, they knew from experience that when the vegetation dried up, there would be a high likelihood of grass fires. That worry proved to be more than justified in mid-March, when a prairie wildfire blackened 298,000 acres of grasslands northeast of Abilene. It was the largest grass fire in the state since the Texas Forest Service began keeping records early in this century.

All winter hardly a week had passed without a serious fire. A few, such as two fires near Barnhart in February and two fires in the Ozona area in early March, burned off several thousand acres apiece before fire departments and ranchmen with cattle sprayers and wet tow sacks managed to snuff them out. Two firefighters had been killed near

Breckenridge when wind shifts changed the direction of a fire and trapped them.

The genesis of the record-breaking wildfire that began on March 10 was a tire-burning fire near Clyde that got out of hand. A local fire department had it almost under control when a second fire broke out a short distance away, that one of suspicious origin. Several cases of malicious arson had been reported in recent weeks. The firefighters had to divide their forces, and both fires got away, soon joining in one front.

A gusty wind ranging from thirty to thirty-five miles per hour made the fire difficult to fight. Water alone was not enough. To remove dry vegetation that would serve as fuel, volunteers on bulldozers and maintainers tried to scrape the ground clear of growth ahead of the flames, but the fire was burning too hot and moving too fast. The heat immediately in front of the fire was intense enough in places to cause spontaneous combustion across the firebreaks, and the wind carried fire brands over the heads of firefighters. Flames would sometimes race along the top of the grass and the volatile dry broom-weed, leaving the lower growth to burn more slowly.

The high wind from the south drove the flames rapidly northward. They jumped Texas Highway 351 between Abilene and Albany and U.S. 180 between Albany and Anson. The concerted efforts of several area volunteer fire departments, ranchmen with cattle spray-ers, and a great many volunteer townspeople and oilfield workers could not stop it. Before the day was over, the fire had swept forty-five miles across Callahan and Shackelford counties, its width averaging six miles.

Wildfire has been dreaded since pioneer times, when the lack of fire-fighting equipment often let it race over vast areas, burning out ranges, farms, and homes until it confronted some natural barrier, such as a river. Early ranchers fought grass fires with the blood of a freshly killed animal, whose carcass they would split open and drag along the fire line. Controlled fires, however, have long been used for range improvement. Indians set fires to manipulate the move-ment of the game, which preferred the new vegetation in recently burned areas. Several generations of ranchmen in the Flint Hills of

Kansas and the Osage area of northeastern Oklahoma have used fire to remove dead vegetation and freshen the tallgrass prairie.

In Texas, ranchers were slow to accept fire as a method of range improvement. The hostility toward burning has lessened in recent years as the range and wildlife management department at Texas Tech University has spearheaded research in the beneficial use of fire. Its chairman, Henry Wright, is known among ranchers as "The Firebug." Many Texas ranchmen have begun controlled burning to stunt unwanted brush and remove dead vegetation that might impede new grass growth. Burning still has its critics and skeptics, but most Texas ranchmen and range scientists have accepted the concept.

Controlled burns are usually carried out from late January into early March, before greenup, on areas that rarely cover more than a thousand acres. First a firebreak is prepared by scalping the grass on the outer edges with a bulldozer. Then the rancher sets a backfire by burning the vegetation at the downwind edge of the pasture he plans to burn. By the time the main fire reaches the backfire area, no vegetation will be left to provide fuel.

The rancher should have water tanks, livestock sprayers, and plenty of help on hand. The humidity should be high and the wind low. When all of these conditions are met, he can climb into the back of a pickup and ignite the grass by dropping burning fuel from a driptorch. But on Thursday, March 10, none of the conditions was right.

By nightfall on the first day of the fire, the heavy smoke had an ominous red glow that could be seen as far away as Breckenridge, some thirty-five miles east. During the night the wind shifted. It began blowing out of the west, and suddenly the leading edge, which had been six miles wide, was now forty-five miles across. So strong was the wind that the smoke could be smelled in Fort Worth.

The most desperate stage of the battle came Friday. By that time nearly forty volunteer fire departments from all over the region—one from as far as Missouri City, near Houston—were scattered along the fire lines, joining volunteer townspeople, ranchmen, oilfield workers, and National Guard units from Abilene. How many people were involved could not be determined. The Red Cross fed breakfast to more than 500 in Albany, and that was by no means the entire force; many were fighting far from Albany.

The turning point came Friday with the arrival of Texas Forest Service personnel and their heavy equipment, portable command center, and expertise at fighting forest fires. They employed observation aircraft and directed the campaign with radios and walkie-talkies. Throughout the day plans were discussed for the evacuation of Albany and Moran. Flames reached within about three-quarters of a mile of some residences on the western end of Albany, the Shackelford County seat. The fire halted about three miles short of Moran, in the southeastern part of the county.

Saving livestock was a life-and-death matter for ranchmen, who threw open gates and cut fences to let as many as possible escape. Those who had time hurriedly rounded up pastures and drove or trucked animals away from advancing flames. But some cattle were overtaken by the fast moving conflagration, which at times raced along faster than a man could run. Some animals were trapped against fences. Others panicked and ran blindly back into the inferno.

Cattle losses could have been far worse. Figuring twenty acres per head, the burned area held 15,000 to possibly 20,000 cattle the day the fire started. Only 300 cattle were killed or so badly injured that they had to be destroyed. Even more cattle are expected to die of pneumonia caused by stress or by breathing smoke and ash. No human lives were lost, and only one house burned.

Though the fire was considered fairly well contained by Saturday, it was not officially declared under control until Monday, the fifth day. It had reached forty-five miles at its north-south axis, with one bulge twenty-six miles wide west to east.

Long before the fire was out, livestock owners had to find a way to feed all those hungry cattle. Some had lost only a portion of their range and were temporarily able to double up. Others had lost all or most of their grass. The Nail Ranch was estimated to have lost 40,000 acres. The Green family interests placed their loss at 60,000.

In much the same way the volunteers had flocked from near and far to fight the fires, strangers began hauling in hay and other feeds, asking for nothing but directions. Singly and in convoys, the trucks, flatbed trailers, and pickups loaded to the limit with feed began arriving in Albany. One feed convoy, put together in Weatherford, totaled fifteen trucks and trailers laden with hay and feed donated by farmers, ranchers, feed mills, and dealers. In West Texas, people may live 200 miles apart, but they're still neighbors.

Ranchman Paul Sims, who operates 5,800 acres southwest of Albany, lost about twenty cows out of a herd of 280. He also lost all his grass. Watching volunteers unload hay from a truck for his cattle he said, "This is the way it's always been done in this country. A man gets hurt, we plow his fields for him. Now we're hurt."

A federal emergency-aid package was announced a few days after the fire, but as is so often the case with such programs, there was less to it than met the eye. Its cost-share limit for rebuilding fences was $10,000 per operator, which might help an Iowa farmer with a 160-acre homestead but doesn't do much for a Texas rancher, since the replacement cost is at least $4,000 a mile. The fire destroyed between 350 and 400 miles of fence. A fifty-fifty cost share was available for emergency livestock feed, but rules require a recipient to deduct for any donated feed he had received.

The dark clouds of smoke had one tentative silver lining. Given a modest amount of spring rainfall, the range that was burned could actually be in better condition after a few months than it was before. The fire removed a heavy, choking cover of dry broomweed, the result of the previous year's bountiful rains, as well as moribund grass growth that had lost most of its feed value. Prickly pear, a particularly prevalent range pest in most of the burned area, was dealt a severe blow, with fifty to sixty percent killed. Ranchers could raise that kill to eighty or ninety percent by spraying the damaged pear with herbicide known as picloram. Mesquite, another range pest, suffered extensive topkill, though rootkill is probably minimal.

More than a century ago, before the Civil War, the first cattlemen brought their herds out to the Clear Fork of the Brazos in the area where Albany stands today. Indian pressure forced them to retreat. They came back after the Civil War, and few have retreated since. Despite their losses from the fire and their worries over how to rebuild, none of the current ranchers as yet has thrown up his hands and said he was quitting.

It has been exactly ten years since Shackelford County endured another natural disaster of major proportions, a flood triggered by rains of twenty-four inches and more within a twenty-four-hour period. An Albany ranchman declared that he had seen flood in 1978 and fire in 1988. He dreaded the earthquake of 1998.

Rancher Use of Range Resource

An address given to the Soil and Water Conservation Society,
San Angelo, Texas, July 9, 1992

IT HAS long irritated me that many of today's self-styled environmentalists and historical revisionists have declared our ranching
and farming forebears to have been despoilers of the land, driven by
greed. I contend that the pioneers made understandable mistakes in
resource management because they brought with them the beliefs
and techniques that had worked well in the places from which they
came. They had to learn the western land's limitations by trial and
error, which sometimes took generations. Their shortcomings resulted not from greed but from lack of experience with an environment that was new to them and more fragile than they could have
imagined.

≈

WHEN early cattlemen from the eastern part of Texas and from
states farther east edged out of the Cross Timbers onto the plains, it
looked to them like a grassland paradise without limit.

For the most part the Indians had been confined to reservations,
and most of the buffalo had been killed off for their hides. The
millions of big shaggies that had roamed the vast region and harvested
its grass resources for untold thousands of years had been removed,
and the ungrazed prairies carried a cover of grass that understandably
misled those early ranchmen into believing it was limitless, that it
would last forever.

Today, nearly a century and a quarter later, it is easy for us to
condemn our forebears as despoilers of the land. Indeed, some of
today's self-appointed environmental watchmen and revisionist his-
torians have done just that—usually from the vantage point of some
large city they have turned into an environmental nightmare.

But we must try to see the new country as *they* saw it. We must try to understand how they thought. To begin with, today's great love affair with nature is a relatively new concept. Thoreau in the mid-1800s, at his idyllic Walden Pond, was decades ahead of his time. This nation's original concepts were mostly brought to these shores by early European immigrants who had no such love affair with nature. On the contrary, in their time nature was to be regarded as an enemy, to be confronted, defeated and harnessed for use by "civilized" man.

The first immigrants looked at the deep, dark forests of the eastern seaboard, shuddered at their threat and set out to cut the forests down. Nature was not to be accepted as it was. Nature was to be changed for the service of man. As Katharine Hepburn's missionary character says in the film *The African Queen*, "Nature is what we are put on this earth to rise above."

We can argue today that they were wrong, but in the eyes of our forefathers it was manifest destiny that the white man go forth into the wilderness and change the face of a hostile earth.

Just as the first settlers feared the forest and felt a religious duty to change it, the first who faced the awesome openness of the Great Plains were cowed by it, and felt that God intended—even demanded—that it be tamed, be changed.

Stephen F. Austin, the father of Texas, was very much of this persuasion. Much of his writing that has survived speaks of the need to "civilize" the wilderness, to develop what he regarded as a wasteland and make it productive.

Most of those who first ventured onto the plains saw them as an obstacle to be challenged and crossed over so they could reach a better land on the other side. Not many Oregon Trail wagon people or Forty-Niners had any intention of remaining a day longer on the plains than they had to. To them it was the Great American Desert, infested by savages, fit only for the Indian and the great herds of buffalo.

Consider this description written in a mixture of awe and dread by Albert Pike 160 or so years ago:

"Imagine yourself . . . standing in a plain to which your eye can see no bounds. Not a tree, not a bush, not a shrub, not a tall weed lifts it head above the grandeur of the desert; not a stone is to be seen on its hard beaten surface; no undulation, no abruptness, no break to relieve the monotony; nothing . . . its sublimity arises from its unbounded extent, its barren monotony and desolation, its still, unmoved, calm, stern, almost self-confident grandeur, its strange power of deception, its want of echo, and in fine, its power of throwing a man back upon himself and giving him a feeling of lone helplessness, strangely mingled at the same time with a feeling of liberty and freedom from restraint."

The Texas plains—and most of the rest of western Texas—remained relatively unknown by white men until after the Civil War. Old maps usually show the high plains only as "desert." One I have seen in archives has a single word inscribed across the top of the entire region: "Comanches." It was a part of Texas for decades before Texans really knew much about it. Aside from the Indians, the first people to venture out upon the high plains in any numbers came from Mexican settlements of eastern and north central New Mexico. These were the *Comancheros*, bold traders who took their lives into their hands and began to trade with the Indians. They were not the bloody raiders of many movies and TV shows, but they did trade for stolen property, taken by the Indians from settlements farther south and east. From the Indians, and from their own adventurous explorations, the *Comancheros* learned where the scarce watering places were.

The history of Texas ranching goes back to Spanish cattlemen who began settling in a cautious way along the north side of the Rio Grande in the early 1700s. As Americans came into the region in the 1820s and afterward, beginning with Austin's colony, they were farmers first and stockmen second. The long distance from markets kept them from developing cattle herds on a massive scale. Sometimes the hides were worth more than the beef.

After the Mexican War, annexation of Texas into the United States helped spur growth in the cattle industry. Texas owners began driving herds east in the 1850s to markets in St. Louis, New Orleans,

Chicago. They did not realize it, but they were setting the stage and training a cadre for the great trail drives that would begin after the Civil War.

In West Texas, settlement had pushed almost to the present site of San Angelo in the 1850s. German immigrants began edging into the hill country in the 1840s and really opened immigration on a significant scale in the 1850s. They were farmers and small stockmen. Other ethnic groups such as the Polish, Swedish and Alsatians set up enclaves. Like the Germans, these were farmers first, stockmen second.

During the Civil War, John Chisum had a large ranch just east of present San Angelo at the confluence of the Concho and Colorado rivers. It was to Chisum's ranch that survivors of the disastrous Dove Creek battle took their wounded in the bitter early days of 1865. Ranching began along the three Conchos at least a decade before it did on the Texas high plains.

The destruction of the Texas plains buffalo began in the winter of 1873–1874 as hunters who had exterminated the Kansas herd worked their way down into Texas from Dodge City. The buffalo slaughter meant the end of the Indian as a barrier to the expansion of white settlement. Without the buffalo, the Indian had no choice but to surrender and go to the reservation. The slaughter also eliminated the buffalo as a competitor to cattle for the grass.

Colonel Ranald Mackenzie and his Fourth Cavalry troops, marching north from Fort Concho, broke up the last great Indian winter encampment in the Palo Duro Canyon in September 1874. In the spring of 1876, barely more than a year later, Charles Goodnight took a herd down from Colorado onto the Texas plains. That fall he moved his cattle into the Palo Duro Canyon. He and a couple of his men rode out beyond the point of the herd, stampeding thousands of buffalo ahead of them, clearing the way for a new era.

Over on the western side of the Panhandle, a number of Mexican sheepmen herded their flocks. Many were former *Comancheros* whose trade had been ruined by the military campaign against the Indians. Goodnight made a treaty with the sheepmen. In effect, they divided the Panhandle between them. But it was not long before other cattlemen drifted into the region, men not party to Goodnight's agreement, and the sheepmen retreated forever back into their New Mexico homelands. For practical purposes, the former buffalo range became a cattle range, and nothing else.

In theory, a range good for buffalo would be good for cattle. The old-time cattlemen firmly believed that, and they would have been right if the cattle had had the same ranging habits as the buffalo. It was in the buffalo's nature to drift with the seasons, with the grass. At times the major migrations involved huge herds running into thousands upon thousands. Between these major movements, however, they broke up most often into small herds and scattered.

Today, we are often misled by old-timers' recollections of grass that reached a horse's belly, and we get the impression it was always like that. Perhaps in some areas to the east it was, but in many accounts left by early travelers we find that these people traveled for days across prairies where little or no grass was to be found. The buffalo had grazed it off, or drouth had turned it to dust, or wildfire had burned it away.

Scouting reports at Fort Concho in the 1870s always described desperate grazing conditions and loss of large numbers of horses because there was not grass enough to sustain them on the long marches. In researching these reports I have come upon many which declared, "Rode so many miles in so many days, lost or abandoned so many horses . . . saw no Indians." As controversial conservationist Allan Savory observed, the buffalo often tended to graze heavily. They could and frequently did grub a place to the ground and churn the surface to dust before they moved on. But it might be months, even years, before they returned to that spot. The grass had time to recover. The white man has always believed in boundaries. This is mine, and that is yours, and we do not encroach on one another. Here I put my cattle, and here they will stay.

It did not work quite that easily in the early days, of course. Cattle drifted, especially when cold northers came howling down from the North Pole and swept across the open prairies that had nothing taller than Indian grass to slow their movement.

The way to keep cattle at home was to build fences. Farmers built them of poles or stones, but that was impractical for ranches because of their size. The invention of barbed wire provided the answer. The first range fences were often drift fences, meant to stop the southward movement of cattle during the great winter storms. What happened sometimes, though, was that cattle would pile up against these fences and suffocate or freeze, and other cattle would walk over them and move on.

The next step, then, was to build more fences. Usually the outside fence came first, enclosing the ranch property. If the rancher was big enough and bold enough, he might enclose some other people's property as well, and deny them its use.

Once the perimeter was fenced, the next step was to begin breaking the one big pasture into many smaller ones. Most of these were still huge by today's standards, but they were a big step forward in the estimation of the people at that time. Cattle could no longer drift with the seasons, as they had done at first, as the buffalo had always done. They did not eat the grass down, then move away and leave it to recover before they came again. They stayed, and all too often they stood over the grass plants and waited to pull off the green leaves as soon as they were long enough to wrap a tongue around. In time there was not enough grass left for the cattle that had been placed upon it.

I grew up on the McElroy Ranch near Crane. An El Paso packer, J. T. McElroy, had put the ranch together around the turn of the century. He sold it to a syndicate after oil discovery in 1926. A few years later he returned to see what changes had been made. One major change was the stocking rate. Lester S. Grant, the ranch manager, had cut cow numbers roughly in half.

After riding around over the pastures, McElroy told him: "I can see that you don't know anything about ranching. You have two grasses for every cow. I always had two cows for every grass."

Nature has a harsh but effective way of teaching her lessons. For many early cattlemen, school took up with the excruciatingly cruel winter of 1886–1887. That was the winter Montana cowboy Charles M. Russell painted the chilling little picture, "The Last of the Five Thousand," which started him toward fame as a western artist.

From the Canadian border to far down into Texas, carrying capacity of the ranges had been sadly overestimated by people whose experience farther east had not prepared them for the realities west of the 98th meridian. The grass was gone. Cattle died by the tens of thousands, and dreams died to match them.

This was a bitter lesson, and the survivors as a group learned it . . . some of it. But as a more benevolent season came and the grass returned, they again overestimated the forage. Not as drastically as before, perhaps, but still too much.

Drouths came periodically, and though it was probably not obvious to most observers at the time, each left the land poorer than it had been before. The deterioration was slow enough that many who lived with it did not see it, or if they saw it they thought it was temporary. They blamed it on having received less rainfall than last year.

White men brought other changes to the range besides an overabundance of livestock. They dreaded range fires and went to Herculean lengths when necessary to put them out. A fire could arouse a defense mechanism as strong as the Comanches ever had. But fire had been one of nature's tools for clearing the old dead grass and keeping brush seedlings under control. The old-timers did not know that the grassland savannahs had developed under a natural fire ecology. They fought fire, and their descendants still do.

A number of old-timers have told me that in retrospect they blame extermination of the prairie dog as much as any other single factor for the great spread of mesquite. Their reasoning, which came as hindsight rather than foresight, has been that the prairie dog kept most mesquite seedlings from ever becoming trees. They have also theorized that the huge prairie-dog towns with their subterranean networks of burrows were a great absorber of rainfall, carrying water down far beyond the sun's heat, beyond evaporation.

Many of the cattle driven up to stock the first ranches in West Texas and on the plains came from brush country to the south. It is well known that nothing prepares a mesquite seed better for germination than passage through a cow's digestive tract.

When old Ab Blocker burned the first XIT brand on the first cow brute just up from South Texas, *her* first reaction was probably to plant a mesquite, then and there.

When I began preparing this paper on early ranchmen's use of the range resource, my first plan was to go back to many good first-person reminiscences of early cattlemen, and to the several excellent cowman biographies and ranch histories by J. Evetts Haley, J. Frank Dobie, W. C. Holden and others.

The project did not turn out as I expected. I found a great deal of history about the adventures of men, the handling of cattle, the business side of early ranching. I found relatively little written about the range as a resource. This probably says something about those times and the men who lived through them. They took the range for granted. It was passive, a gift from the Almighty, a gift that at first seemed to have little practical limit.

The range as a resource was seldom addressed at any length except in a negative sense—in the times when drouth came and there *was* no resource. Then it was mentioned in terms of its effect upon men and cattle, not in terms of a resource having a value in and of itself.

Most of the early cattlemen—just as had been the case with early farmers—came from areas farther east where they were used to more generous rainfall. When they came west they brought with them the concepts and practices that had served them in that other land. They held to them until experience—the most unforgiving of all teachers—showed them they had to adapt to a different country and different ways.

I have referred mostly to cattle. The early sheepmen always *herded* sheep, moving them with the grass and water. Actually, though sheep carried a reputation for ruining the range, the truth is that these husbandry practices were more beneficial to the range than continuous grazing by cattle. So long as there was fresh feed, a *good* herder took his flock to it. He did not willingly take his sheep back too quickly where they had already grazed. My cattle-raising forebears would disown me for saying this, but the early sheepmen as a group took better care of the range.

Robert Maudslay was an Englishman who came to West Texas in 1882 and stayed the rest of his life. Even in his old age, when sheep were turned loose to range free within net fences, he still firmly believed in seeing his sheep from their own level, afoot. He *walked* his pastures.

As a young man he went into the Big Lake country. The sheepmen who ranged their flocks there soon informally parceled out their individual claims and kept their flocks within those unmarked boundaries. Later they leased or bought the land to protect their grazing rights.

Maudslay had a fine contempt for the "drifter" sheepmen who trespassed on others' land, camping wherever they found the grass and water good, no matter who it belonged to. Usually if challenged they had some excuse for not moving on.

The late Mark Nasworthy of San Angelo told me that as a boy he saw such people carrying a broken wheel tied up under the wagonbed. When they found a likely camp, they removed a good wheel and hid it. They put the broken wheel out where it could be seen. When they had grazed off all the grass, the broken wheel would mysteriously mend itself, and they would be on their way to live off someone else's land.

Not all herders were good shepherds or good range men, by any means, and the irresponsible might leave a place "sheeped out." But usually the same things happened to them that happened to cattlemen who grossly overstocked their ranges. Nature caught up with them.

Robert Maudslay in later years wrote about a twenty-month drouth which spanned 1892–1893. It happened to coincide with the great money panic of 1893 and the lifting of tariff barriers against imported wool. The result was devastation for sheepmen. His word picture of the drouth is as good a one—and as sad a one—as you'll find:

"It had rained so much in the fall of 1891 that we were sure the bottom had fallen out of the sky. And we must have been right, because after that there wasn't any rain left in it for almost two years, except a little spot on the Plains two miles square. Every day a hot, glaring, cloudless sky seemed to mock the dreams we'd had. Around us, as far as we could see, was dust.

"What little vegetation there was left was covered with layers of dust so that it took on the color of the parched earth around it. It was a burnt world, dull brown and gray in spots and blinding white in others. There was no green in it. If there was feed to buy, it wasn't for us. . . . Money was hard to get and banks were calling in their loans. We cut out about 2,500 head of sheep and sold them for a dollar apiece, but this money was soon swallowed up in debts and running expenses. . . .

"Instead of raising lambs we had to kill them as they came. The ewe mothers, in fact, realizing their inability to raise them, generally went off and left them. . . . Did you ever look at a hot yellow sky every day for months and see nothing in it but buzzards? Not a cloud, not even the promise of a cloud, and the sheep you'd thought you were going to make a fortune on dragging around in front of you bleating weakly at you for grass, and finally, too weak even to bleat, just lying down by you and dying—dying by the hundreds. Every day more dead sheep, and every day another hot yellow sky."

Maudslay took a wagon and went to San Angelo to see what he could do about a fresh start. His brother Harry stayed behind . . . and put a bullet in his brain.

It is easy for us, using a century of hindsight built up at the expense of others, to criticize our forebears for their misunderstanding of the range and its proper use. Most were doing the best they could with the knowledge they had at the time. They were in a new land they did not fully understand. A hundred years or so later, we still do not fully understand it. We are still casting about for the proper way to use the range without depleting it as a resource. We have tried the Merrill four-pasture rotation system, the HILF system, short-duration and the Savory method. For every answer, we find another question.

Today's range managers are more knowledgeable than their forebears. In general, ranges across the West today are in better condition than at any time in this century. But let's don't be hard on Granddad. Most of what we know, we learned at *his* expense.

Let's make the best of that painful investment, and not let our descendants have to say of us what some of us have unjustifiably said about our forefathers.

59

Plows and Cows

Old-time 'Sheep Rustler' Respected, Except By Owners of Cow Outfits

Livestock Weekly, June 12, 1968

PHILIP THOMPSON loved to talk, and I loved to listen. He remembered the days when sheep were still drifted under herd across West Texas, a practice that died out once fencing of privately owned land became prevalent. Arthur G. Anderson, of whom he speaks, was said to be the state's largest sheep owner in his time. Once, when Anderson was drifting his flocks in the Davis Mountain country, cattlemen had him arrested and imprisoned in a dry well in Fort Davis. He never forgave them. It was said that years later, mention of the incident would still arouse him to anger. Though West Texas cattlemen initially ridiculed sheepmen, most eventually recognized that sheep were the better investment most of the time. If their vegetation was suitable, they began raising sheep themselves. It was cattle for respectability and sheep for a living.

≈

SAN ANGELO Philip Thompson, eighty-four, of San Angelo, believes he's probably the last old-time West Texas sheep rustler still alive.

The word "rustler" isn't as bad as it may sound. To earlier generations a sheep rustler, in Thompson's words, was a man who could "count sheep and talk Mexican." He would be in charge of several flocks of sheep and their herders.

Thompson spent eight years working for Arthur G. Anderson, pioneer Texas sheepman who established the big Hat A ranch in southern Pecos County. Those were drouth years, 1905 to 1912, and he put in a great deal of his time ranging sheep from one part of West Texas to another, wherever Anderson could find grass.

Thompson recalls those early days in detail and enjoys telling about them. He is proud of being, as he says, "the first baby born in Abilene," in 1884, three years after the railroad briefly terminated construction there and decided it was a good place to start a town. It was out on open prairie. The only feed and water was that which the railroad hauled on its cars. The first building of any account was the big Texas & Pacific Railroad Hotel, which the company built so its employees would have a place to live. Thompson's father was a railroad bookkeeper, and Philip was born in the hotel.

Upon coming of age, Thompson worked first in a bank but decided he wanted to become a rancher . . . a sheep rancher at that. He went to an old friend, Col. J.H. (Jim) Parramore, pioneer Abilene cattleman, and asked him to help him get a start in sheep. The old cowman gravely chewed his tobacco awhile, told Thompson he had no use either for sheep or sheepmen, and advised him to go see Arthur G. Anderson, who had made his start ranching in neighboring Mitchell County. Parramore didn't care for Anderson's sheep but had great respect for the man.

Anderson put Thompson to work first as a bookkeeper at the Hat A headquarters. After a year Thompson decided he knew plenty about bookkeeping but little about sheep and asked to be allowed to go out as a herder.

Though Anderson was no relation, Thompson still speaks of him as "Uncle Arthur."

"Uncle Arthur had 200 sections down there in two pastures, 100 sections apiece. During that time (that Thompson rustled for him) it never did rain. Uncle Arthur had to get out and rustle grass. He had 30,000 sheep, 200 saddle horses, 3,000 cows. And he raised stock horses during that time . . . had lots of stallions and 300 mares."

The first year on the road, Thompson had charge of 6,000 sheep, trailing them to grass Anderson had found west of San Angelo, not far from Knickerbocker. He had a cook, a wagon man and three herders. Each morning he and the wagon man would spend about an hour counting the sheep off into three flocks of about 2,000 each.

"It took me months to make these trips, going about six, eight or ten miles a day with 6,000 sheep. You can't specify how many miles they'll go in a day; it takes different times. If it was a brush country, they'd stop and graze on brush. If it was a grass country, they'd graze a-walking."

Sheep always moved better drifting east than drifting west. They disliked going into the afternoon sun, so they would move and graze at oblique angles to it, zigzagging back and forth. A trail drive west always took days longer than the same mileage east.

By that time most of the Texas ranchland was taken up, though fences were still not numerous enough to be a great problem. When the flock came to a barbed wire fence, the rustler would ride ahead and unstaple the wires from the posts for a considerable distance, raising the wires so the sheep could pass under. If there was a gate within reach, the wagon would go to it. If not, the wires would be held to the ground to allow it to pass over. After the flocks passed, the fence would be stapled back.

Drifting flocks of sheep were sometimes an annoyance to ranchmen unless prior arrangements had been made. Thompson had no real trouble in his days of trailing, though he recalls several instances of ruffled feelings. Once after he had put a flock across at Horsehead Crossing on the Pecos, a cowman rode up accompanied by several cowboys, all of them carrying rifles. In a loud voice he demanded to know whose sheep these were. Thompson told him.

"Well, get them out of here. This is my ranch; I don't want them here."

Thompson was a small man, and those Winchesters looked awfully large. He replied that the sheep were on their way off and would clear the range in due time. That wasn't fast enough for the rancher. "Let's help him, boys," he said. He and the cowboys started firing their rifles into the air, figuring the sheep would stampede like cattle.

They didn't. Instead of running away, they turned inward and ran together in a knot. The cowboys shouted and fired their rifles for upwards of an hour without budging the sheep. They finally rode off frustrated and left sheepherding to the sheepherders.

Another time, one of the few instances Thompson ever saw Anderson angry, a cowman on a ranch west of Pecos—Thompson still calls it Pecos City, as many old-timers do—changed Thompson's route to keep him from passing through a pasture where he was feeding cattle. Anderson was trying to catch up to Thompson's flock in a buggy, riding far into the night, following the sheep tracks. In the darkness he missed the place where the flock was turned around the cow pasture.

Next day, tired and cross, he caught up to the flock as it was nooning. The cowman was there and explained the situation, but a long night's searching in a buggy had been too much, and Anderson gave vent to the little profanity he ever allowed himself to use: "By jings, dammit!"

On that trip Thompson got his introduction to Pecos City water. Anderson brought another rustler to relieve him so he could go to Abilene and spend Christmas with his family. "I had been on the road three months and hadn't had a bath or a shave during that time," Thompson recalls. "I got in the bathtub, then in the barber chair. The barber took the comb to my whiskers."

He made a couple of stabs at it, then asked if Thompson had washed his face and head in the bathwater. Thompson had. Belatedly the barber told him the water was too hard for that purpose and charged him a dime a quart for the three quarts of hauled-in spring water it took to wash his hair and beard over again.

At lambing time the ranch needed extra help, so Thompson would go to Del Rio to find about fifty Mexicans. "I'd get with a Mexican commission man there and give him a dollar a head to get herders for me. That was before there was a bridge across the Rio Grande at Del Rio. The little town across there (now Ciudad Acuña) was named Las Vacas, which meant 'the cows.' They had a raft, an iron post on each side of the river and a wire cable across. We'd drive the horse and buggy onto the raft, and the Mexicans would skim it across the river 300 feet."

Thompson and the commission man would make all the cantinas

and tell the men interested to meet them the next day across in San Felipe, which was the Mexican name for Del Rio. Out of the 250–300 men, Thompson would pick fifty who looked as if they would do. He was paying eighteen dollars a month and usually had to advance a man up to a month's wages to get him.

"I'd go to the bank and get a thousand dollars worth of silver and currency. I'd put it in two pockets and walk about three blocks down to the store, looking like a milk cow with those bags hanging out."

The Mexicans would take the advance money back across the river and leave most of it for their families to live on. "They would stay with us. In seven years of going to get them, I never lost a Mexican by advancing them money."

He would take the men by train to Sanderson. There a freight wagon would be waiting to haul their bedding. Thompson and the men would walk beside the wagon the 100 miles or so to the ranch.

Each morning as the flock drifted from the bedground to graze, those ewes which had lambed during the night would be left there in place. No attempt would be made to move them for a week or so until the lambs were big enough to follow. Then they would be gently thrown into *manadas* of about 1,000 each. A seventy percent lamb crop under herd was considered good.

"The 100-percent lamb crops are made in the drugstore, not on the range," Thompson comments.

Usually during lambing, and again during shearing, a Mexican merchant would come along in a hack drawn by two burros. His merchandise would include tobacco and smoking supplies, shirts, shoes, sombreros and anywhere from two to four pretty Mexican girls. Whatever advance money the men had left usually went quickly, and the ranch would have to advance them some more on their wages.

The vehicle that brought the girls was known to the herders as the "honey wagon."

Anderson bred 15,000 ewes every fall. Much of the time he had an additional 15,000 dry sheep. There was no market for lambs in those days. Wethers were kept until they were up to three or four years old. Finally, some fall, it would rain, and the next spring the weed crop would fatten the dry sheep. Then it was time to ship everything on the place except for the ewe flock.

Before Joe Kerr built a warehouse in Sanderson, the wool had to be shipped to Boston for sale. One year, Thompson recalls, Anderson shipped about 160,000 pounds of wool by boat out of Houston. Coming out of bone-dry Pecos County, it picked up $2,500 worth of extra weight in moisture absorbed from the sea air.

It took Anderson about five years to get rid of sheep scab. "If he could ever have gotten all his sheep together," Thompson says, "he could have killed it in two or three dippings. But he had so many sheep, sometimes a herder would lose sheep that had scab, and they would get in a clean herd and cause the herd to get scab. We would mix a barrel of lime, two barrels of sulphur, and we'd boil that all night. We'd work all day and boil dip all night. We rustlers got twenty-five dollars a month, day and night."

When Anderson sold out, he gave Thompson permission to use his sheep brand and his distinctive nose mark, which was obtained by cutting a slit across the bridge of the lamb's nose at marking time. When it healed, it would leave a raised roll of skin that could be seen from a distance and identify the sheep.

Using the wages and the knowledge he had earned from Arthur Anderson, Thompson went into sheep ranching for himself after 1912. He ranched on leased country mostly, including one place in Sterling County which he leased thirty-two years from E.D. Parramore and heirs. In 1951 he bought a ranch twenty miles northwest of Roswell, New Mexico, selling it ten years later to Floyd Childress, Roswell banker.

It took him a long time to decide to quit. He felt, perhaps, like his mentor Arthur Anderson, who once turned down an offer to sell his Hat A ranch for a good price. "I don't want to sell it," Anderson said. "I want to keep it till I get twenty-five cents for my wool."

Thompson doesn't believe Anderson ever saw wool reach twenty-five cents.

Leo Richardson Started Small, Worked Hard And Built Solid

Livestock Weekly, April 18, 1974

LEO RICHARDSON was among the most influential men in the Texas sheep industry in his heyday, the 1930s, and well into the 1970s. Operating along the Pecos River on some of the most unforgiving rangeland Texas offers, he had one of the most sought-after flocks of registered and purebred Rambouillet sheep, built up through years of struggle and personal sacrifice. His experience went back to the days when Texas sheepmen still kept their flocks under herd. Together, he and Philip Thompson told me more about early sheep operations than anyone else I knew. He was one of the models I used in creating the character of Charlie Flagg in my novel, *The Time It Never Rained*. I treasure his memory.

≈

IRAAN   Leo Richardson of Iraan is known far and wide for his registered sheep flock and his leadership in the Texas sheep industry.

Not so well known is the slow, hard way he started, trapping coons and ringtails for the pelts and saving his ranchhand wages for more than fifteen years to buy sheep; trading his mutton lambs for ewe lambs year after year to let his flock increase; and finally cutting loose in the depth of the Depression in 1931 with the 1,300 head he had built up.

Even before he started his sheep flock, he had built up a small herd of Angora goats out of his ranch wages, only to lose three years of work in a single cold rainy spell.

Richardson, now seventy-eight, pulled out on his own at about seventeen. Born at Junction, he first worked for the Schreiner family on ranches between Junction and Rocksprings and in the Kerrville area. He saved his wages more than three years to buy a little bunch of Angora goats. A long wet spell set in just after April shearing, and they froze down even under a shed.

Determined to start over, he drifted west to Sonora. He heard that Roy Hudspeth needed a hand but was warned that Hudspeth was a demanding man to work for. Hudspeth himself even warned Leo of that. But Leo needed a job, and he figured Hudspeth needed a hand who wasn't afraid of work.

One of the rules of the Hudspeth ranch was that the small varmints belonged to the men who worked there. As an adjunct to his ranch work, therefore, Richardson started trapping and skinning, saving not only part of his salary but all of the pelt money. By the end of three years he had saved enough to buy a small flock of sheep. There was no place on the Hudspeth ranch to keep them, however, so he went to work for Massie West at Ozona. West let him run his Rambouillet sheep in the horse trap. He spent two years on the West ranch, then moved over to Frank Friend's, also near Ozona, and spent four years.

His deal with Friend was that he could have the use of a certain pasture plus his wages. And he never let up on the trapping. "A ringtail," he says, "just didn't stand much chance."

By that time the big varmints such as coyotes and bobcats had been well cleaned out of that country, and the land was sheep-fenced.

Richardson never sold any of his sheep. Each fall he traded his mutton lambs to Friend for ewe lambs, keeping all the increase.

By 1931 he had enough sheep to go out on his own. He leased thirteen sections of Ira Yates' land north of Iraan, taking with him 800 bred ewes and pairs, and 500 yearling ewes.

He and Mrs. Richardson by then had been married almost ten years. She had been teaching school at Copperas in Kimble County. They had two sons, Leonard and Rod. Rod still ranches in partnership with his parents, but Leonard died in 1952.

In the earliest years, Leo and Mrs. Richardson did most of the work themselves, occasionally hiring temporary extra help for special times such as marking or shearing.

Since he came to Iraan he has ranched entirely on his own, although for awhile he held a part-time job taking care of some of Ira Yates' pasture and town lot leases at thirty dollars a month. He began putting that thirty dollars a month into registered Rambouillet sheep. His first were bought from Ozona breeders Wilse Owens and Vic Pierce, and Utah breeder John K. Madsen.

Over the years he gradually bred out and phased out his original grade sheep. Today he runs about 1,500 registered ewes plus a large commercial flock which is of the same blood, and in his estimation, equal in quality to the registered ewes. The size of the operation and some of the pastures dictates that many ewes be group-bred to several bucks, so that the specific sire of an individual lamb cannot be known. The bloodlines, however, are the same as in the papered sheep.

He also gradually increased his lease holdings and bought a couple of tracts, so that he now operates about 100 sections. Rod, besides the family partnership, has deeded land and university leases of his own.

Leo has spent most of his career ranching in and around an oilfield, none of it his, so he pretty well knows the ropes. The principal problem is traffic, particularly at lambing time. For this reason he alway tries to save back some pastures in which there is little or no activity, using these through the lambing season. Of course he and the oil companies don't always check signals, so they may start drilling about the time the ewes start lambing. That happened this year, an effect of the energy crisis.

The sheep industry has undergone drastic changes in the sixty-one years Richardson has followed it. His first job with the Schreiners was as a "rustler," overseeing three Mexican herders and their three flocks of sheep. He would count a flock a day, getting around to counting each individual flock every third day. If any sheep were missing it was up to him to round them up and get them back to the flock, or to account for them at least.

"Few people remember anymore how we counted sheep in flocks in those days," he says. The herders would move the flock out to an open area and set up two sticks about eight to ten feet apart. The sheep would be moved between those two sticks at a pace that allowed them to be counted. Through conditioning, the sheep knew to go between the sticks and not around them.

Herders weren't allowed to keep dogs, which were considered too hard on the sheep.

A wagon man kept the herder in grub and moved his camp for him, on average about once every two weeks. The West Texas herders slept mainly in tents, rather than the more elaborate wagons used in the mountain country. Sometimes it was not even a tent; it might be no more than a wagon sheet and a brush windbreak.

At lambing time two flocks would be thrown together, two herders tending one. Outside men would pick up the ewes with fresh baby lambs and separate them from the ewes still to lamb. As lambs got to be about three days old and hardy enough to travel, they and their mothers would be thrown into small bunches.

It took lots of extra help at lambing time, usually five or six men for 1,500–2,000 ewes. Ninety percent of those used in West Texas were Mexicans. Lambing would be completed in about two months, the extra help turned loose and the flocks divided back into their normal size.

Herding had about died out in far West Texas when Richardson moved to Iraan; it had already phased out in the Hill Country, where rough terrain and heavy brush made herding more difficult.

Back in the herding days, shearing was done by hand. Leo recalls that he was about fifteen when he saw his first shearing machine. It was hand-cranked, one crank to each drop, one cranker to each shearer.

Some people might be surprised at his judgment that the Iraan ranch country is better today than when he first saw it. He credits this to lessons learned in brush control and proper grazing. He remembers when ranchmen in that area considered 125–150 sheep per section to be a proper stocking rate. By the end of the 1950s drouth the rate had dropped to about fifty. Today a more common rate is about eighty per section.

Leo and Rod have done extensive rootplowing and reseeding in overflow and flat areas of their country where it seemed to offer the most promise.

In recent years they have not run any cattle, preferring to keep a straight sheep operation. In other years they used to run commercial Herefords, and a few years ago they had about 250 Brangus cows.

Leo was one of the several Rambouillet breeders responsible for instituting the ram performance test at Sonora more than twenty-five years ago. He had shown sheep for ten years, boxing up 1,200 show ribbons in that time. But he and a number of other breeders worried that the show ring wasn't providing real answers to many of their breeding problems. The program was set up under supervision of the late Wallace Dameron and more or less played by ear at first. But Richardson feels that it has had a far-reaching effect upon the breed, producing a bigger and smoother sheep and opening up the faces without taking away from the wool clip.

That the Richardsons are popular people is attested to by the fact that when they had open house for their fiftieth wedding anniversary in October 1972, and Mrs. Richardson feared that nobody would show up, 240 couples signed their guest book on one Sunday afternoon.

A Few Chuckwagons Still Operate,
But It's a Far Cry from Old Days

Livestock Weekly, July 8, 1971

WHEN I was a very small boy, the McElroy Ranch still used a traditional team-drawn chuckwagon. Soon after Dad became foreman he started putting the chuckbox on the back of a flatbed truck, which was faster and more mobile. The food was still basically the same, and the cowboys slept at the wagon during the ranch's two roundups each year. Sometime in the 1950s Dad updated the chuckwagon for the last time, mounting the chuckbox on a trailer that could be pulled behind a pickup. An extra-large water barrel was a permanent part of the trailer, enabling camp to be made wherever it was needed without concern over the availability of drinkable water at the site. Today the old-time chuckwagon is being revived for show purposes, at least, at various chuckwagon cookoff contests around the country.

≈

STAMFORD   Don't mourn too long for the old-time chuckwagon, says wagon cook Richard Bolt of the Pitchfork Ranch, Guthrie; he believes the modern version is better.

Bolt, to be fifty-nine in September, could hardly be called an old-timer. Yet he has been helping and cooking around ranch wagons off and on for almost fifty years, between regular cowboy jobs and with fourteen years out while he served as a Baptist minister.

His father, W. J. "Bo" Bolt, who died when Richard was twelve, was a wagon cook before him. Much of what Richard knows about the chuckbox culinary art was learned while he was chopping wood, washing dishes and peeling spuds for his father in various cow camps. When a heart attack knocked him out of the pulpit and the doctors told him to get back to the out-of-doors, he returned to the trade he had learned in an earlier time.

The Pitchfork wagon was one of the only three genuine old-time mule-drawn rigs set up here during the traditional Cowboy Reunion last week. The others were from the neighboring 6666 and from the Swenson Land & Cattle Co. Only the Pitchfork and the 6666 actually use their wagons outside much anymore.

Visiting the wagons like a sailor renting a boat on a holiday was Waggoner Ranch cook Jerry Allen, sixty-three, of Vernon. He didn't bring the Waggoner wagon, partly because it isn't really a wagon anymore; it's a big long truck with a non-traditional type of chuckbox and with sideboards that let down to make long tables.

Allen doesn't view the modern trends in quite the same light as Bolt does; he is a traditionalist. "The sideboards are strictly for the dudes," he declares. "If I catch a cowboy eating off of them, that's a dishwashing job." He still looks back with some fondness on the days when cowboys thrived on salt pork, beans, sourdough bread and, if they were lucky, some raisins.

"You know what these Waggoner cowboys are doing now?" He demanded. "They're keeping ice and Kool-Aid at the wagon. Kool-Aid! Next thing you know they'll be wanting sweet milk."

Allen estimates that he has cooked a total of about fifteen years, not counting straight cowboy jobs sandwiched in between. He has cooked at various times for the Pitchfork, the Sixes and for the X Ranch at Kent. He says he differs from the normal old-time wagon cook in one important particular: "Most wagon cooks were always cranky with the boys. I'm not cranky. My only fault is that I lie to them. I still ride more rough horses than anybody—under the tent flap."

Allen and Bolt put their heads together and couldn't think of more than three big ranches that normally use a wagon any substantial time anymore: Pitchfork, the Sixes and Waggoners. The Waggoner wagon stays out virtually the year around, coming in for about two weeks around July Fourth.

By contrast, Bolt's Pitchfork wagon is used about two months in the spring and two in the fall. The rest of the year he cowboys for the outfit.

Even the Pitchfork wagon isn't "out" in the traditional sense. Most of the time it stays firmly anchored at the headquarters colt barn, occasionally being moved to one of the outlying batch camps. Cowboys and horses are hauled out to the work each morning and hauled in at night. Even during roundup, the cowboys get to sleep in their own beds at home most nights. Bolt frequently hauls the noon meal to them in a pickup.

Whatever violence this might do to the romance of the old West, Bolt spends no time mourning.

"People always talk about the good old days," he says. "I was there, and I remember them too well to want to go back."

He says the big ranches feed their hands much better today than they used to; good help is hard to find. The menu is broader and better balanced. "Cowboys don't put up with the stomach trouble they used to have."

He can remember when a crew killed a beef every few days, wrapping the quarters in tarps and hanging them off the side of the wagon. Sometimes toward the end the beef wasn't as good as it might have been.

Now the Pitchfork feeds its own beeves, sends them to a custom slaughterer to be cut, wrapped and frozen, and keeps the beef in a big walk-in freezer, to which Bolt can go each day to pick up what he needs.

Bolt is one of a few ranch cooks who still makes traditional sourdough biscuits three times a day. He says most make yeast bread or use what he terms "zip-open" biscuits.

His recipe is one he learned helping his father around the wagon when he was a boy. He never did put it on paper, however, until a while back when the Marlboro cigarette people used him as the central figure in a chuckwagon cookbook they put out as an advertising piece. Reducing it to writing was something of a chore. "I never did actually measure anything," he says. "I just poured till my conscience said quit." And he also made it up in big quantities for lots of men. It took Bolt and his wife quite a while to whittle it down to family size.

His recipe for sourdough biscuits calls for two cups all-purpose flour, one tablespoon sugar, one tablespoon baking powder, three-fourths teaspoon salt, two cups sourdough starter and two to three tablespoons softened lard or butter.

Sift flour, sugar, baking powder and salt into large bowl; pour in starter. Mix to make firm dough. Grease twelve-inch iron skillet with lard. Pinch off balls the size of walnuts. Place in pan. Set biscuits in a warm place ten to fifteen minutes. Bake in 400 degree oven twenty-five to thirty minutes.

The sourdough starter is made in a large crock, at least three quarts. Soften a package of active dry yeast in a quart of lukewarm water. Add two tablespoons sugar and four cups sifted flour and beat to mix. Cover, let it rise until light and slightly aged, twenty-four to forty-eight hours. Starter may be kept in refrigerator seven to ten days without attention, then should be stirred and equal amounts of flour and water added. To keep starter, pour off amount needed for recipe, then add flour and water to remainder. Amount will depend on amount of starter left.

The Marlboro cookbook—actually a pamphlet made up of full-color ranch photographs—is being distributed free in tobacco shops around the country and was an insert in a recent issue of *Life*. Since it appeared, Bolt has been receiving letters from all over the country, including one proposal of marriage. He says he tried to get Mrs. Bolt to answer that one for him, but she wouldn't.

Unlike many a traditionalist, Bolt does not put down the modern cowboy. Though today's cowpuncher does not have to put in the long hours and endure many of the hardships of his father and grandfather, Bolt believes he gets the job done quicker and with considerably more efficiency, thanks to mechanization.

"Forty or fifty years ago, when this was still an open country without the brush we have today, it would take twenty to thirty men to do the job that eight or nine can do now, even with the brush."

Plowing Up Treeless Prairie,
Schwartz Found Burned Stumps

Livestock Weekly, June 26, 1975

OTTO SCHWARTZ was a good example of the frugal, hard-working farmers who broke out open pastureland on Lipan Flat east of San Angelo and put it into crops in the 1920s. He became a friend of mine during the years I worked as an agricultural writer for the *San Angelo Standard-Times*, helping educate me about farming as it was done by the German- and Czech-heritage plowmen of that era. Though he is gone, his descendants still farm the land he put together. They do it with a love for the soil and a strong conservationist ethic bred to the bone, not simply tacked on because it seems the politically correct thing to do.

≈

SAN ANGELO   When Otto Schwartz first started breaking out farmland on Lipan Flat south and east of San Angelo in 1923, it was mostly open rangeland, hardly a mesquite anywhere in sight. Yet, every so often his plow would bump against an unseen stump, sometimes a big one, invariably burned.

In later years, that which didn't go into farmland grew up so heavily in mesquite that it was sometimes hard to walk through. He remembered those burned stumps. It has been his contention— shared by many of his generation—that when settlement stopped the prairie fires, it set the stage for mesquite to be planted by fenced-in cattle.

Though always first and foremost a farmer, Schwartz kept a cow herd for many years and considered it a vital part of his operation. He had to sell his cattle in 1964 after a heart attack forced him to cut down on work. There are few cattle on "the Flat" today. You can drive for miles along farm roads in the area and seldom see a fence.

"These boys with their big six-row equipment have taken all the fences out," Schwartz says. "They need half an acre to turn around in."

He regards this as a necessity of mechanized times, but he believes it has contributed to production problems. One function of his cattle—and those of other farmers—was to salvage growth which would otherwise be wasted. It was always customary to turn cattle in on cottonfields to glean what the hand-pickers had left.

"As long as we grazed those fields, we never had any problem with boll weevils or the pink bollworm," he declares. Now these pests have a firm hold and must be fought every year.

Use of chemical defoliants for mechanical cotton harvesting has made it impossible to graze cotton anyway; the defoliants are usually poisonous.

At seventy-four, Schwartz has turned almost all his land over to his three sons and two daughters, keeping only a very small tract near the house to "piddle on." He still likes to work as much as his health will allow; he has always been a hard worker.

He came to the San Angelo area to live in 1923—having seen it in 1919 and liked it—and went to work building houses and barns for W.H. Wilde for a dollar and a half a day and dinner. Very little of the flat had yet been broken out for farming. Wilde offered to furnish a tractor, fuel and seed to Schwartz and a cousin, Joe Berger, if they would farm for him on halves. This was fine, except that it cut out the carpenter salary. They worked five days a week on the Wilde land, then worked Saturdays and Sundays for other people on a cash basis so they could buy enough to eat. They lived four months in a cellar they had dug. Otto says, "There were more rattlesnakes in it than there were of us."

They made a couple of crops, but the picking was still thin. One day, desperately needing some tiding-over money, he went to a San Angelo bank to try to borrow fifty dollars. He was wearing work clothes, the only kind he had. He sat on a bench, waiting while better dressed people kept going ahead of him to visit with the banker. Finally about noon, when he was the only one still there, the banker beckoned him over and asked what he needed. Schwartz told him.

"What have you for security?" the banker asked. Schwartz didn't know what security was. The banker explained it meant farm implements, anything tangible. Schwartz didn't even have a cotton hoe he could rightly say was his. He had ten cents in his pocket, and at that he was a dime better off than his cousin.

The banker said he couldn't help him. Schwartz walked out bitterly disappointed, not sure how he would survive. He swore to himself that unless it came to dire necessity he would never borrow a dollar from any bank, anywhere.

He never has. Though he bought land nine times in his life and eventually built up more than 1,100 acres of the best farming land in the San Angelo area, he never did so until he had the cash in hand to pay for it.

Things were still tough when he was married January 6, 1926, to a Moulton girl he had known for five years. "I brought her home," he says, "and she asked me where the bed was. I pointed to a mattress on the floor. She asked me where the chairs were, and I pointed to some boards nailed across the top of wooden kegs."

But he managed to buy her a little furniture out of the crop he had just made, and bought some horses and implements as well. Owning his own equipment, he was able to start farming on better shares, getting two-thirds of the feed and three-fourths of the cotton instead of the fifty-fifty split he had taken before.

He was able to buy his first land, 180 acres, in the fall of 1927. After that it was a gradual climb upward.

Schwartz has vivid memories of the area as it was when he first saw it. When he came out to Runnels County in 1919 to visit relatives, he saw bleached buffalo skulls and bones at the bottom of bluffs on Pony Creek near Ballinger. Hide hunters had run buffalo over the

81

bluffs in the 1870s, a cheap method of getting them in large numbers.

Lipan Flat, once a huge prairie dog town, still had a scattering of prairie dogs when he went to it in 1923, though the majority had been poisoned out several years earlier under Texas law. Only a relatively few tracts of land had been broken out for farming; the influx of German and Czech farmers who eventually put that whole area under cultivation was just beginning. Earlier settlers had had little luck raising even Johnson grass and didn't think the land was suitable for cotton or maize. For the last forty or fifty years those have been its principal cash crops.

Otto Schwartz is keenly aware of his heritage, not only the pioneer spirit in general but the story of his own ancestors and their struggles. Other family members call on him for information about history; he has a keen memory for names and dates. His forebears came from that part of Czechoslovakia known as the Sudetenland, although at the time it was still part of Austria-Hungary, so that he considers his background Austrian.

His maternal grandfather, Karl Loika, landed in the U.S. on December 8, 1873, accompanied by his wife and his aged father, and set out by train for Schulenburg, Texas, where relatives lived. He was told the railroad ended at Schulenburg, but in fact the road had been extended to Flatonia. He rode to the end of the track, then had to walk back. He bought some horses, but thieves quickly stole them. He finally had nothing left but a muzzle-loading shotgun, which he traded for a horse. Thieves came for the horse but only succeeded in breaking its neck against the tree to which it was tied, leaving Loika destitute. A blacksmith, he forged a spade and spaded out ten acres for a crop, then built a brush fence around it. Cattlemen burned the fence and let their cattle in on his crop.

He finally sharecropped until he had made a start and settled his debts.

Schwartz's father, Joseph, set out from the same European area in 1890, bound for the U.S. with others of his family. He was arrested in Bremerhaven because he had not served his required military time. The family went on without him, leaving him his ticket. One night, by accident or design, a coat hanging by the cell door jammed the lock so that the door didn't close. The prisoners all skipped out. Schwartz hurried to the docks, explained his problem to ship's officers, and was allowed to hide in a coal bin for three days until the ship left harbor. He landed in New York on his twentieth birthday.

He had been educated for the priesthood in the old country but didn't really care for it. He settled at Moravia, Texas, learned to speak and write English fluently, and gradually built up substantial land holdings. The Schwartzes raised fourteen children of their own plus two belonging to others of the family. Otto remembers his mother baking several loaves of bread each day and cooking potatoes in a huge pot.

Besides farming, the family operated a custom cane mill, grinding cane and making molasses for other people on either a cash basis or for a percentage of the molasses. They also operated a custom threshing machine; they had a sizable working crew of their own raising.

Otto took all the schooling that was available: nine years, seven months of the year. He left home at twenty-three for the same reason that his father and grandfather had left the old country; custom dictated that the land went to the eldest son, and the younger ones had to go their own way.

It bothers him today to see so many farm boys who want to stay and farm but can't raise the capital it takes to start and to meet the tremendous overhead required by heavy equipment. He still remembers that trip to the San Angelo bank with ten cents in his pocket.

Boom In Midkiff Farming Area
Caused By Younger Generation

Livestock Weekly, October 18, 1979

SOON after moving to San Angelo in 1947, I became aware of the high caliber of farmers who operated on Lipan Flat east of the city. Most were of German and Czech heritage. The Lipan Flat region had been broken out for farming in the 1920s and early 1930s by young farmers who had migrated from Central Texas, most representing only the second or third generation of their families in this country. Each generation helped the next to get started. When Lipan Flat filled up, the next generation pioneered the St. Lawrence community. Many of the young people who grew up at St. Lawrence moved to the Midkiff area, each generation leapfrogging farther west. These were never "windshield" farmers. They were conservative, hard-working people who irrigated their land with sweat as well as water. They persevered and survived while many others were falling by the wayside.

≈

MIDKIFF Most people outside of the immediate area have never heard of Midkiff. Many who live within a relatively short distance have never been there. Somewhat out of the way, southeast of Midland and north of Rankin, it is not a place you casually drive through on the way to somewhere else.

But this tiny town just inside the northeastern corner of Upton County—a veritable stone's throw from the point where Upton, Midland, Glasscock and Reagan counties corner together—is headquarters for what some observers call the "hottest new farming district in Texas."

Land long regarded as cow country is falling to the plow at a steady pace. Just this year, says county agent Kent Powell, cotton acres in

84

Upton County jumped to 13,375 from last year's 6,300. That addition was entirely in the Midkiff area.

This new farmland is being broken out on clay loam mesquite flats which soil specialists say are an extreme northwestern extension of the Edwards Plateau. Range conservationists set the "normal" stocking rate at fifty sheep and seventeen cattle per section, though sheep aren't numerous because of the coyote threat.

Other irrigation areas like Pecos-Coyanosa boomed a generation ago because of strong water. The Midkiff area's boom is based on a tight water supply that most irrigationists would not have given a second look in the past. As a whole, says Kenneth E. Lindsey, extension service area agronomist at Fort Stockton, the wells are 250–300 feet deep and yield only fifty–sixty gallons a minute. It takes careful management to get the most out of so modest a supply.

The big Pecos boom of the late 1940s and early 1950s drew a lot of people who were investors first and farmers second. Many had never farmed before. For a few years, plentiful water and good crops covered up a lot of management deficiencies. But diminishing water, smaller crops and higher costs eventually drove a majority of farmers out of that area.

The new Midkiff area development is different, insist such observers as Lindsey, Powell, district agent Ray Siegmund and area economist Gary Condra.

Most of the new farmers in the Midkiff community have come over from the St. Lawrence community, which lies about twenty miles east in Glasscock County. Some are from around Wall, east of San Angelo. With few exceptions, they come from families who have been farmers for generations.

The St. Lawrence community could probably make a strong paternity case, if necessary, and in a sense Wall could be considered the grandfather.

A large group of returning World War II veterans, natives of the Wall area, found it hard to buy enough land at home to set themselves up in farming. In the late 1940s and early 1950s they began breaking out ranchland south of Garden City. This became the St.

Lawrence community. The farmers were so young that for many years—until the postwar baby crop became old enough—the community did not have a single high-school student riding the bus to Garden City.

Now that second generation has grown up and is branching out, mostly west into the Midkiff area, a few to the largely abandoned Coyanosa farming area near Pecos. But where the Coyanosa group is trying to rejuvenate old land, the Midkiff bunch is breaking out and planting new land.

The surnames testify to the strong link with the older farming communities: Hoelscher, Halfmann, Gulley, Wilde, Dusek. . . .

Agronomist Lindsey thinks the youth of this community is one of its strongest assets. "Midkiff probably has more young farmers under thirty-five than any place I know of," he declares. "When you go over there you're not talking to an audience that is thinking about retiring."

At the same time, however, he sees these farmers as atypical. They grew up on a tractor seat and have the strong work ethic that has long marked the Lipan Flat farming area east of San Angelo. "These are not like a lot of young people today, looking for an easy way," he adds.

By today's standards they are, as a group, following the conservative precepts of their forebears. There aren't many big houses in the Midkiff community. In fact, mobile homes probably outnumber the rest. These young farmers are living on their places and doing most the work alone or with minimum help.

Because of the limited water, most are stretching it as far as possible, wasting little, and trying harder for minimum cost input than for maximum crop yield. Cotton is far and away the major cash crop. Grain sorghums and wheat are planted in rotation, more to boost the future cotton crops than for their own cash values. These are grown most often on what amounts to little more than a dryland basis, perhaps given a preplant watering and then nursed on through with little or no additional irrigation.

Livestock is a minor item.

Though the farming is being done in the midst of an area long developed for oil and gas production, most of the irrigation pumps are electrical. Inasmuch as these were new installations, and farmers had a choice, they opted for electricity. It is simpler, and compared to today's gas prices, no more expensive. These young men have not overlooked the fact that some farmers in the Pecos area were cut off from gas service even though gas wells were numerous all around them.

Recently, raw rangeland has been offered at around $200 per acre in this immediate area. Average cost to clear and break it and drill and equip the wells is about $200 more.

Though these young farmers have inherited a strong but old work ethic, they have some modern ideas about organization. For instance, they get together on cropping plans to keep everything as uniform as possible. About forty farmers decided to buy cotton module builders. They bought them all at one time in a package deal, all identical, easing the problem of stocking spare parts and also simplifying repair. Anyone who can fix one can fix them all.

Total cultivated acreage in the four-corners area is estimated at around 90,000, mostly in Glasscock, Upton and Reagan counties, a little lapping into Midland.

Midkiff itself is not a new town. It was born in the early 1950s as an oil town, serving the needs of what was then a booming new drilling area. The new farmers are using the water that the oil men passed on their way down to deeper formations.

For that matter, Midkiff wasn't the town's original choice for a name. Early residents called it Hadacol Corners, after a highly advertised tonic popular in the first decade after World War II. Postal authorities regarded the name as frivolous and refused to certify it. Residents then settled for the name of a pioneer ranching family.

It's probably just as well. Hadacol seems largely forgotten, but the Midkiff family is still around.

John Smith Uses Guard Dogs and Mules To Run off Coyotes
Livestock Weekly, April 8, 1982

THE USE of guard dogs and mules has grown considerably among small and medium-sized sheep and goat operations to protect against coyotes and other predators, though it remains difficult for large ranches and large pastures. John Smith was an early advocate. A while after this article was printed, John told me a story that was sad, yet almost funny in its irony. A man drove up to his place one day and proudly announced that he had saved a bunch of John's sheep. "There was two big white dogs out there amongst them, but I shot them before they could kill any!"

≈

MULLIN If you were a coyote and had a strong taste for mutton, you might be smart to go around John Smith's place. He has some most disagreeable guards posted in his pastures.

Smith ranches several scattered places in northern Mills County, south of Brownwood. Few people to the north of him keep sheep or goats anymore; coyote losses have driven them out of that business. Coyotes gave Smith a hard time, too. He won't go so far as to say his is the final answer, or by any means the only one, but it has brought a sharp reduction in his predator losses.

He uses Great Pyrenees guard dogs in several pastures and donkeys or mules in five others. Coyotes may enter a mule pasture, but they tend to leave it faster than they came in. Smith finds that mules have a strong aversion to canines of any form and will chase them out in a hurry. He can't even use his sheep dogs to work stock in most of the mule pastures unless he pens or ties the mule first.

Coyotes evidently won't even enter a pasture where a Great Pyrenees dog is stationed. The dogs lie up and sleep much of the day, but at night they roam, barking and raising a general ruckus, and go marking the fence posts. Evidently even their scent makes a coyote go the long way around.

Unlike sheep-working dogs, the Great Pyrenees don't require training to do their job. The guarding instinct was bred into them for centuries in Europe. Smith, and other people who raise or use them, simply keep them among sheep or goats almost from the time they are born. The guarding instinct then makes them highly protective when they are turned out into a pasture with sheep or goats.

Smith has three milking nannies on which he and Mrs. Smith raise the pups. One of these nannies willingly accepts the pups as if they were her own baby kids. The other two have to be held while the pups suck. This imprints the pups with a fierce loyalty they never lose.

Great Pyrenees, white in color, grow rapidly and have a voracious appetite. Even as pups they develop an aggressive personality. On occasion they will shed litter mates' blood fighting over food. As disconcerting as this might be to an owner, it is a mark of a potentially good guard dog, Smith believes.

The pups are friendly to people, but Smith does not encourage this much. He feels that the more standoffish a dog is, even to his owner, the better job he will do. "The worst thing you can do is make a pet out of them," he declares.

He raises the pups amid sheep and goats so that they will remain with them by choice. He turns a pup out into a pasture with the stock at about five months of age. By the time the dog is a year old it is mature and doing its job, if it is ever going to.

Smith has been raising Great Pyrenees about two years, both for his own use and for sale. He buys and sells sheep and goats over a lot of country besides Texas. He brought back his first Great Pyrenees female on a sheep truck making a backhaul from an out-of-state delivery.

He sold all but one of the pups out of the first litter, then decided he should have kept them for his own use. He finally bought some of them back for prices up to three times what he had been paid. He sold that first female, another mistake, though he kept three pups from her first litter.

He has seven grown dogs now, either working or breeding. Four are actually out with sheep and goats; two more will go out shortly.

Fully grown, his males have averaged about 150 pounds, his females about 100. They have an appetite to match. He feeds them Alpo, which isn't quite the cheapest ration around, and dry commercial dog food. He also buys large quantities of sheep livers from the Swift lamb plant in Brownwood.

He usually, but not always, gets around to feed his pasture dogs once a day. The other day he was carrying feed to one of them. A baby lamb had died of natural causes, and a couple of buzzards were feeding on it. As the dog came up he saw the buzzards and charged them with blood in his eyes. He came within an inch of catching one before it sluggishly lifted itself from the ground. "All fuzzed up," as Smith puts it, the dog stood guard over the carcass and dared the buzzards to come back.

A point that worries some people about guard dogs is that sheep and goats don't stay in one bunch; they scatter out, and one dog can't be with all of them at the same time. Smith has not found this to be a real problem. He finds that just having a dog in the pasture, somewhere, seems to make coyotes keep their distance.

Some people have found guard dogs so possessive that they won't let other domestic animals approach sheep or goats. Smith runs cattle in many of the pastures and has not encountered trouble between his dogs and the cattle. They seem to get used to one another in a few days. The dogs soon learn there isn't any harm in the cattle and at least tolerate their presence.

Sheep that aren't used to having a guard dog around are not exactly overjoyed the first time Smith puts a dog out, especially when the dog seems to feel he is a sheep and wants to get in among them. This, too, levels out in a few days. After a time the sheep seem to sense that the dog means protection. Now and then Smith sees a sheep and a dog licking each other's faces.

He has never seen one of his dogs offer any real threat to the sheep other than to chase them away from its feed, firmly but bloodlessly.

The dogs have no tolerance for wild animals. "You won't see a rabbit, or a coon, or even a deer in the pastures where the dogs are," Smith says. "They kill and eat the smaller animals they can catch. They chase the others away."

Smith has not been trying the mule or donkey method quite as long as the dogs, but he feels they are doing him a good job. A number of ranchmen around the country have reported that the system works. Smith has been told that jennies are the best, though he has not proven it one way or the other. Turned into a pasture without other company, they have a tendency to take up with sheep or goats. They may not have the guarding instinct of the dog, but their natural dislike of dogs and coyotes brings much the same end result.

Smith is a fixture at West Texas sheep and goat auctions, making four or five most weeks. He buys on order as well as to trade and ships a lot of packer sheep and goats to Mexico.

His name occasionally brings a look of disbelief. A Mexican packer smiled broadly when introduced to him awhile back and said, "John Smith is the best known American name in all of Mexico."

In his case he has had that name all his life, unlike some who have conveniently assumed it at a later age. In fact, the Smith family has lived in the Mullin area since before the Civil War. One of his forebears, riding with split reins tied together, lost a race with a Comanche raiding party near one of the places where Smith is running sheep and cattle today. The reins caught on a limb, jerked his horse down and let the Indians swarm over him before he could defend himself.

Outlaw Steer, Fighting Mad, Finally Penned By Helicopter

Livestock Weekly, May 5, 1983

YEARS after my father retired from his job as general manager of the McElroy Ranch at Crane and the ranch had changed owners, I began hearing stories about a wild steer there that refused to be corraled and challenged all comers to combat. The steer was finally captured, but only with the aid of modern technology. The ranch people's respect for this moss-horned old fighter led them to retire him to grass in a horse pasture rather than send him to slaughter. There, like his outlaw mother before him, he eventually died in the fullness of his years, unrepentant.

≈

FOR MOST of ten years, the big crossbred steer with long upswept horns was the terror of the Tudic Pasture. He had successfully fought off horses and men year after year, and not once had he allowed himself to be driven into a pen.

It took a helicopter, finally, to bluff and bully him into captivity, and then only after a sparring match that continued on and off the better part of a day.

Whoa, you're saying. If he was never penned, how did he come to be a steer? We'll get to that.

The steer, part Brahman, part Hereford, part Beefmaster, was born about ten years ago in a big, sandy, brushy ten-twelve section pasture known as Tudic on the McElroy Ranch. He came by his wildness naturally. His mammy was a big red motley-faced cow of the same lawless persuasion, penned only a time or two herself. She was left to raise calves, and she finally died in that pasture, in the fullness of her years.

True to his upbringing, this particular calf with strong Hereford influence in his markings and coloration was missed in the first roundups, either by accident or by his own design. He was a two-year-old bull by the time he came into sudden confrontation with three horsemen working the pasture. They were Fletcher Freeman, Linton Brem and Gaylord Russell.

Bill Boyd, who is joint foreman along with his brother Bob, tells the story. The young bull resisted being pushed toward the pens and went on the attack. To avoid injury to their horses, the cowboys decided to stretch him then and there. They castrated and earmarked him but had no way to brand him. (He still does not bear the ranch's Jigger Y brand.)

They decided to free him but quickly found they were not free *of* him. Russell took the rope off his horns and started back for his horse. The bull, now a steer, didn't give him time to make the saddle. He got to his feet, kicked off the heel rope and charged. Russell dove for his horse and landed on his stomach across the saddle as the horse wisely took to the brush to get out of the way. Russell managed to hang onto him—the alternative was unthinkable—until they were out of the steer's reach.

From that time on, the big steer resisted all efforts to pen him. Confronted by a horseman, he would usually retreat just a little way, then turn and come out fighting. Sometimes he was a solitary outlaw; other times he would stay with a young bull or two. At sight of a vehicle he would fade away into the catclaw and mesquite.

That big brushy pasture has always had a tendency to outlaw cattle, as do some others on this big ranch of some 230 sections. For those which refused to be penned, the answer has always been to ride them down, rope and tie them, then bring a trailer and haul them away. A spiderweb pattern of oilfield roads over much of the ranch has helped.

But Tudic Pasture has few roads, and much of it is impassable for vehicles because of sand and brush. So there seemed no practical way ever to bring the steer to heel. As the years went by, it became easier and easier simply to tolerate him.

In the spring of 1982, a helicopter was pressed into service to help clear Tudic. The big steer was brought up within sight of the pens before he turned and bolted, taking much of the herd with him. The rest of the cattle were finally gathered, but not the big one.

The Boyds and ranch owner Vannie Cook, Jr., of McAllen, finally decided early this spring that something had to be done. They had developed a grudging admiration for the old adversary and didn't want to do him any harm, but by now his big, curved, upsweeping horns had reached a size that would offer a tempting trophy. Sooner or later, they feared, somebody would kill him just to have that head.

Moreover, he remained a hazard to anybody who rode a horse into that pasture or ventured far away from a vehicle afoot. Most steers have a tendency to become docile. This one had never yielded an inch.

Russ Hill, who operates Hilco Aviation in Odessa, was called upon to round up the pasture with his helicopter. This time, he was told, they wanted the steer brought in no matter what it took.

What it took was most of the day, sparring with the big old fighter, hazing him ever closer to the pens, losing him, bringing him back, gradually wearing him down. Little by little the steer gave ground. Just before dark, Hill finally badgered him through the gate.

The fight was far from over. The steer went on the prod against everything that moved, including the other cattle in the pen. He picked up a 400-pound calf on his horns and sent it rolling. The ground crew managed to get him into a crowding pen with some other cattle, but they could not force him into a chute.

They tied two forty-five-foot nylon ropes together, got a loop on the horns, then ran the other end of the rope through a gooseneck trailer and tied it to a pickup with four-wheel drive. Fighting every foot of the way, the steer was dragged into the trailer and hauled to ranch headquarters nine miles east of Crane.

Put into a strong steel pen with several bulls, he refused either to eat or drink for about a week. Estimated to weigh close to a ton, he looked for a while as if he might starve himself to death. But finally he began to follow the bulls' example and go to the trough, or to whatever was pitched over the fence.

He has gentled down considerably in the weeks since his capture, though he still will not allow anyone in the pen afoot. "It isn't enough just to get on top of the fence," says Boyd. "As tall as he is, and as long as his horns are, he can still reach you on top of a seven-foot fence."

When a *Livestock Weekly* reporter prepared to take his picture through the fence the other day, the big steer came halfway across the pen to meet him, tossing his head belligerently. He stopped, confident of his bluff, and posed as if he had been doing it all his life—on his own terms, of course.

After dropping a good deal of weight, the steer is putting it back on again, working up to the good flesh he was carrying the day he finally lost to the machine age. Cook and the Boyds have no intention of shipping him off to a packer. He has their respect, if not their trust. They hope daily feeding in the pen will finally gentle him to a point that he will submit to handling and they can turn him out into a small trap or pasture. There they intend to let him live out his life and die of old age, like his mother did.

Where Have All the Cowboys Gone?
Family Weekly, October 30, 1983

MANY people declare that ranching changed more in the generation or two after World War II than it had changed in all the years before the war, from trail-drive days forward. A big part of this resulted from advanced technology. But one factor which has struck me over and over again has been the transformation of the typical working cowboy from his usual bachelor status of old to today's family man. The reasons—at least as I see them—are outlined in this article.

≈

WHEN I was a youngster in West Texas in the late 1920s and on up to World War II, the bachelor cowboy remained the hub around which the ranch wheels turned, as he had been from trail-drive times. He fell into one of two categories: young bachelor, from the late teens through the twenties; and the old bachelor, from about thirty on up. If a cowboy didn't marry by his early thirties he was considered too set in his ways to get along with a woman. The cowboys I remember who married in their middle years tended to prove the rule: Like a horse not broken until seven or eight years of age, they took poorly to domestication.

On the McElroy Ranch, known then and now as the Jigger Y, a large L-shaped bunkhouse provided small individual rooms for four or five bachelor cowboys. There was no place for a married cowboy unless he was a foreman, which Dad was, or could hold down one of the ranch's two outlying "camps" which had houses adequate for a family.

The drifting cowboy of fiction was not a myth. In an earlier time, such men might roam from the Texas-Mexico border all the way to Wyoming and Montana looking for work, staying a while on each job, then moving on to scratch an itch and see what wonders awaited on the other side of the hill.

My grandfather, Bill Kelton, was one of these drifters early in his life. Oldest of six children, he was not yet twelve when his homesteader father died. Granddad went to work to help support the family. He broke horses and mules and worked as a cowboy around his home in Callahan County, then drifted away to hunt for better pay. At one time or another, before he married, he worked from the lower reaches of the Pecos River to as far north as the XIT Ranch in the Panhandle.

My father, Buck Kelton, grew up on the Scharbauer ranches north of Midland and, in his teens, wage-worked on many outfits in the Midland-Odessa region, usually for a dollar a day or less. Accommodations were usually Spartan. He used to recall that one ranch put him in a small sheet-iron shack so hot on summer days that he could not enter it until after sundown. That fitted the owner's purpose; he did not want his cowboys in camp between sunrise and sunset anyway. Dad married my mother on his twenty-fourth birthday and for the next few years took ranch "camp" jobs that furnished a house for a couple. Such jobs were by no means plentiful, and many a cowboy who chose matrimony was forced to change his occupation.

By the time I came along, the drifting cowboys were much less likely to travel on horseback than in a beat-up old coupe, with a saddle, bridle and bedroll stowed in the rumble seat. Even so, their mode of transportation was about the only essential difference from the days when my granddad was young. They dropped in often at McElroy headquarters in those tight Depression years. Occasionally a lucky one found Dad needing help. More often they got a square meal in the bunkhouse dining room, perhaps slept the night on a spare cot, then traveled on to some other ranch the next day.

Every part of the ranching country had cowboy hangouts where a ranchman needing to hire could find bachelor hands looking for work. In our case it was Midland, specifically the Scharbauer Hotel, where jobless cowboys would hang around waiting. If the weather was pleasant, several were likely to be squatting on their boot heels, leaning against the outside wall near the entrance. In inclement weather, they would be in the lobby, sometimes sitting in the big, overstuffed chairs, sometimes hunkered against the walls, campfire style. Few actually roomed in the hotel or even ate in its coffee shop; they could not afford it.

Midland had many day-working bachelor cowboys who preferred temporary employment to steady jobs. Day work paid better if a man could keep reasonably busy. Usually this involved the semi-annual roundups, when a cowboy was more likely to sleep on the ground near a chuckwagon than in a nice dry bunkhouse. Roundup days started long before daylight and usually did not end until dark.

It was no place for a married man. The cowboy spent weeks or months away from home and suffered much uncertainty about his next job. Finding day work was usually hard in winter, when ranchers trimmed payrolls. Often two or more bachelor cowboys would share the rent on a small house in town and spend the winter huddled around a pot-bellied stove, eating their own crude cooking and hoping last summer's saved-up wages would stretch until the grass began to rise. A winter or two like that got a cowboy to thinking about more compatible companionship, especially if she could cook.

Of the bachelor cowboys I knew when I was a boy, most eventually married, then found jobs that offered better pay and more security. Oilfields became the most common alternative for Texans. While the Jigger Y in the 1930s paid bachelor cowboys forty dollars a month plus room and board, "roughnecking" in the oilfields paid $200 or better. Several cowboys I knew took up oilfield work so they could marry and raise a family.

Some, of course, remained confirmed bachelors. To me, the epitome of bachelorism was Wes Reynolds. He was a Scharbauer cowboy in the early years of the century when my grandfather was a foreman, and he helped teach my father the cowboy trade. Much later he tried to do the same for me, with disappointing results.

Wes fit the stereotype of the cranky old bachelor deeply set in his ways. He stood in awe of no boss and no boss' son. Once, when my father was perhaps nine or ten years old, he helped Wes move a herd of cattle down a long lane north of Midland. In that country a windmill stood every couple of miles. The day was warm, and every time they approached a mill, Dad spurred away to get a drink of water. He would take a sip or two and return to the herd. Finally Wes went with him. When Dad took a sip from the end of the pipe and backed away, Wes said, "I don't believe you've had enough. Drink a little more." Each time Dad tried to quit, Wes made him drink again, until the boy was about to burst. Wes, a man of few but potent words, gave him an important cowboy lesson. "Next time, dammit, you'll water out before you leave the house!"

As far back as I remember, it was routine for Dad to saddle his horse in the early morning, then drink a generous quantity of water to stand him against the day. He made us buttons do likewise. Even now, I rarely drink water—or anything else—between meals.

In the 1940s, Dad had a small ranch leased for his own cattle and hired Wes, who was by then quite elderly, to watch over the place. Wes' housekeeping seemed without order or plan. I went to the leased ranch with my younger brother Myrle once, to relieve Wes while he had a summer visit with kinfolks. As a favor we cleaned his house thoroughly and set it in good order. Wes was dismayed. He couldn't find a thing. Worst of all, we had scrubbed his old coffeepot. It was weeks later before he could get a tolerable flavor in his coffee, he said. Even then he considered the pot permanently damaged.

It's easy to allow romanticism to cloud the realities of this bachelor life, but it had a dark side. Many of these men became old without a family for comfort, without a home to call their own. The fortunate ones might become "pensioners" of a sort, holding down some easy caretaker job on a ranch, as Wes was doing for Dad. The less fortunate might spend their final years ill and alone, living on the bitter edge of poverty in some detested town, exiled by their age from the only kind of life they knew or cared about.

One half-senile old cowboy I remember from my boyhood used to drift around on a raw-boned black horse. He'd stop at my grand-parents' small ranch north of Midland to beg a meal for himself and feed for his poor, tired animal. Because he was a stranger to soap and water, Mammaw would try to feed him on the porch. If Granddad had some old clothes to spare, the drifter received a change, and then

Mammaw, her arm extended as far as it would reach, carried away the castoffs to be burned beneath her washpot. In his day he had been an open-range cowboy, but he was a pathetic remnant of a long time ago.

With little change except for his name, I used him in my book, *The Good Old Boys*. In real life and in the book, he stepped down from the saddle to open a gate and suffered a heart attack. He died as he had lived, alone on the prairie.

My grandparents moved from the ranch into Midland in the early 1940s when it became clear that Granddad was terminally ill. They had spent most of their lives without electricity or indoor plumbing. They owned an automobile for traveling the twenty-five miles to town, but he never had a pickup for ranch work. Until the day he sold his cattle, he worked on horseback or with a wagon.

Ranches were forced to undergo traumatic changes because of a wartime labor shortage. Tens of thousands of cowboys went off to fight in World War II, and most never returned to their old ways of life. Ranchers learned to mechanize to a degree they had once thought impossible. My father, for instance, liked to build horse-trailers. In an earlier time, we often spent hours riding to some far pasture on horseback to work cattle, then rode hard to reach home before dark. Trailers made it possible to haul horses and men to the farthest part of the ranch in a half-hour, do the work and be back at headquarters by noon. We could work somewhere else the other half of the day. New fences cut pastures into smaller units that could be handled by fewer men.

Most ranches discarded the chuckwagon. They hauled men home at the end of the day to sleep in their own beds. To compete against other demands for the labor force, they built better housing and hired married men for their stability.

On the average ranch today, the bachelor bunkhouse is as rare as family houses were forty years ago. The average cowboy goes out to work each morning much like his city counterpart. Chances are that he has had at least some exposure to a college education, that he is a fair-to-middling mechanic and electrician, that he knows a smattering of veterinary medicine, can discuss nutrition, artificial insemination and perhaps even embryo transplantation. At the end of the working day he probably goes home to central heat and air conditioning.

His sons are as likely to become accountants or lawyers as cowboys. And should they become cowboys, the odds are slim that they will ever share a bunkhouse with a half dozen other young bachelors as Dad or Granddad once did, or eat chuckwagon grub and sleep on the ground.

They might vicariously enjoy the fantasy, but few would seriously care—or now be able—to live that life for long.

Idaho's Ray Hunt Demonstrates
Gentling Horses Without Fear

Livestock Weekly, September 25, 1986

IF THERE is one thing virtually all ranchmen share, it is a love of good horses. One of the most popular attractions in ranching circles across the West in recent years has been horse-gentling demonstrations by Ray Hunt. I have seen him perform several times and have watched with interest the reaction of ranchers and cowboys in the crowd. Invariably, it is one of admiration for his skill and puzzlement over his quick results.

≈

LUBBOCK Horsemen the last few years have heard a lot about Ray Hunt of Mountain Home, Idaho, and his smooth, gentle horse training techniques. He demonstrated them at the annual Golden Spur Livestock Day at the Texas Tech University livestock arena.

He drew a standing-room crowd, and hardly anybody left during his two lengthy demonstrations. His handling methods are better seen than described, but his comments were often straight to the point:

"I'm not doing this for you (the crowd); I'm doing it for the horse."

"The horse is my friend, and I treat him like a friend, not a slave."

"If he runs away with you, throws you off or kicks you, it's your fault."

"The horse will tell you when it's right. He won't lie to you or cheat you. I go to humans for opinions, but I go to the horse for the facts."

"The biggest trouble with a lot of horse breakers is that the human always thinks he has to win every time."

"Make the wrong thing difficult for him (the horse) and the right thing easy."

"Most people don't teach a horse how to be caught but only to be captured."

"I don't know anybody who sends a child to a 'breaker.' They send them to a teacher, to be taught."

About books on training horses: "The horse didn't write the book of rules. Go to the horse for the answer. He'll tell you."

"Don't teach a horse like a human being; he's better than a human being. Don't let him get into a rut just because you are."

"The only time Thoroughbred blood hurts a horse is when he doesn't have any of it in him. The reason the Quarter Horse is so good is because of the Thoroughbred in him."

Hunt expressed a regret that to most horses today, "it's a phony world." A majority are kept for hobby or show purposes rather than for useful work, which would be their more natural element.

He worked with three different horses during the demonstrations. He had seen none of them before. The first was a small brown horse, thin, a bit snorty because he had been handled very little, and some of that had been for some recent painful tooth work.

Hunt said the trainer should always give the horse "a place to go" to keep him from feeling trapped and work always with a gentle hand rather than brute force. Don't rush or "overexpose" the horse, he cautioned.

He also reminded watchers that the horse "has two sides, so you have to teach both of them." Lessons learned from the left side have to be taught all over again for the right side. They do not transfer automatically.

A horse may get used to something being done from the left side, such as saddling or mounting, and accept it calmly, yet react with fear or violence if the same thing is attempted from the right side without his first being conditioned to it.

During his short training sessions, Hunt repeated each move from both sides until the horse came to accept it.

"You never know when you may need to saddle him from the right handed side," he commented.

All his moves were slow, gentle and repeated again and again until the horse, extremely wary at first, accepted them without flinching or fear. He had the brown bronc leading in a relatively short time.

"I've heard people say, 'I've drug my horse around the block with a tractor and he still won't lead.' All they've done is teach him how to drag," Hunt declared. "If you're not careful you'll have to drag him the rest of his life."

He gently flipped a long halter rein around the horse's forefeet, around his hind feet and over his head, ears and rump until the animal came to accept the moves without fear.

Before he quit, he was picking up the brown's feet and holding them. When he tried it with the hind feet, the horse would start several times to kick, and Hunt would let go before the animal could follow through. After several repetitions, the horse accepted without resistance.

Asked what to do if the horse bites him, he said, "Try not to let him, but if he does, bear the pain and try again."

The second horse was a dun, a bit fleshier and possibly a little older but not broken. As with the first horse, Hunt kept playing with the rope and the halter rein, casting it around the legs and rump until the animal settled down and accepted.

The horse kept running around and around the circular pen, trying to get away from him. Hunt kept following him, letting him run in only one direction. In a bit the horse did just what Hunt predicted: he turned and faced Hunt, and let Hunt ease up to him in a non-threatening manner. After a breakaway or two, the horse finally let Hunt rub his nose and halter him.

Presently Hunt saddled him after first letting him feel the blanket thrown over his back and both sides several times. Finally Hunt mounted him, standing awhile in the left stirrup before bringing his right leg up and over. When the horse acted as if it might jump, Hunt stepped back to the ground. When he seated himself, the horse appeared confused but made no move to pitch.

A horse reacts with fear to the new and unknown but accepts it as he learns that he will not be harmed, Hunt stressed. This takes patience and gentleness on the trainer's part and a willingness to move at the horse's pace, not necessarily at his own, he said.

Everything he did, he repeated many times. He acknowledged that he was moving much faster in the demonstration than he normally would at home in his own pens. He said he would be happy to make as much progress with a horse in a week under normal circumstances as he made during the one day's demonstrations.

After a lunch break, he worked some more with the second horse, then worked for a short time with an older sorrel already gentle to demonstrate a little about advanced training.

"You want a horse to keep learning, always," he said. "Don't try too much too soon, or he may quit you. The horse gets discouraged and starts looking for ways to rebel."

Too much equipment used by trainers is designed to hurt the horse, to force him into doing things instead of leading him into it, he said. Of this equipment, he declared, "It's the human who needs it, not the horse."

He put a lot of emphasis on the horse's mental attitude. Mental stress can break a horse down physically, he said. Too often the horse remains under severe stress during the "breaking" process. Adverse reactions become so deeply imprinted that it is difficult and perhaps impossible to erase them.

"Try to keep the horse from being afraid," he said. "You have to demonstrate to him that he won't be harmed."

With both of the broncs, he demonstrated that in a relatively short time he could have them quit running from him and actually turn and come to him. They reached a point that as he walked away they followed him.

He said horse and man are two minds and two bodies, but the horseman's task is to make them perform as if they were one mind and one body: "mine." "The only way to do this is to get in harmony with the horse," he commented.

He compared horseback riding to dancing. Dancers either move apart, each doing something different, or they move together in harmony.

With the mature sorrel he demonstrated his way of dealing with a high-headed horse. Cables and tiedowns are the wrong approach, he said, because they don't cure the habit; they only put a physical restriction on it. When the horse held its head too high, he simply pulled up on the reins, drawing the head even higher. After a long moment the horse did exactly what Hunt predicted: he gave way and dropped his head until his nose touched the ground, seeking relief from the upward pressure. The instant Hunt felt him start to give, he released the pressure and let the horse have all the slack he needed. That, he said, was a demonstration of his No. 1 maxim: "Make the wrong thing difficult and the right thing easy."

Nub Wilde Worked Wherever Sheep Are Raised in the United States

Livestock Weekly, May 25 and June 1, 1989

PACKINGHOUSE buyers are often unjustly abused, both by the ranchers and feedlot operators who feel they are being underpaid for their lambs and cattle and by the packing-company bosses who feel that the buyers are paying too much. Jim Taylor, who spent his adult life purchasing lambs for a major packing firm, declared upon his retirement that he had never been able to fulfill one lifelong ambition: to buy a load of lambs that made money for the company. Nub Wilde was a longtime lamb buyer for Swift. A native of Utah, he made friends everywhere he worked despite the "stigma" of being a packer buyer. Though in particulars his story is unique, in its generalities it is typical of all those in his trade.

≈

SAN ANGELO Nub Wilde says he may have bought and loaded sheep in more places than anyone still living.

He has bought lambs in Texas for Swift Independent for about the last dozen years. He will soon be shifting his base of operations to the mountain West, working from Salt Lake City. Retired from Swift since February, he has become a contract lamb buyer for ConAgra, which bought both Swift and Monfort.

Now sixty-one, he was born in the Wasatch Mountains east of Salt Lake City "on a poor little sheep outfit" at Oakley, Utah. He grew up there, leaving home at eighteen.

His first vivid recollection of the sheep business was in being sent to Nevada to the winter desert range to stay in the wagon with a sheepherder and relieve the camp tender through the holidays. There was no water and no practical way to carry any to the camp ("We were too poor to have water wagons"), so the camp depended upon melted snow.

When the herder took the sheep out in the morning to graze, he told Nub to melt down enough snow for the camp and the horses. There had been just a thin skiff of it, so the quantity and quality were limited. Nub built a fire with sagebrush and scooped snow into a tub with a small coal shovel.

Each time he melted down the snow he found sheep pellets in the bottom, so he would throw it out and start over. When the herder came in that night, he found the tub empty. Nub explained.

The herder declared angrily, "A little sheep manure won't hurt you!" (He did not actually say "manure.")

The family had a winter range on public lands near Gold Hill, Nevada, when World War II began. The government took the land for a bombing range, so Nub's father had to sell his sheep.

Nub went to work in California for George Luckey of San Antonio, Texas, who at the time was running cattle in California's Imperial Valley.

Nub in 1949 was working on a ranch in Utah. Swift was pasturing lambs in the Imperial Valley, where his father was also running sheep. "They asked my dad where they could get some help. He said he had a dumb kid over in Utah."

Nub started his association with Swift October 1, 1949. The company was putting 25,000 to 30,000 lambs on alfalfa fields. "They just said, 'Here they are; take care of them,'" he recalls. The lambs always arrived on the train in the middle of the night and had to be unloaded and trailed or trucked to the fields. A herder was sent out with every band, so there were twenty to twenty-five men, and none spoke English.

"I learned to speak Spanish in about two weeks," he says, "as much of it as I know."

To compound his other problem, immigration officers were picking up his helpers every time they saw them.

When spring came and the lambs were all shipped, he declared that he wanted no more of that, and he quit.

"The next August, Swift asked me to come back. I was making $7 a day. They asked me how much I wanted, and I told them some ridiculous figure. They told me to be there next week."

He ran lambs for Swift in the winter of 1950–1951 and next spring started helping Swift buyers to ship lambs they had bought. He worked from the Imperial Valley to Bakersfield, up to Sacramento and over into Idaho.

In 1951 he started buying lambs, working out of Swift's Los Angeles plant. At that time the company had more than thirty plants slaughtering sheep in the U.S. Armour and Wilson had some fifty million ewes.

About 1955 he was transferred to Columbus, Ohio. Swift had killing plants in Cleveland, Brooklyn, Nashville, Summerville, Massachusetts and Evansville, Indiana. He was one of three lamb and veal calf buyers who made up the eastern buying department, based in Chicago.

In the spring the office would move to Lexington, Kentucky. A series of lamb pools were put together in Ohio, West Virginia, Pennsylvania and New York State, and he attended an auction every day.

About 1957 a sheep-raising movement started in North and South Carolina and Georgia, where land cottoned or tobaccoed out was being put into legumes to try to rejuvenate the soil. Nub was asked if he could buy crossbred ewes for these operations. Swift thought the idea was good but did not want the company involved, so he was given permission to do it during his vacation. The state of North Carolina paid his expenses to Lewiston, Montana.

He sent about 5,000 to 6,000 Hampshire cross ewe lambs to Ohio to spend the winter. In the spring they were moved down to North Carolina and scattered out to various county seats where farmers could buy them in lots of fifty or more. He bought rams in Virginia to go with the ewes.

He did this for three years and figures he put out about 50,000 to 60,000 ewes in the two Carolinas. He remembers the first load at Piedmont, North Carolina. They were unloaded at a cattle auction for dispersal to farmers. Those people had not seen sheep before. A county agent with a clipboard and a pocketful of pencils asked Nub if he could guarantee them to be breeders. Nub said, "All I can tell you is that their mothers and fathers were."

A series of lamb pools was set up through the extension service. County agents would mark out the fats, and Nub would bring the trucks. It worked well for a few years because this was fresh, clean ground for sheep. But eventually parasites found them, and the sheep industry there went into decline.

He was still working out of Columbus when the lamb packing plants began closing in the mid-1950s. Sheep numbers were declining and could no longer maintain all the plants.

He figures the biggest factor was the cutbacks in grazing allotments on public lands in the West. Other factors were shortage of herders, abundance of predators and the proliferation of synthetic fibers.

He recalls that in 1951 the wool market had gone way up. Swift had about 100,000 lamb fleeces in a San Francisco warehouse and was offered about $1.40 a pound. The lamb buyers wanted to sell, but the company wanted to hold out for a little more money. It eventually wound up selling the wool for about forty-seven to fifty cents.

One of the big pluses that he sees, looking back, was the industry's getting away from dependence upon the railroads through a shift to trucks.

Buying lambs in Idaho recently, he saw one of the long iron bars used to inch freight cars into position at the loading chutes, one by one. That reminded him how glad he was not to be depending upon the railroads anymore.

He was shipping lambs at Flagstaff, Arizona, one time. The Santa Fe livestock cars, already antique, had a wheel on top which operated the brakes. After finishing loading a car of lambs, he got the cars moving by using a bar, intending to put the next one up to the loading chute. The track was on a slight downgrade, however, and the cars kept moving. He climbed up on top to set the brakes, but the wheel would not turn. The cars ran all the way down the hill, finally tipping over at a switch.

He was at Sugar City, Idaho, once, loading eight cars of lambs off beet tops. He finished loading four cars, then had to leave to receive lambs elsewhere. He had billed the first four cars, fats, to New York, and the last four cars, feeders, to the Imperial Valley.

After he left, a beet train came along. The sheep cars had to be moved to make room. When they were brought back, their order had been reversed. The feeders went to the New York packing plant, and the fats went to the Imperial Valley. He had a hard time explaining that.

One of the hardest places he ever loaded lambs in those days was at Tocaine, North Carolina. There were no loading facilities and no proper scales. He went there to receive two cars of lambs. They were weighed one at a time on a set of cotton scales. A man balanced the scales with his own weight on them. Then the lambs were brought to him one at a time, and he held them while they were weighed. The lambs were placed on a pickup, hauled up beside the waiting freight car and put inside by hand, one at a time. It took all day.

He shipped a lot of lambs to the New York plant. The cars would go to Jersey City, then had to be ferried across the Hudson River, where an engine would pick up the cars and deliver them to the plant. This maneuver added about a day to most shipments, especially if the lambs had to be unloaded and rested before the ferry trip. The packing plant was at the present location of the United Nations Building. Armour had a plant there, too.

When its eastern lamb packing plants closed in 1964, Swift transferred Nub to Scottsbluff, Nebraska. He remained there thirteen years, buying lambs in all the western states. After the Scottsbluff plant ceased operations, he moved to Swift's new plant in Brownwood, Texas, in 1977, then to San Angelo in 1983. He says, "I suspect that I have probably been involved in the sheep business in more places than anybody still alive."

He remembers a lot of fun, and a lot of tribulations. Buffalo, New York, used to have a stockyards. All the livestock had to be kept inside in the winter, cattle on the first floor, sheep and hogs on the second, poultry on the top floor. He went to Buffalo one night to buy lambs and was stuck there for six days because of deep snow; nothing could move.

He has loaded lambs on the Pacific Ocean at Camp Pendleton, and on the Atlantic on Pimlico Sound, North Carolina. Buying lambs in the West was much different from the East because of the large numbers. One of the best sheepmen he ever consistently bought from, he recalls, was the late Ray Smith of Craig, Colorado. "He was probably as good a sheepman as there was in the West," Nub says. Smith took great pride in his operation and the quality of his sheep.

One of the first things Nub always looked at on a ranch was the horses. If the horses were in good shape, he figured the sheep would be too. If the horses had saddle sores and their hipbones stuck out, he could usually figure the rest of the outfit was not well run either.

One sheepman he always tried but never managed to buy from was a man named Covey, who operated out of Cokeville, Wyoming. Covey told him, "I always sell lambs to Armour and buy Swift stock. You guys buy them cheaper than anybody else."

Covey founded the Little America motels and truck stops. Once as a boy, herding sheep out in the Wyoming desert, he was caught in winter blizzard. He declared that if he was ever able, he would build a good hotel where he had spent such a miserable time. He did, several of them.

Nub notes that the lamb business, like many others, is seasonal. He has spent a good part of his life following the lamb-shipping season as it develops across the West.

The first time he ever bought any Navajo lambs was at a trading post near Cameron, Arizona. The sale was handled like some of the pool sales back east. A delivery day was appointed, and Indian women brought in the lambs to be weighed one at a time, the weight credited to each individual owner.

Nub would weigh the lambs out of a pen one at a time, then put them in another pen. Out of the corner of his eye he noticed two

Indian men lifting lambs from the weighed pen and surreptitiously moving them back to the other pen to be weighed again. He started marking the sheep with chalk, which put a stop to that manuever.

He was a little puzzled over the fact that the lambs seemed to be weighing about twenty or so pounds more than he guessed, but the scales had checked out all right.

Later, while he sat on a pine stump with the trading post operator, figuring up the totals, he noticed cigarette smoke coming from beneath the scales. He found two Indians hiding there. Each time sheep had been weighed, they had pulled down on the beam to make the scales show a heavier weight.

Nub halted the delivery then and there. "I told the trader we would wait a day and then reweigh them," he says. "He was mad, but we did it."

The lambs weighed eighteen pounds less the second day.

His first experience in Texas was a hard lesson in listening to good advice. Through a commission company, he bought about 17,000 mutton lambs out of some 35,000 that a Texas ranchman had put together to winter in the Fort Stockton area.

Some people tried to warn him to be careful, but he saw nothing wrong with the deal. The lambs averaged fifty-nine pounds when they were turned out in the fall. He bought them for April 1 delivery out of the wool, at about $18.50, as he recalls.

At delivery time, by his description, they were as flat and thin "as an empty hot water bottle." The first load or two went to George Temple at Lamar, Colorado. They weighed just fifty-eight pounds, one less than in the fall, and Temple turned them down. Nub found a home for them in Terry Turner's feedlot, also near Lamar.

The lambs had done worse than poorly; they showed no gain for the whole winter, and he had not thought to put a minimum weight clause in the contract. He contacted the Swift lawyers in Chicago about his grounds for turning them down as unmerchantable. One of the lawyers asked him if they would be worth $5 instead of $18.50. Nub thought they would.

"Then they're not unmerchantable," the lawyer said.

The seller had become none too keen on delivering the lambs, and

Nub was certainly not keen on receiving them, but the commission men insisted on the deal going through because they wanted their fee. The government inspector looked at the lambs in Turner's feedlot and declared them to have bluetongue disease.

"Needless to say, I had a lot of sleepless nights."

He wound up taking 10,000 head and paying the commission on the rest, while the owner kept them in hopes of a better season. The deal lucked out. When the lambs went on feed they straightened up and made a lot of money for Swift.

One of the things he always admired about the Swift organization was that it stood behind its work. "I've made a lot of dumb deals, but I never made a deal that Swift didn't pay for. They stood behind me every time."

His father, in the sheep business all his life, was killed in a tractor accident. He had a bad case of arthritis and could not straddle a tractor; he had to sit on it sidesaddle-style. A tractor got away from him, tipped over and killed him.

Nub married when he was nineteen, his wife seventeen. She was from Kama, Utah. They have three sons, two daughters, thirteen grandchildren and expect "two more before the snow flies." One son is a lawyer in Brownsville, one is about to graduate from the University of Texas at Arlington, and one is a jeweler in Salt Lake. The daughters both live in Salt Lake, one a registered nurse, the other an accountant in the same hospital. None has followed in his footsteps as a sheepman.

Nub has been listed as a missing person a couple of times in his lamb-buying travels. Once he was staying in a hotel in Phoenix and drove south to Casa Grande to load lambs. While he was gone a burglar stole all the clothes in his room. The thief went to Tucson, checked into a hotel but left without paying his bill. The clothes evidently did not fit him, so he left part of them behind. Among them the hotel people found a letter from Mrs. Wilde.

Assuming Nub to be the one who had skipped out on the bill, the police put out an APB on him. Nub's father-in-law, a Utah sheriff, got the APB. Meanwhile, Nub had moved on to Sacramento, still loading lambs. His father-in-law notified him of the APB, so Nub called the sheriff in Tucson, got things straightened out and recovered what clothes had been left behind.

Another time, while he was working out of Scottsbluff, he started for Rawlins, Wyoming, to take up lambs. He liked to fish and always carried his fishing rod. Where the Sweetwater River crosses the highway, he pulled off to the side of the road and decided to try his luck. Almost as soon as the hook hit the water, he had a three-pound rainbow trout. Encouraged, he moved on upriver, losing track of time.

A highway patrolman noticed his car. When it was still there the third time he passed, he reported it. Swift was notified. Over the years Nub has taken a lot of ribbing about being a hard-working lamb buyer who fished so long that his car was considered abandoned.

He says the greatest pleasure of being in the sheep business has been the caliber of people he has worked with. Noting that there are occasional exceptions, he declares that livestock people in general and sheep people in particular are honorable; their word is good.

He declares that Texas has the best people and the poorest sheep of any state in the West. He finds it the easiest place of all to buy and trade. "I'll miss that," he says. He notes that there are a lot of good sheep in the state, but overall he finds their quality below that of most mountain states. He believes the difference is that in Texas the sheep are run loose under fence, whereas in most of the other western states they still have to be herded on open range. Under herding, the sheepman sees a lot of them, and the general level of husbandry is better.

"Ray Smith once said that sheep have been herded since biblical times, and they still need to be herded," he says.

He has seen many changes in the way sheep are handled. When he was a boy the family used to trail their sheep to Goldhill, Nevada, about 200 miles or more, each spring and trail back in the fall. The trip took forty or fifty days each way. Everybody there trailed sheep the same way.

There used to be a Salt Lake City policeman whose only duty in season was to see the sheep bands through the city. There were about thirty or forty miles of fenced sheep trail through the city's watershed, only about twenty-five or thirty yards wide. The first band through would get all the vegetation. The other outfits had to carry along hay and push the sheep hard to get them through as quickly as possible. Horsedrawn vehicles and commissary were common. Now the pickup reigns.

In California, every band had a sheepherder with a pack-carrying burro. The sheep followed the burro. He knows of only two or three outfits still trailing that way. Most now truck them from one irrigated patch to another, a considerable expense.

In Idaho Falls the other day he was asked when he was going to quit buying lambs. "When it quits being fun," he said.

The nickname "Nub" comes from the fact that he is missing about half of one forefinger, caught in a washing machine motor when he was eighteen months old. He has been called Nub ever since.

Old-timers Remember

Cowboy Warnie May 'Retired' at Seventy-Five, Now Nearly Ninety, He Still Hasn't Quit

Livestock Weekly, March 12, 1970

PEOPLE had been telling me for some time that I should visit Warnie May, one of the last turn-of-the-century cowboys left in the area east of Abilene. I had some difficulty in finding his place, not far from where my grandfather had grown up. Though May was nearly ninety, he had a saddled horse tied in front of the house, just in case he decided to go somewhere. We had visited a few minutes when he suddenly frowned and asked me to repeat my name. "Any kin to Bill Kelton?" he demanded. I told him Bill Kelton had been my grandfather. He grasped my hand tightly enough to make it hurt and declared that he and my grandfather had grown up together, cowboyed together, and that they had remained close friends to the end of Granddad's life. Later I took my father over to May's ninetieth birthday party, which I believe may have been his last.

≈

OVALO   J. W. "Warnie" May, approaching ninety, became a cowboy for wages when he was only twelve. Somewhere around fourteen years of age—he says he never had much memory for dates—he shared a bedroll with outlaw Black Jack Ketchum one night at the 6 Ranch chuckwagon near Knickerbocker west of San Angelo.

As May remembers it, Black Jack was on the dodge. He would drift in to the wagon occasionally to eat or sleep, then like some wily old steer slipping up to and away from water, he would quietly drift out of sight. This particular day, Black Jack's horse was given out when he came upon the "button," Warnie May, riding a fresh 6 horse. Black Jack made the youngster swap horses with him, then disappeared. May had to lead the horse two miles to camp. Along about ten or eleven that night, Ketchum and Bill Ike Babb rode in. Black Jack crawled into the bedroll May was sharing with wagon boss Oscar Finney and laid his Winchester down between himself and the boy.

"That thing felt like it must of weighed 200 pounds," May recalls. "I didn't sleep much. Them was rough fellows those days."

May lives today at the same Cook Waterhole where his family first came in a wagon to settle about 1888. He was about eight then and remembers an old fallen-in picket house covered with dirt which had served as a cow camp. It was too far gone for the family to use; they stayed in a tent awhile. May's father had bought 250 acres at $3 an acre sight unseen and had some time finding just where the land was.

The place still isn't the easiest for a stranger to find.

May was earning wages long before he was old enough to shave. Even before the Black Jack Ketchum experience he was working for a couple of brothers out in the Pecos River country. They stole a flock of sheep, but May was too young and green to realize it; he did what he was told to. When the matter came to light, the brothers sent him away to keep him from people who might ask embarrassing questions; that was when he wound up working for the 6s on Dove Creek west of San Angelo. For a time he drew two paychecks: one for working 6 cattle and one from the brothers for staying out of sight.

"For a long time," he says, "I was like a coyote wolf; prowled around wherever I could get a job."

He spent nineteen years on the Harris ranch near Eula in Callahan County. That ranch was owned by contractors and was devoted to raising and training horses and mules, many for work on the contractors' various road and railway construction jobs. The rest were for sale. May's specialty was riding broncs.

"I never had no secret. I just slipped down under the fork and gripped my knees and sat there. When somebody else had a horse he couldn't ride, he would bring it to me and I'd be the one had to ride it."

He took up a job as a fever tick inspector for Taylor County and stayed two years. Then he moved to Palestine in East Texas and spent a year cleaning up ticks in Anderson County. He recalls that it was often troublesome work, for many people didn't want to dip their cattle. The only time he ever called for help, though, was once near Palestine when a woman carrying something rolled up in her apron served notice that he wasn't just about to dip her cattle. May strongly suspected she carried a gun. He got the law to take care of that problem before he went on with the dipping. He returned to Taylor County to finish up the project and was the county's last tick inspector.

Besides his own livestock raising, he has worked for various other people as a cowboy through the years. He used to bring in wild two- and three-year-old steers for the big Windham ranches at so much a head delivered to their pens; that was no job for an amateur. "Cowboy work is all I ever done," he says. "I always liked it."

He decided to retire at seventy-five and sold his livestock, but that didn't mean he quit. Three sons ranch in the area, and he helps them regularly, still riding horseback just about every day at eighty-nine. "We still work stock in the open a lot, like the old days; rope them and drag them out and brand them like we always did."

Not long ago he had a chance to find out he could still ride a bad one. A six-year-old mare accidentally took him into a yellow-jacket nest and went into panic. "She pitched all over that country with me, but I stayed on her. I didn't get scared till she started to bawling."

He didn't feel he could afford to be thrown off and risk breaking a leg or an arm. In his long cowboy career he has suffered only two bad breaks—his right arm when he was a youngster at the 6s near Knickerbocker, and a leg when a cinch ring pulled loose as he was dragging a cow out of a bog at the Harris ranch. At the 6s, the wagon cook broke up an Arbuckle coffee box for splints and set the arm so well that it healed almost perfectly straight; it shows only a tiny rough ridge today.

Go to a doctor? "There wasn't no doctor," says May. "I just laid around camp three or four days, then went back to work and learned to rope left-handed. I got so I could rope about as good left-handed as I could right-handed; could forefoot them or anything."

He doesn't think horses are as good as they used to be. "The higher they're bred the sorrier they are, I believe. They just ain't got the staying quality those Spanish horses had; they don't stay in there."

He gets impatient with modern cowboys, too. "They don't know how to do nothing."

A highlight for May these days is his annual birthday party, usually a two-day affair on the Saturday and Sunday nearest his actual birthday, June 24. Over the two days as many as two or three hundred guests will show up to wish him well, eat barbecue and perhaps have a drink or two. On Saturdays they can have their drinks at the grove where the barbecue is; on Sundays they take them to the barn "because the preacher might come." Some cowboy friends who come from a distance bring their bedrolls and sleep on the ground.

One brother, Tom, still lives; a longtime cowboy, he is in a rest home in Abilene. Tom went off to the Spanish-American War with some other cowboys from the Suggs Ranch west of San Angelo; they joined the Rough Riders. Warnie May stayed home. "I never did like to fight," he says. "Oh, I always liked to wrestle, but that was in fun." Around the cowcamps, cowboys used to wrestle for recreation. Any newcomer was likely to have to prove himself on a cowhide. Rules specified that the combatant's feet must never step off of the hide. Wrestling and an occasional game of seven-up were about the only real cowboy entertainment. As May remembers, there wasn't much time for recreation.

"We had to stand guard every night, so we had to sleep every chance we got."

The three sons ranching close to home are Waldon, G. T. "Cotton" and Jack May. A fourth son, J. W., Jr., lives in Abilene. Alton Kelton May is a deputy sheriff at Panhandle, and Oma "Slick" May is with Scharbauer Cattle Co. in Vega. A stepdaughter, Mill Minta Keeton, stays with Warnie May at the homeplace in Ovalo.

Mitch's Trading Wasn't Glamorous,
But It Was Unmatched For Volume

Livestock Weekly, September 12, 1968

FOR YEARS I watched E. L. Mitchell engage in one of the most unglamorous facets of the livestock trade, buying old sheep and goats out of San Angelo auctions for a packer contract. He sat quietly in his accustomed chair, making his bids methodically, without fanfare or flamboyance. Wearing khakis and a little snap-brim hat, he was hardly a colorful figure in the classic western tradition. But he bought uncountable thousands of sheep and goats in what was essentially a salvage market and put millions of dollars into the pockets of Texas ranchers when they needed the money most.

≈

SAN ANGELO   Many a time in the last twenty-five or thirty years, E. L. Mitchell has stood in the background and watched some sheep buyer get his picture made in a pen of fancy lambs or good yearling ewes bought for a market-topping price. "Mitch" has seldom ever had either his name or his picture in the news columns, but for years he was considered the biggest sheep buyer in Texas. He probably still ranks close to the top of the list.

The trouble is that his specialty lacks glamour. He buys old ewes, old bucks and goats for the packer market.

His biggest years were in the early 1950s, when drouth blistered the Southwest and ranchers were having to whittle herds and flocks season after season. He bought 100,000 head a year at the peak. And though the price was not spectacular, the packer market was a lifesaver for many a ranchman. Other buyers were in and out, but Mitch was in the market at some price day in and day out, week in and week out, during those long, unhappy years.

Mitchell has been trading in cattle or sheep most of his adult life. He was born southwest of Nashville, Tennessee, where his father operated a steam shovel and steam locomotive handling iron ore. The family moved to San Angelo in 1907, when Mitch was about fourteen. He owned a few cattle by the time he was called to France in World War I. After the war he ran 300 to 500 mother cows on leased country, selling calves for $8 to $12 per head. Land leased then for fifty cents or less. He could put a cow on ten acres for $5 and squeeze a little profit out of her.

He was forced into trading by a market break. He had bought a string of cows to go on a leased place. A disastrous market in 1921 caught him owning cows for which he had turned down $70 a head and which he wound up selling to packers in Fort Worth for a nickel a pound. Only by trading was he able to keep his head above water and his family fed.

For a while after he started trading, he wondered why he hadn't been doing it all the time. It seemed to him that he had the Midas touch. For a time, everything he bought found a ready market and usually a profit. "I'd buy something from somebody, start walking down the street and run into somebody I could sell them to," he recalls. It didn't last.

He became interested in sheep because of their two-way pay, wool and mutton. He could usually get enough for the wool to pay expenses, and the lamb was profit. But not always. He vividly remembers the two-year-old ewes he shipped to Kansas City and netted only $2.30 per head after paying the freight. And he won't ever forget the load of three-year-old ewes he trucked to Fort Worth for a net of $1.12 per head.

"I never did have any that failed to pay the trucking, but I thought a time or two they weren't going to," he says. "She was sure rough in those Depression days."

In the 1930s he started trading in breeding bucks. One year he bought and sold more than 7,000 head.

Anybody who trades usually winds up holding some remnants too old or too thin to carry any farther. Through the years Mitchell built up a clientele for old sheep and goats, as well as some cattle, among packing plants in the San Antonio area and south Texas. He was buying these sheep by the thousands before Melton Provision Company built its plant and made an exclusive arrangement with him more than twenty years ago. During his early years with Melton he attended auction sales six days a week, and he bought in the country when he could.

He has been taking it easier the last few years, usually attending a couple of auctions a week and buying some country offerings.

"I never did try to pull any big deals," he says. "I always limited myself to what I could handle and keep from getting too far out on a limb."

That doesn't mean he has lacked the spirit of adventure. Always remembered as a high point of his life was a thirty-day boat trip he and a young uncle made down the Pecos River one winter when Mitch was just twenty. They went in at the mouth of Liveoak, near Sheffield, and took their time drifting along for a month. The river was deep and clear, though salty. They hunted for most of their food, game being plentiful. They trapped ringtails and foxes and skinned them. They left the river near Langtry and sold their catch of furs for $270 or $280 at a time when a good cowboy couldn't make but about $30 a month. During the whole trip they saw just two people, one Anglo and one Mexican.

Looking back upon the vast changes the livestock industry has made during his active years, he believes the biggest single factor has been the growth of the auction sale. "Auctions revolutionized livestock movement." he declares. Yet, the auction couldn't come of age until transportation and communications had advanced to a point that made it possible.

He has seen a lot of improvements since the time a ranchman at Rocksprings offered to round up his goats and put them out into the lane if Mitch would just drive them away. "I couldn't accept the deal," he recalls. "I didn't have anywhere to put them."

Hugh Campbell Was a Pro Ball Player, Cowboy and Four-Section Homesteader
Livestock Weekly, January 9, 1969

HUGH CAMPBELL, better known as "Red," was an earnest, talkative little fellow who in some ways reminded me a lot of my rancher grandfather. A young cowboy at the turn of the century, then a homesteader and in later years a leading West Texas Hereford cattle breeder, he had a wealth of good stories to tell. I wish I could have heard them all. Here are a few of them. Incidentally, my grandfather also broke horses and mules for Scott & Robertson in his youth. Movie actor Cliff Robertson, whom I have never met, is descended from the Robertsons of that partnership.

≈

BALLINGER   At just short of ninety-one, Hugh Campbell still dislikes being called Mr. Campbell. He'll tell a visitor, "Mr. Campbell was my papa's name. Mine is just Hugh . . . Red, better known."

There's probably not a Hereford man in Texas who doesn't know him. He still shows much of the wiriness that made him a top bronc rider in his early cowboy years. There is still more rust color than gray in his hair. He has always loved to talk, and the years have not dimmed his memories; he has seen plenty to talk about.

He still attends an occasional stock show or bull sale. Not long ago a cattle magazine featured a cover picture of him with John Wayne. Campbell is proud of the picture, but he confesses he's never seen a John Wayne movie. He sees no need in watching fictional westerns; he was there for the real thing.

"Papa turned each of us loose to make our own way when we got to be eighteen," he recalls. He left the Milam County farm determined to go west and become a cowboy. A good country ball player, he delayed his cowboy career long enough to play pro baseball for a New York Giants farm club in Houston through the summer of 1895.

Heading west to seek his fortune late that year, he came to Ballinger, where a sister lived. The town had too many saloons and too many plows to suit him. His goal was Midland, but he stopped over in Abilene and took a job breaking mules. When he was done he bought the mules for $25 apiece, shipped them to a first-Monday sale near his hometown and sold them for $75, his first trading profit. The money went in his sock.

During those early years he broke broncs and cowboyed for several big outfits, notably Scott & Robertson north of Stanton. He got to know the whole country from Abilene west to Midland, Odessa and Pecos, plus much of eastern New Mexico. He wound up running the A. S. Hawkins horse ranch in present-day Winkler County and in 1906 took out a four-section claim on land the state opened for homesteading. The land was valued generally at $2 an acre, the sandhills at $1.

In 1903 there were just fifteen men and one woman living in what today is Winkler County, Campbell recalls. Later on when the people decided to organize the county, a company laid out a townsite to be called Duval. But most of the other residents favored a different townsite (they had all been given lots by the man who owned the site). To make their town official they had to have a post office. Government red tape was as entangling then as now in such matters. The post office department kept turning down one application after another.

Theodore Roosevelt was president. Mrs. Campbell came up with the idea of naming the town Kermit, for Roosevelt's son. Within a week after the name was submitted, the town had approval for its post office. And Kermit won the county seat election.

During the early years of proving up his claim, Campbell continued to work outside for supplemental income. He worked cattle, ran wagons and broke horses. His brother, the late Seth Campbell (father of Lee Campbell, former president of the Texas Hereford Association), had come to the same country and also had claimed land under Texas homestead laws.

Hugh Campbell left one ranch job because of the beef. One day before riding off on business, the boss told Campbell and another cowboy to kill a fat beef. Next morning the boss noticed one of his cows walking the fence and bawling; he wondered aloud what could be the matter with her.

"You'd bawl too if your calf had been killed for a beef," Campbell told him.

The boss almost did. He said irritably, "Don't you know that around here we kill strays?"

Campbell put his bedroll in the wagon and asked to go to town. He said he wasn't going to work for $30 a month and then have to steal his beef.

He was acquainted with Jim Miller, a notorious West Texas gunfighter whose career eventually ended under the rafter of an Ada, Oklahoma, barn in one of the Southwest's more spectacular lynchings. The acquaintanceship started this way:

Working cows in the Monahans shipping pens, Campbell was badly hooked under one arm. The cowboys carried him to a hotel near the tracks, where the doctor treated him and told him he would have to stay close until the danger of blood poisoning was gone.

Shortly before this, a rancher had hired tough Jim Miller to run a bunch of four-section homesteaders off their claims along the Pecos River. Miller had done quite well at his job until one day he rode up on a man who didn't care to move. The settler neatly parted Miller's hair with a .30-.30 slug.

The morning after being hooked, Campbell decided to go out for air. On the hotel's front porch he met a stranger whose head was wrapped in bandages. The stranger pointed to a butcherbird on a telephone wire and offered to bet $5 he could hit the bird with a pistol shot. Campbell declined the bet. The stranger demonstrated anyway, and down came the bird.

Campbell walked across the street and asked a friend who was that crazy so-and-so firing the pistol. The friend asked in surprise, "You don't know Jim Miller?"

Campbell did from then on; he made a point of it. The first thing he did was find himself a bed in a rooming house and move out of the hotel.

He recalls that there were many tough men in far West Texas, some legal and some not so legal. Inadvertently he got on the bad side of one when he found a couple of calves wearing one rancher's brand and following another rancher's cows. One thing led to another until cattle inspector Lod Callahan of Midland was called into the case and got shot in the leg. The hot-iron artist fled into New Mexico. Some time later Campbell accidentally got his hands on a letter in which the thief vowed to get even with him. He worried, because he knew the man was capable of it.

Sitting in his house one day, he glimpsed a rider passing the window. Certain it was the thief come to settle up, he stepped quickly to his back porch, got a rifle and told Mrs. Campbell to open the door. Campbell held the rifle ready to fire as soon as the thief stepped into view.

The man in the doorway turned out to be a friendly cowboy. Campbell quickly put the rifle away, and the cowboy never knew how close he came to being shot. The incident haunted Campbell for years, because he always felt that had it happened at night instead of in daylight, he might have fired before he realized his mistake.

Anyway, the man he worried about never came back. An argument over a poker game in Arizona resulted in a gunfight, and he came out second.

Campbell made a few cattle drives in the waning days of the trailing industry. He went on a drive from Midland, Texas, to Spearfish, South Dakota, that took three months and sixteen days. He made several shorter drives to Kansas for Scott & Robertson. They had to cross Indian Territory. Winfield Scott gave his men orders that when the Indians asked for beef, they should always be given one. In return, the Indians would help the drovers in any way they could.

Right behind one Scott & Robertson herd came a McKenzie herd from Fort Stockton. The trail boss refused an Indian request for beef.

That night his herd was stampeded, and he lost a week gathering cattle.

Campbell says he "never was stuck on the Kermit country."

He homesteaded there principally because it was one of the last places open. It was a good grass country when he first saw it, for the early ranchers stocked it within its limitations. He believes the big decline came with the four-sectioners, who had a hard row to hoe financially and tried to get more out of the land than it was capable of producing.

He owned fifteen or sixteen sections when he decided to sell in 1917 and move back east. The war was on; he feared he might have to leave a wife and two sons on land still far from paid for. He sold out, then bought 827 acres about five miles north of Ballinger. The place was much smaller than his Winkler County ranch, but at least it was free and clear. Though it had quite a lot of farmland on it, at thirty-eight he was no longer so intolerant of farming as he had been at eighteen.

Through the years he added to his holdings. At one time he owned land in Concho and Schleicher counties but sold it. He still owns a section he bought some years ago in Brown County.

He bought his first registered Herefords in 1927 from Tom Schulz of Paint Rock. He added to the herd until finally he owned only registered cattle. The Campbell cattle gained quite a bit of fame in the 1950s because of steers fed and shown by his grandsons, Mark and Hugh, III. Hugh Campbell was always around when the steers were shown, and anybody who didn't know the boys were his grandsons just wasn't paying attention.

A son, Rollin, and the two grandsons are running the Ballinger places now. Another son, Randall, has a place in Hamilton County, where he runs Angus cattle.

Hugh Campbell still rides horseback occasionally. "I finally had to sell my old horse," he says. "I just couldn't keep off of him."

A couple of years ago he should have. In a hurry to catch a cow, he jumped on the horse's bare back. Startled, the horse bolted out from under him. Campbell wound up hospitalized, several vertebrae broken. Crowding ninety, he decided it was time to quit riding bareback.

Rachel Bingham Cooked For Cowboys Thirty-Three Years; Would Never Do It Again

Livestock Weekly, October 16, 1969

A FICTION writer never knows where the next idea will come from or the solution to a worrisome story problem. I had written much of my novel, *The Day the Cowboys Quit,* but was having difficulty with a hired-gun character named Lafey Dodge. I could not seem to bring him to any kind of reality; he remained a two-dimensional villain of the old pulp-magazine variety. Then ranchwoman Rachel Bingham told me her story about an old-time gunfighter named Pink Higgins. He was much like the character I had been trying vainly to create. I interpolated Mrs. Bingham's story about the cattle thief's grave into my novel, and suddenly Lafey Dodge became a real human being with all of a real human being's contradictions. I have always been grateful to her.

≈

SPUR   The finest Texas cowboy photographs ever done were those Erwin E. Smith made on various Panhandle ranches around and just after the turn of the century. For three generations they have been widely printed and circulated. A number of them hang on Rachel Bingham's wall. Mrs. Bingham, seventy-eight, can identify a great many of the cowboys because she cooked for them during the thirty-three years she and her husband, the late Al Bingham, lived and worked on the Spur Ranch. Most of those years she cooked for an average of about three cowboys besides her own family, and at special times a dozen or more.

"We moved four times in thirty-three years and never left the ranch," she says. "I lived in one house at headquarters twenty-two years and never broke a windowpane."

Not that she didn't sometimes feel like it. When they finally left the Spur in 1942, she was still cooking on a wood stove and finishing the night-time chores by lamplight. A visit to the bathroom was still an outdoor trip. She saw the ranch industry move from horse and wagon to a pickup and truck economy, but she never had hot and cold running water until she finally moved to town.

Her father was W. W. Ellis, early-day Spur rancher. In 1903, at about twelve, she helped him drive his cattle to the area around Spur from Wellington. She rode horseback a lot until recent years and never any way but sidesaddle. When she was a girl a woman who rode astride, drank whisky or smoked cigarettes was not highly regarded. She has never done any of the three.

They had some colorful neighbors in those days. Most noted was Pink Higgins, still remembered as a gunman and survivor of the Higgins-Horrell family feud in Central Texas. Rachel says he was a kind and thoughtful neighbor, whatever his past might have been. He freely admitted a number of killings and said they were all justified. The last came during Rachel's girlhood, when the Spur Ranch hired Higgins to do whatever was necessary to stop some cattle stealing. What was necessary was the killing of a cowboy, done, however, in self defense. The cowboy was buried in a open pasture not far from where he died.

In later years Rachel's husband noticed that cattle were walking over the grave and had knocked the headboard down. He decided to haul some wire and posts over there and fence off the little plot to protect it. While he was digging, Higgins came along. For a nervous moment or two, Bingham thought Higgins was going to contest him for what he was doing.

Instead, Higgins said, "I believe I'll help you." He tied his horse, took hold of the posthole diggers and helped fence off the grave of the man he had killed.

It was told about Higgins that he was scarred from head to toe from his many battles. When he died of a heart attack in his later years, Al Bingham went over to help prepare him for burial. He said the only scar the man bore was a small one just above one wrist.

Perhaps one reason for her good feelings about Higgins was that one time when she was still a girl, she went to town with her father for supplies, riding sidesaddle on a mule. At a river crossing they met Higgins on his way to Snyder to stand trial for the death of the cowboy. Higgins commented to Ellis that he should be proud of his daughter. "I've got four daughters," Higgins said, "and not a one of them can ride a mule." Rachel Ellis felt ten feet tall.

Al Bingham had worked for the Spur Ranch since 1904 and stayed on when the Swenson Land & Cattle Company bought the 480,000 acre place in 1909. He and Rachel were married in 1909 and spent $90 setting up housekeeping. That bought them a bedstead, mattress and springs, cookstove and dresser. "I was prouder of that than of anything I have now," she says.

The company put them in what was known as the South Spur Camp. It was a small frame house without screens or linoleum. They bathed in a Number Three washtub (and did the whole thirty-three years) but at least had good spring water to put in it. Three cowboys wintered at the camp, and she cooked for them. In those days when a ranch hired a married cowpuncher it was considered that the wife was hired too, though she was seldom paid.

The town of Spur was born in 1909. The Binghams rode in eleven miles on horseback the day the town lots were put up for sale and bought one for $50. When they sold it three or four years later for $100, they thought they were rich.

It was mostly big-ranch country in those days, the Spur, O Bar O, Pitchfork, 6666s. But there were still many small landowners, mostly people who had filed under the Four Section Act. Some ranches paid cowboys to file and turn the land over to them. A lot of horses, dogs and cats filed on land and got it. Faulty surveys led to disputes and vacancies; Mrs. Bingham knows of one section of land that had 800 acres instead of 640. Section lines were often irregular, the bulges commonly known in those days as "landslides."

Through the years the Binghams were moved to the Red Arroyo Camp and later the Slaughter Camp. She had running water of a sort. "I'd grab two three-gallon buckets and run to the spring." She has little use for people who enjoy modern conveniences and still complain.

Ranch fare consisted mostly of staples, including beef, beans, canned goods and dried fruits. There was never fresh fruit or vegetables beyond what they grew in a garden. She always made it a point to can lots of fruits, jams and jellies.

She wearied of it, as might be expected. One Christmas, after she had cooked, fed and washed dishes for about a dozen "cowboys, comers and goers," she declared she was quitting. Al Bingham could go or stay but she was through cooking. In fact, she stayed in bed and let the men fix their own breakfast.

Range boss Joe Erickson, known as "Judge," talked her into staying until he could confer with the Spur office at Stamford. When he came back a few days later, he offered to move the Binghams to ranch headquarters. Reluctantly she agreed. She had a better house there, though she says she could have thrown a dog through some of the cracks in the siding. She still had to cook for three cowboys. "I was still carrying water, too, but I didn't have to climb up into a wagon to get it like I had done at dry times in the camps."

For twenty-two years they lived at Spur headquarters. She fed, mothered and nursed more cowboys than she can count. During what she calls "that other depression," when cowboy wages dropped to $18 a month for a time, she washed clothes and mended socks because the cowboys couldn't afford to buy clothes or hire laundry done. She would fry down 150 jars of sausage every winter. She jerked beef and preserved fried steaks by pouring grease over them and sealing the jars.

The hardships have left some marks. "I've got a misplaced gallbladder that I think comes from trying to hug a wire gate shut so many times when the wire was too short."

At headquarters she had no electricity for a refrigerator but bought ice in 100-pound blocks for an icebox. The men at the ice plant always put it in the car for her, but she usually had to lift it into the icebox herself when she got home. Now when her back hurts, which it often does, she remembers the icebox. Ranch entertainment in her early years was limited mainly to two events: all-night dances and brush arbor camp meetings. The same people went to both and saw nothing incompatible in them. Rachel Bingham calls herself a "dancing Methodist."

"Al Bingham and me won twenty-eight prizes dancing after we were old people," she recalls. Her father was a fiddler and taught all his children to play fiddle, guitar and mandolin. Mrs. Bingham still goes to square dances and fiddling contests. She has a rare ability to pat her foot to the music as she dances.

The Binghams left the ranch in 1942 and bought a house in town. For a time Al Bingham was a fencing contractor. After a few years he rejoined the Spur but lived in town. Rachel had had all the ranch life she wanted. She cherishes the memories but wouldn't do it again for anything.

"I'd get me a bill and peck with the chickens; I'd get me a cup and pass it before I'd ever cook on another ranch," she declares.

Her later years have been made lonely by the loss of much of her family. Her husband went first, in 1951. Then one of her only two sons, Newt, died in a bunkhouse fire at the Matador Ranch. Rachel adopted and raised her grandson, only to see him die in a tractor accident at eighteen. A few years ago her youngest sister, whom she helped raise, was killed in an automobile accident in San Angelo.

"When you bury that many of your own," she says sadly, "the sun goes down in the middle of the afternoon."

Snoring Mules, Muddy Roads
Bothered Old-time Freighters

Livestock Weekly, April 30, 1970

DURING my twenty-two years with *Livestock Weekly* I frequently visited small-town livestock auctions to find out what was new and to pick up possible leads for feature articles. One of my favorites was the auction in Mason, where almost invariably I would run across Irvin Ellebracht. He had a smile that was like a whole chandelier lighting up. He almost always had a story that was worth sitting and listening to. I have gotten a lot of mileage out of retelling his story about the *old* trail drivers.

≈

MASON   The teamster of old faced many problems largely unknown to his truck-driving counterpart today—bad roads, swollen rivers, snoring mules.

Irvin Ellebracht, to be seventy-five June 3, spent several years as a freighter before the curtain came down on that profession. He was also a cowboy and for many years made a considerable part of his living driving cattle at $4 a day from Mason and environs north to the railroad shipping pens at Brady, or east to Llano.

Biggest event of his freighting career was the moving of the huge Max Martin two-story ranch home by wagon six miles to a new location across the Llano River.

Ellebracht had grown up around a wagonyard and worked as a

cowboy for $1 a day during spring and summer, hauling stovewood at $3 a load during the off seasons. Later on, his father-in-law, A.J. Lindsay, had several unemployed mules, a big freight wagon and a smaller trail wagon, and Ellebracht needed something to do. They decided to go into freighting. Ellebracht teamed up with John Owens, an old-time Mason freighter. They began hauling cotton and cottonseed from the Mason County gins (at one time there were eleven, now there are none) to Brady, backhauling steel, cement and lumber for Mason bridge jobs. Ellebracht and Owens took a contract to haul eighty-four carloads of building materials from the railroad at Menard to the big Junction bridge project in 1915. That took them about seven months.

The house-moving job was the most challenging and interesting project they ever undertook, however. About the turn of the century Max Martin had built a fine big home on his ranch south of the river at Hedwig's Hill. Later he moved to Mason, and the house stood empty. His son, the late Seth Martin, was about to be married and needed a house on the ranch where he lived. Max Martin hired a Brady carpenter to see if he could get the house moved.

Nobody knew if it could be done. Ellebracht recalls that the house then must have been about forty by sixty feet, built to last forever. Its builder recalled that he had put a ton of square forged nails into it. Martin told the carpenter to take the chance; the house was of no value to him where it stood, and if it fell apart they would simply salvage the lumber and start over.

Owens and Ellebracht took on the moving contract. The carpenter sawed the house half in two, right through the center gable and around the heavy staircase so the house could be hauled in two sections.

It was six miles to Seth Martin's location. A crew moved ahead, cutting timber and clearing a forty-foot right-of-way. Ellebracht brought his ten mules; Owens brought all he had and some he borrowed from brothers. They took the beds from four wagons and made up several forty-foot 12 x 12s by binding 2 x 12s together, lashing these between the wagons as coupling pole extensions. They used screw-type jacks to raise the house up, then lower it onto the 12 x 12s. They had thirty-six mules, eighteen to each front corner.

The very first obstacle was the river. They stuck the wagons as they tried to move up the north bank and had to winch them out with steel cable blocks. Then they hit a stump in the newly cleared right-of-way and broke a wagon wheel. Jacking the wagon up and replacing that wheel was no small chore.

The betting was that the house would fall to pieces somewhere en route, but it didn't. They set the first half down on oak blocks and went back for the other half. The whole moving job took ten days, for which Ellebracht earned a total of $100 for his labor and the use of his ten mules.

When they finished, the mules had left the two halves of the house only about a foot out of line. The final alignment was accomplished by winching. The carpenters patched up the sawed sections, and the house was as good as if it had never been touched.

In fact, it still stands today, owned by Homer Martin, son of Seth. It has been bricked up and modernized and is considered one of the finest ranch homes in Mason County. In the whole move, not even a window was broken.

Looking back on it, Ellebracht can see that it was a hard life, though he didn't realize it at the time. Muddy roads were a teamster's nightmare, and they seemed to be muddy a lot of the time. Ellebracht spent a lot of hours doubling and tripling his teams to pull wagons through bad places one at a time. Feeding, watering, shoeing, hitching all those mules was a time-eating chore. And when it was all done, he usually had to drag his bedroll well away from the mules to get any sleep.

"Some of those old mules could really snore," he recalls. "They'd be up and down all night eating, stirring around, then going back to sleep and snoring."

After four years of freighting, he and Lindsay decided it was time to move on to something else and sold their mules. Ellebracht remembers the day he took the mules to Brady and delivered them to the buyer. He turned right around and came back to Mason the same day; he says if he had stayed over and had looked at those mules, he would have cried.

After that, Ellebracht spent much of his time driving cattle the thirty or so miles to the railroad at Brady and at Llano. Most of the cattle came from south of Mason. He had two good horses. One he would use in helping gather the cattle and start them. As he passed his own house six miles north of Mason on the way to Brady, he would leave that horse and pick up his coal black trail horse, Cyclone. Often when delivery was made at Brady he would catch a ride back home in a wagon or hack. He would simply turn Cyclone loose; the black would come home by himself.

One landmark on the Mason-Brady trail was the old Bird Trap, a few miles north of Mason, originally owned by George Bird. Fenced early, it was used as an overnight stop for cattle drives as far back as the 1880s when the destinations were much farther north than Brady. The front gate was of wire, strung between two post oak trees just far enough apart that a wagon could move between them. Those two trees still stand though the fence has long since been moved. Some wire and a piece of chain still cling to them.

One of Ellebracht's most memorable drives was to Llano in the mid 1920s; he was helping move 1,000 yearlings to the railroad. The night a disastrous tornado destroyed most of Rocksprings, Ellebracht and his crew were watching the lightning and moving among the herd, keeping them up. So long as the herd was kept stirring, it was less likely to take fright and stampede. Several old-time cowboys went with Ellebracht on that drive. The late Jim Brandenberger, who had gone up the long trails in the great cattle driving days, said sentimentally that he wanted to make a final trip with "one more bunch of cattle." Ellebracht rode among the cattle, singing to them all night. Several other veteran cowboys far older than Ellebracht were also along, including Emil and Alec Durst.

When they reached the Llano River, they found it on an eight-foot rise. Ellebracht and a couple of others got some of the steers into a bunch about twenty cattle wide and rushed them into the water. The rest followed, the current moving them into a half circle.

When the last of the cattle were crossed, Ellebracht started looking around for the old-timers. They were not in sight. He worried until they showed up in camp awhile later. When they finished pushing the cattle into the water, they had sensibly ridden upriver and crossed over on a bridge. That, Ellebracht reflected, was probably one reason they had managed to live so long and become known as *old* trail drivers.

After his cowboying days, Ellebracht became a range inspector for the federal Department of Agriculture in 1937 and spent twenty-five years and a month working for Uncle Sam, staking tanks, measuring allotments, checking brush-clearing projects, and so on.

Retired, he still operates 435 acres north of Mason and comes to town on auction sale days to watch the cattle sell. He considers himself part of the unofficial "entertainment committee" at the weekly auction.

Otto Jones' Suit Caused Joke
To Be Played On Horse Jingler

Livestock Weekly, August 19, 1971

THE GREATEST benefit of the forty-two years I spent as an active agricultural writer was in getting to know so many wonderful people in the ranching and farming professions. None of these memories do I treasure more than the delightful hours I spent on one occasion or another in the company of Otto Jones. I had known his brother Freddy when I was a boy; he day-worked for my father a time or two on the McElroy Ranch. I never met Otto until later years, however. I only wished I had come to know him much earlier. When my son Steve wrote his book, *Renderbrook: A Century under the Spade Brand*, he was able to use my notes and tapes of Otto's reminiscences. I regret that he never got to know Otto.

≈

COLORADO CITY When Otto Jones hired on as a cowboy at the Spade Ranch in 1907 at $25 a month, manager D.N. "Uncle Dick" Arnett told him the wage wasn't the thing that really mattered anyway. "He told me 'The man that stays is the man that wins,'" Jones recalls. Jones figures he won, for he stayed more than sixty years.

Wagonboss in 1910 and manager in 1912, Jones was active until a heart attack forced his retirement in 1966. Even then, he continued to live at the ranch until he moved to a house in Colorado City in

1969. He still drives a Spade car out to the ranch every few days to check the rain gauges and look around.

Cowboys always loved practical jokes, and Jones' arrival at the Spade chuckwagon that first day gave Fred Rodway, second wagonboss, a chance to pull one on the horse jingler. Jones owned one good suit, and having no place to pack it, he wore it that day. As Jones rode up, Rodway told the jingler the dressed-up fellow was W.L. Ellwood, the Spade owner, and that he had better trot out and hold his horse for him. Jones was impressed right off by the ranch's hospitality; the jingler obligingly held his horse all the time Jones ate dinner and applied to Dick Arnett for a job.

Arnett had been a friend of Jones' father, W.C. "Black Bill" Jones, who in the 1880s and early 1890s was a range boss for the H Triangle Bar at the head of Sweetwater Creek three miles northeast of Maryneal.

The Spade Ranch started as early as 1878 but has been in the Ellwood family since 1889. The Ellwoods—pioneer manufacturers of barbed wire—bought the brand and cattle from an early Donley County rancher named J.F. "Spade" Evans.

The home ranch was the Renderbrook Spade south of Colorado City, then 200 sections, later 250, now 215. Jones' first job was to help trail cows from there north of Gail to the ranch's "49 Pasture," so-called because it contained forty-nine sections. Farther north was the 450-section "Plains" ranch, fifty miles long and nine or ten miles wide, in Hockley and Lubbock counties. This was used primarily as a big steer country, though in dry times it pastured cows and heifers when the home ranch herd had to be thinned.

In the early years before the final tick cleanup, all cattle had to be dipped twice before they could move from the Renderbrook to the 49 or Plains ranch. As soon as the second dipping was completed, they hit the trail. It was about four days to the 49 or ten days to the Plains. The nicotine sulphate dip had a tendency to heat the cattle, so they couldn't be pushed too hard. They were usually driven in the morning, rested through the heat of the day, then moved again in late afternoon and into evening.

The general routine was to take yearling steers to the 49, pasture them till they were two-year-olds, then take them to the Plains. There in the early years they stayed until they were fours; later they began selling as threes. By the early 1940s they were selling as twos. The 49 pasture by then had long since been sold.

There was already a fair amount of barbed wire in the country when Jones began his cattle driving career. If a gate wasn't handy, the practice was to pull the steeples out and lower the wire to cross a herd. When Spade began putting red plank gates at regular intervals in its fences, some of the old cows never could learn to use them. They would pass an open gate, looking for a place where the wire was let down.

Jones remembers that though steer herds would occasionally run, dry cows were most likely to pull off an old-fashioned stampede.

About the most troublesome cattle problem he ever encountered involved a steer herd that the cowboys were pushing up to the shipping pens at the Smyer siding on the Plains in 1942. Tom Arnett loped ahead to ask the train crew not to blow their whistle. Just before he reached the engine, they did it. The cattle disappeared in one grand rush into a nearby field of tall cane, where they suddenly realized they couldn't see each other and went into a panic sure enough. It took a long time to drive them out of that cane.

Another time, a herd was being held overnight in a jog at the Rattlesnake Tank in a Slaughter pasture. Several horses in the remuda wore bells. In the night, after a little rain, the horses got to running and playing. The cattle tore up a considerable amount of Slaughter fence getting away from those bells.

Jones delivered 800 head of two- and three-year-old heifers into the young town of Lubbock in 1913, watering them in a lake outside of town. That lake is now the site of a large apartment house on South University, where water still collects when it rains. Jones rode up to the courthouse square, where all the business then was concentrated, and counted thirteen automobiles. They impressed him most because of the wooden spokes, which reminded him of buggy wheels. He says on a recent trip to Lubbock he saw an estimated 1,300 cars on Avenue Q alone, all competing for one parking space.

He drove the herd across open country between town and the

present site of the Tech campus, delivering them at a canyon now on the north edge of Tech.

Night guard was in three shifts. Some men liked the first or last because they got all their sleep in one piece. But others liked the middle guard because they had a chance for a little more sleep afterward. The middle guard was usually the most active because it was the nature of many cattle to get up in the middle of the night and move around. If a cloud came up, the wagonboss lost the most sleep; he was likely to be up all night. A lighted lantern was left tied to the top of the chuckbox so the night herders could find the wagon in the dark.

The cattle drives stopped after the railroad was built from Sweet-water to Lubbock. But some years later, when times were hard and money tight, W.L. Ellwood asked Jones if he could again drive cattle afoot to the Plains ranch and save shipping expense. Jones said he would like to try; he had several young cowboys who had never had the pleasure of standing night guard. For about three years in the early 1920s, Spade again went back to trailing. It was even tougher by then to work out a route because so much more land had been fenced and had gone into farming. But on the other hand the tick problem was over, and the cattle no longer had to dipped.

Jones regards the elimination of the tick as the biggest single job of his career. The cleanup began in earnest in 1914 and was not finished until 1917. The Spade wagon went out in April and stayed until December. The goal was to dip every animal every twenty-one days. But invariably some cattle were missed, and sometimes it took thirty days to get around.

The big drouth from 1916 to 1918, bad in other ways, helped the tick work because it trimmed the Spade cow herd from 6,000 head to about 1,500, allowing large pastures to be vacated for long periods to break the tick's life cycle, and making it possible to get everything dipped on schedule.

He says screwworms never were a bad problem on the Spade until about 1914. Up to then cowboys branded mavericks year-around, whenever and wherever they found them. Screwworms hit hard again in 1919, another wet year, and remained a problem off and on until the eradication program of the early 1960s.

He didn't begin noticing mesquite encroachment until the 1930s. There had always been some of it in the bottoms and on old roundup grounds, but it was not a problem. He blames it on drouths, overstocking, and on prairie dog eradication, though he regards the prairie dogs as being as hard on grass as the mesquite is. Prairie dog flats never had much grass.

He says through the years the Spade was always fortunate in having good cowboys, in some cases whole families of them like the Arnolds, Russells, McClellans, Boatrights, Northcutts and Swanns.

When times became good enough that every cowboy had a car, the end was in sight for the old-time roundup and chuckwagon. At first the married men would leave the wagon at night to go home. Then the bachelors started pulling out. When even the cook left, letting raccoons steal all the bacon out of the chuckwagon, Jones retired the wagon and built a trailer to haul the noon meal out from headquarters.

He says retirement doesn't bore him. "At eighty-two, you find it takes up a lot of your time just living," he declares. He sleeps real late in the morning, usually to 7:00 A.M. He reads several daily papers plus some weekly papers and magazines. It takes a certain amount of time to keep the grassburrs pulled out of the yard. He takes a nap every afternoon and drives out to the ranch a couple of times a week. That doesn't leave him much time for boredom, he says.

Big Lesson For Would-Be Cowboys:
Learn How To Stay Out Of The Way

Livestock Weekly, December 16, 1971

I SAW old-time cowboy Porter Myers first in a Tom Ryan painting. Later I recognized him on sight at an OS Ranch steer roping near Post and arranged to interview him at his home in the edge of that Caprock town. He had the kind of understated humor common to so many cowboys. He also had the many accumulated injuries which are a mark of a cowboy who has spent so many years at his trade. Though I talked with him only one time, I felt I had known him always. I have known his type all my life.

≈

POST   The first lesson a young cowboy needs to learn is how to stay out of the way, says Porter Myers, who was a young cowboy himself fifty or sixty years ago.

"When an old kid starts to learn how to stay out of your way, he's learning to cowboy," declares Myers. "Some never can learn that, and when one of those rides up it's like two good men leaving."

Myers retired from the 6666 Ranch at Guthrie almost three years ago after having worked on that ranch steadily for twenty-nine years, never missing a paycheck. A broken hip was the contributing factor to his decision. Afterwards he found boredom a lot more formidable than a broken hip, so he went back to light cowboying on a day-work basis when he felt like it, and lately to taking care of a ten-section ranch for a Lubbock owner.

Myers, to be sixty-nine in January, has lately come into two claims to fame. He has been the subject in two prize-winning art works by noted cowboy painter Tom Ryan, who has spent much time on the Four Sixes. One, done about 1967 and shown widely around the country since, is entitled *Sixty Years in the Saddle*. It depicts Myers on horseback, pushing cows and calves across a winter-dormant mesquite pasture. Newest, entitled *The Heritage*, shows Myers and his grandson, Rooster Swartz, pointing the way for a small herd. It was a gold medal winner at the National Cowboy Hall of Fame in Oklahoma City.

Myers and Ryan recently signed a contract with a calendar firm, so these pictures may start showing up on ranchhouse walls.

Until his retirement, Myers had spent all his life in Stonewall and King counties. He grew up on a stockfarm which his parents had settled in the early 1890s.

"Cowboying was all I ever wanted to do, the height of my ambition. Other people might have had jobs that made more money, but I never envied them. I always enjoyed what I did.

"A man ambitious to make a lot of money wouldn't ever want to be a cowboy; that's the wrong place for it. I was a cowboy because I loved the work. I worked hard and took a lot of punishment, but I had a lot of fun."

He did farmwork as a boy, and he tried it again for awhile after he and Mrs. Myers were married, fifty years ago last May 29. "Every day I ever ran a plow, I begrudged it. I told my wife I had taken it as long as I could, and I went back to cowboying for a living." He worked on several area ranches before joining the Sixes.

Through the years he acquired the cowboy's trademarks: a broken bone here, another there, a stiff neck, rheumatism from old injuries unseen but always felt.

Not since the late 1940s has he been able to turn his head and look back over his shoulder. He doesn't remember what happened, but witnesses told him about it. The last thing he remembers is loping up to go around some cattle; the next thing, he woke up in the Paducah hospital. It happened a long way out in the pasture, and he got back on his horse and followed the cowboys to camp, completely out of his head, two vertebrae out of line.

Some years later a horse fell and crushed his right ankle. The doctor told him he had worn his last cowboy boot. Myers took a pair of his boots to a saddleshop and had one boot split down the front, all the way to the toe, and laces put in. Later he replaced the laces with a zipper. Eventually he was able to slip a normal boot on and off.

The worst injury was the broken hip. The outfit was loading cattle in a set of brand-new steel pens. Myers had been doing the counting and was jotting a note in his tally book when a steer took a flying jump at a steel gate that someone had left unlatched. The gate slammed into Myers, knocking him down, and then the steer landed on top of him.

Myers says, "Every time they called the hospital that they were bringing in somebody from the ranch, those nurses knew it was either me or George Humphrey." Humphrey is the longtime Four Sixes manager.

Mr. and Mrs. Myers spent most of their 6666 years in either the ranch's north camp or its south camp. Myers raised two sons and two daughters more or less on horseback, trying to keep up with a fast pace. He shudders now when he thinks of the chances he led the youngsters into. "I never looked at the ground, I just looked at whatever I happened to be running. I didn't get grown till I was past fifty." He says he is teaching his grandchildren more caution.

One of the benefits of working on a big outfit like the Four Sixes was that a man hired to cowboy could spend most of his time cowboying, Myers says. Men were hired special for windmilling, fence building, etc. That was not always the case on smaller outfits. The chuckwagon usually went out about September 1 and stayed out until mid-January. It went out again April 1; the cowboys were lucky if they were through by July 4, when the 6666 wagon was traditionally due in Stamford for the Cowboy Reunion. Sometimes when the reunion was over the wagon had to go back out for a short while.

Myers says people didn't realize they were undergoing hardships. "We seemed to enjoy ourselves and our friends more than we do now," he comments.

Just the same, he concedes that it would be hard to go back to that life after having today's conveniences. He didn't have electricity and butane until the early 1950s. Later, he and Mrs. Myers moved to a camp where the REA (Rural Electrification Administration) had just installed a line. By then they had gotten used to electrical appliances. The REA was a week late getting the electricity turned on. "We hurt," he says. "I mean, we really hurt."

In his younger years he enjoyed riding broncs. "As a kid, if I heard about a horse that had been bucking people off, I couldn't rest till I had taken a seat at him. Sometimes I rode them, sometimes I didn't."

After Myers had recuperated more or less from the broken hip, he had some trouble getting around, particularly getting on and off of a horse. The cowboys wouldn't let him do anything strenuous, always telling him to stand back and let them take care of it. Myers says he decided he had as well quit officially as unofficially, so he took voluntary retirement.

He moved to Post but soon found retirement bored him. He worked a while at the Lubbock auctions, moving cattle up and down the alleys on horseback. He found it didn't take long to see all there was to see of an alley. It was too much confinement for a man used to big pastures. "You were in a lope all the time but not going anywhere."

He started day-working for Jim Prather and other ranchers around Post. Lately he has been looking after a ten-section ranch for W. T. Sharp of Lubbock. He has an eleven-year-old that the Four Sixes gave him, the last "hackamore bronc" he ever broke, turned over to him as a three-year-old after having been ridden a few saddles.

Myers lives in town and drives out to the ranch every day in his pickup. He wears his spurs the way he wears his boots—all day, every day.

He has seen lots of improvements in recent years in living conditions for both man and beast. "Even the cattle are spoiled now," he declares. "We used to have nothing but old gyp water on a lot of the ranch; those old native cows would drink it like it was good. These cows now, they've been fed so long, and given good water so long, they'd starve to death before they would drink any of that gyp."

He and George Humphrey both took a dim view when cowboys began to demand iced tea at the chuckwagon; it came in spite of them. Myers never did learn to like iced tea, but he puts away a lot of coffee.

Fish Martin Traded Colt for Hen; Learned Lesson In Economics

Livestock Weekly, April 27, 1972

FISH MARTIN was one of my grandfather's generation, those people who were a link between the first West Texas pioneers and my own time. He witnessed the coming of railroads, carried a surveyor's flag for the laying-out of a new county, helped catch some of the last wild horses, spent years working as a cowboy and ended his days operating a little second-hand shop on San Angelo's north side, where he placed more value on good conversation than on making a trade.

≈

SAN ANGELO   Fisher "Fish" Martin missed the disastrous Ben Ficklin flood of 1882 by two years. His father, mother and four sisters got out by the skin of their teeth, or Martin would never have been around to observe his eighty-eighth birthday coming up Monday.

His father, Bit Martin, had come to the Concho country from Gonzales in 1872, first establishing a ranch between Knickerbocker and Christoval. Sometime during the 1870s he freighted lumber with an ox team and built a hotel in old Ben Ficklin, which was the Tom Green County seat and a far more respectable town than wicked San Angelo, then considered largely a sin center for the soldiers at Fort Concho.

The flood came up during the night and would have swept the

family away had an uncle not brought them a warning. Water was up to the bed of the hack they used to beat their retreat. The hotel went down the river, as did about sixty-five people. The town of Ben Ficklin never recovered.

The family moved back to the ranch, where Fisher Martin was born in 1884. When he was still a baby his father sold out and moved to the later site of Sherwood on Spring Creek, and bought a ranch at Arden. Sherwood was founded when Irion County was organized in 1889. Martin grew up there.

His father was livestock inspector for Irion County. The country still had lots of mustangs running wild. The father, who always rode good horses, would ride into a band of mustangs, rope a colt and hold it until the mustangs were out of sight. Then the colt would follow his horse home. At one time Fish was bottle feeding five mustang colts his father had caught that way. Once his father brought home two at one time. He had roped one, then jumped off and grabbed another around the neck, holding both until the rest of the band was gone.

The last mustangs he saw were in the 09 Ranch's 100-section south pasture soon after the turn of the century. People by then were shooting the ones they couldn't catch. They were also shooting a lot of wild burros to remove them from competition for the grass.

He remembers the mustangs as small and not very pretty by modern standards. Their manes and forelocks grew so long that when running they had to sling their heads from side to side to see where they were going. Their tails dragged the ground, often accumulating a considerable knot of burrs and other trash. Sometimes that knot got big enough that it would bounce up and down when they broke into a run.

His early education toward a sense of values was helped along by a mustang colt he had raised on a bottle. In the presence of his father he traded it for a speckled hen that had caught his eye. When his mother later protested, his father said the boy was old enough to learn that a deal was a deal, and he made it stand. That lesson served him well in later years when trading became a means of livelihood.

He began working on area ranches at sixteen. His first steady job was on Ed Jackson's 09 Ranch about halfway between Sherwood and

Ozona at the turn of the century. He jingled horses for that outfit three years before they ever gave him a cowpunching job. He recalls that there were often 200 or more horses in the remuda. The wagon was out a good part of the year, the ranch having perhaps twenty hands of its own plus several "outside" men from neighboring ranches. Each man customarily had seven horses in his mount. Using two a day, a cowboy let a horse get three days' rest between rides.

Ordinarily a man would get about four decently gentle horses and three young "broke" horses—"broke" meaning the ranch had hired somebody to ride them five "saddles" and pronounce them ready. The broncs would be dependable horses to work the herd.

In 1904 he helped as a flag man in running the survey for Reagan County after it was cut from Tom Green County. People have often wondered about the odd, long panhandle that extends westward from the north part of Tom Green County the full width of Irion. Because Irion was organized well ahead of some counties farther west, the panhandle was left for a legal connection between the eastern and western parts of Tom Green. It is hardly wide enough to sweat a good saddle horse in a lope.

Martin remembers seeing eight-to-nine-year-old big steers in the heavy brush of Centralia Draw, wise old steers that had eluded the Bar S roundups year after year. He recalls that the brush was confined mostly to such draws. He attributes the brushless condition of the prairies then to periodic grass fires. He says in the early mornings his boots would sometimes be wet in the stirrups from dragging through dew on top of the tall grass. When dry, that grass made a fire hot enough to destroy any kind of brush.

His longest lasting ranch job was with the Cargile Company, organized by J.S. Cargile, who bought the Bird & Mertz ranch at the head of Rocky Creek northwest of San Angelo in 1902. Martin had put up the Cargile crew for the night at a house he was living in near Water Valley. A few days later Jess and Howard Cargile, sons of J.S., hired Martin to go to the ranch.

He says he never could forget the day he went on the payroll: the twelfth day of the twelfth month of 1912.

He stayed there eighteen years, most of that time as boss and roustabout for the various Cargile ranches. After six years, still working for Cargile Company, he went into partnership with Jess Cargile on sheep. Their first band was 1,400 good young ewes bought for $14 per head. They ran them twelve months, paying the Cargile Company for the grass, got a clip of wool which brought fifty cents a pound (it was little or no better in 1972) and a lamb crop which sold for $11 per head. After paying all expenses they lacked only fifty cents per head clearing the ewes. Later they made a deal to run three bands under herd on the John Abe March ranch at five cents a month per head, sixty cents a year.

Among other Cargile operations was the buying of unbroken young mules, growing them out and reselling them. Martin still has a scar on his side where a big outlaw mule grabbed him and pulled him down from a fence with its teeth while he was showing a string of mules to some buyers for the Texas penal system. He was sure they would want to cut that mule back, but to his great satisfaction they bought him. They said they had a big black convict who would chew both ears off of that mule.

Jess Cargile and Martin finally sold out their sheep operation, and Martin left the ranch. "I was getting up in years, or thought I was," he explains. He had decided it was time to find a gentler life. He didn't know he still had more years ahead of him than he had put behind him.

For many years he and Mrs. Martin moved around the country, living a while here, a while there, settling a few months or a few years in any place that struck their fancy "until one of us got the itch to move." He traded in real estate or anything else that showed promise of a good return.

For the last several years he has been back in San Angelo, near where it all started for him. He operates a small second-hand store on North Chadbourne. "It gives me something to do," he says.

He never did forget the lesson he learned swapping that mustang colt for a speckled hen. The other day while a reporter was visiting him a man came in with a pulley he wanted to swap for a kitchen faucet set and $2 boot. Martin thought $1 boot was enough. When the reporter left after an hour, they still hadn't come to terms over that extra dollar.

Jethro Holmes Has Two Work Oxen
As His Answer To Energy Crisis

Livestock Weekly, March 28, 1974

I FIRST met Jethro Holmes at one of San Antonio's annual folklife festivals on the grounds of the Institute of Texan Cultures. He had his team of oxen hauling logs for the building of a pioneer-style cabin on the institute grounds. I made it a point a few months later to visit him on his home grounds in the East Texas piney woods and found him a delightful person, in many ways a throwback to my grandparents' generation.

≈

WOODVILLE   It's hard to find many East Texas occupations that Jethro Holmes hasn't tried at one time or another, and usually managed to make a living at.

Most people in recent years tend to think of him as an ox trainer. His ten-year-old twin oxen, Tom and Jerry, have been seen in shows and parades over much of the country as well as working for real up and down logging roads here in deep East Texas.

But in his eighty-two years he has been at one time or another a cotton hauler, a farmer, a cowpuncher, a coppersmith, a concrete man, a hearse driver, a logger and a tree surgeon. Once in 1914 he helped drive more than 3,000 cattle from Sonora to Eden, then helped drive 1,562 turkeys to a packing plant in Brady.

Today he keeps busy mainly as a tree surgeon and concrete man. Among other things he uses his two oxen to level off foundation sites for new houses and to haul off trees that he cuts down.

Holmes started training work oxen when he was ten years old and had trained seventeen yokes by the time he went to World War I in 1917. He still owned eight yokes of oxen when he went into uniform. While he was gone, his father sold them.

He thought about training some more, but the gasoline engine had made oxen look hopelessly old-fashioned by then. He never tried to train oxen again until he got his present pair from a dairyman here the day after they were born. They were twins, a Holstein-Guernsey cross. He raised them on a bottle, made a small yoke to put on them when they were two-and-a-half months old and didn't castrate them until they were past two years old. He wouldn't have done it even then, but there were too many heifers in the neighborhood, and the pair were getting a shade unruly.

He says he was afraid that after fifty-four years he might have lost his touch, but everything came back to him easily. After all, he points out, oxen don't change much.

"I can walk out into a herd of cattle and tell you every bull calf that would mind and break and not be mean," he says.

He finds Jerseys the meanest, Holsteins the easiest to handle and train. "They never forget nothing," he declares.

In training Tom and Jerry he used to drive them to town and back, a distance of perhaps two miles or a little more. They still want to stop everywhere he stopped then, and turn everywhere he turned. On one of his trips to town he pulled in at Jesse Mills' house and tied the two calves at the gate. He still has to pull at the oxen to keep them from taking that road.

His oxen know the town of Woodville about as well as he does. If he gives them their head, they'll go straight for the tree where he customarily stakes them. Turned loose on the town, they'll graze around but eventually come back to the tree and wait.

He makes his own yokes and so far has had to make several for this pair as they grew. He used to like willow, but it is hard to get anymore, so he uses curly maple. Birch is the best, but he can't get it. A well-made ox yoke, he says, can be balanced on the point of a nail.

Jethro Holmes is considered one of Woodville's great natural resources, promoting his town wherever he goes, both with his oxen and with his outgoing personality. He is one of those eternal optimists to whom a stranger is just a friend he hasn't gotten around to visiting with yet.

He grew up in San Augustine County, where his family had large farming interests. As a boy he helped take family cotton to the gin at Martinsville, four oxen hauling two bales to the load—about 1,100 pounds of lint cotton and 1,400 pounds of seed. He vividly remembers "Eggnog Branch," a favorite wagoners' campsite, well named for an inclination to put away a few nips of homemade whiskey to fight off the chill of the fall night air.

His great-grandfather had originally settled there on a Spanish grant and built one of the earliest water-driven mills in Texas for grinding wheat and corn.

Holmes was working in Houston in 1914, driving a hearse among other things, when the people he was working with got a call from the bank in Eden to send 300 cotton pickers. Holmes was sent out with a cashier's check to recruit them, get them on a train and see them to Eden. There they were parceled out to individual farmers. While he was in Eden, B. M. Badgen and C. W. Call bought a big string of cattle in the Sonora area, and Holmes went down to help bring the cattle to Eden. He remembers them as totaling about 3,000 Herefords and 250 Mexican steers. When he got back to Eden, somebody there was buying up turkeys for a processing plant in Brady, and he signed on to help drive the birds.

He says he drove those turkeys just the way they drove the cattle except somewhat slower. The main bunch would move down the road while a buyer went off on side trips picking up turkeys. These would be driven up to the road and thrown in with the others. There was little or no night time traffic then, so the turkeys were allowed to bed down in the lane. Holmes recalls that 1,562 head were delivered to Brady after a loss of only five on the trip. They were too fat and died of the exertion.

Holmes has spent most of his life around farming and livestock, at least off and on, but he developed mechanical skills that put him in demand over the years for other work. During World War II he was called on by the government to do copper work on ships in Houston. He says he's the oldest remaining coppersmith in the state. It's a lost art, almost, like training oxen.

He gets a lot of calls as a tree surgeon. Not long ago he was called to Jasper to see if he could save that town's historic old Tavern Oak, under which the Confederate veterans used to have their meetings. The tree, estimated to be 250 years old, had much rotten wood and mistletoe damage. He trimmed out a lot of dead wood and put five yards of concrete into the tree. He has pictures of himself standing far up in that tree working; he was fully eighty years old at the time.

Since he has had the two trained oxen, it has become standard procedure for him to play Santa Claus at Christmas time, putting lighted deer antlers on Tom and Jerry and passing them off as reindeer.

People who have known him for years say Holmes used to play Santa Claus in a different way in flusher times. They say it was his habit to spend considerable money making up food and gift baskets, which he delivered to the front porches of the needy in the dark of the night.

Today those two oxen not only are rare show pieces but help him make a living. He works them to plows, slips, fresnoes and a log wagon.

The best—or at least easiest—way to locate Holmes is to catch him at the drugstore in town. The last mile or so to his place is down a rough, high-centered, extremely crooked logging road far out in the tall timber where you'll think you are hopelessly lost. But his pack of hound dogs will come out and meet you, accompanying you the rest of the way in full cry. When you leave, they'll convoy you halfway back to the pavement, bidding you goodbye.

Old Family Tradition Kept
Frank Austin In Cattle Trade

Livestock Weekly, December 16, 1976

FRANK AUSTIN was a lanky little West Texas rancher who had as engaging a smile as I ever saw. When I would visit an Abilene bookstore for book-signing parties, he would come to visit and share with me stories of his cattle-raising forebears. His story about his grandfather, John W. Day, taking his children up the trail in a cast-off army hearse, showed up in one of my novels, *Eyes of the Hawk*. His story about breaking bronc horses and mules was interpolated into a sequence in *The Good Old Boys*. He also told me a couple of stories I have not had the nerve to use anywhere. The last time I saw him was shortly before he died. He showed up, as always, at one of my book-signings in Abilene, and we had a good visit. After he left, the store received a worried call from his home. He was not supposed even to be out of bed, much less to be driving his pickup over to the shopping center to sit and talk for an hour about old times.

≈

ABILENE   That Frank Austin of Abilene has always been most interested in livestock and ranching is understandable. He comes from a long line of cattlemen, both on his mother's and his father's sides of the family.

On his mother's side was Jesse Day, born in Tennessee in 1804. Austin says Jesse Day was an original Texas trail driver. He was trailing cattle to Missouri before the Civil War. In fact, he was drowned in 1860 while crossing a herd over the Brazos River at Waco.

Austin's great-uncle, Tony Day, a son of the trail driver, did not like feeling crowded. He left Callahan County and operated the Turkey Track Ranch near Tascosa in the Panhandle until he began to feel hemmed in by barbed wire and settlements. He moved up to Spearfish, South Dakota, and in partnership with Englishman Hank Cresswell set up a new Turkey Track Ranch. When that country too began to fence up, he sold out his interests and moved on north to Alberta, Canada. At one time he was reputed to be leasing two million acres from the Canadian government. But he had strayed a long way from Texas. He fell victim to a monstrous freezeup which cost him 15,000 cattle. He retired to sunny San Diego, California, where he bought some land and kept an orange grove the rest of his life.

Austin's grandfather, John W. Day, ranched originally in the Kyle area. He was gathering steers for a trail drive when his wife died, leaving him several children including Austin's mother, then per-haps eight or nine years old. Day still had to make that drive and decided to take the children with him. In San Antonio he bought an old military hearse from the army and put bunks in it for the children. He took an old black woman named Aunt Rose to care for them on the trail. They encountered no particular trouble, though Austin's mother had one bad scare. Indians came along and demanded a beef. One of them saw the little girl and jokingly offered to trade a paint pony for her. She took it seriously and hid in the hearse.

Grandpa Day brought his money home and hid it. One day three or four men rode up to the house and called him out. They put a rope around his neck, lifted him up on a horse and threatened to hang him if he didn't give them the money. He refused, and they led the horse out from under him. He dangled there, strangling. Either the rope was not tight or it stretched, for his toes touched the ground.

Old Aunt Rose was watching from the house. The moment the men turned to ride away, she ran out with a butcherknife and cut Day down. Austin remembers the scar that remained on his grandfather's throat the rest of his life. His neck was always a little crooked too. Aunt Rose had a home as long as she lived.

Sometime after the hanging incident, Grandpa Day moved west to Callahan County, landing at old Belle Plain, at one time a county seat, today a scattering of old stone walls and rubble. He and the Austin family happened to buy adjoining ranches there, south of present Baird.

Grandpa Austin was an inveterate tinkerer, always inventing something. He invented a movable washing machine, took it to the St. Louis Fair and won a prize. It was hand-agitated and had a firebox beneath to heat the water. He invented a gate, one of which is in the Baird museum. A horseman or wagon driver simply pulled a long rope to open it, went through, then pulled another rope to shut it. Later, when Baird was a division point on the Texas & Pacific Railroad, he invented some gadget having to do with the tracks and made money out of that.

Frank Austin has an old tintype made of his own father at Coleman in 1885, when he was helping gather steers for the noted Ab Blocker to take up the trail. After he married neighbor John Day's daughter, Cora, he moved to Baird, by then the county seat, and put in a butcher shop and meat market, and later a hardware and furniture business. When oil play began, Austin's father did well in that too. In later years he moved to Abilene and went into the refrigeration business, handling butcher supplies, commercial cooler storage, and so on.

Growing up in Baird, Frank Austin did cowboy work every summer, starting out at fifty cents a day. As he became older he started riding broncs. He worked three summers on the Dick Cordwent ranch south of Baird. The owner had a big horse ranch in far West Texas at Salt Flat. He would ship horses and mules to Baird to be broken for sale. One year Austin helped break 250 wild horses shipped by rail from Toyah.

They would hitch a gentle mule to a flatbed wagon, then tie the tongue to a stump with a slipknot. They would bring a bronc up, put it into harness by the mule, jerk the slipknot and take off. The gentle mule would run, and the bronc either ran with it or got dragged. By the time they had made a good round with the wagon the bronc was usually too tired to pitch much. They would take him out of harness, saddle him up and ride him.

They cut oats with a self binder, usually working three gentle horses and one bronc horse or mule. Outnumbered, the bronc could do little but go along.

The better horses would be paired by sizes and colors for buggy horses. A good matched buggy team would bring considerably more money than two individual saddlehorses.

Austin never contested as a roper or rider, but he liked to go to early-day steer ropings and bronc riding shows. He says he is probably one of the few men still living who ever saw the famous Booger Red Privett get thrown. Booger Red traveled about the country with his own string of broncs and a set of cowboys. They would put up a tall round canvas screen, like a tent without a top, and inside it build a temporary corral out of posts and heavy well rope. The crowd would pay to go in and watch the riding exhibitions. Besides riding his own outlaws, Privett would advertise for local people to bring their worst broncs.

When Privett hit Baird with his show, one of the Austins' neighbors, John Hancock, brought in a smooth, good looking bay mare. There were no chutes. Broncs were snubbed to a saddlehorn and saddled in the arena. Booger Red climbed aboard, made a little speech and jabbed spurs to the mare. She went straight up and Booger Red came straight down, over her shoulder. He had been taken by surprise. His legging strings caught on the saddlehorn but broke and freed him. Angry and embarrassed, he got back on the mare and made a good ride. "He could be thrown," Austin says, "but not often."

Austin cowboyed until he went to Europe in World War I. Upon his release in Fort Worth in 1919, a friend got him a job at Armour & Company. He intended to work there only a little while until he found something more to his liking, but he stayed sixteen years in the dressed beef plant. He bought some land near Rhome to satisfy his itch for the country. He would buy thin cattle on the Fort Worth yards, fleshen them up and resell them. He had always been interested in horses and got to raising Quarter Horses. He was one of the organizers of the American Quarter Horse Association.

He finally sold out at Fort Worth and Rhome and went to Abilene to join his father in the refrigeration business awhile. He formed a partnership with Dr. Phil Smith, and together they opened the first veterinary supply house in that part of the country.

He and son-in-law Bob Cockrell leased a Stonewall County ranch together and operated it about twelve years, then leased and bought land closer to home. Last year Cockrell bought a ranch in the southern part of Callahan County. Austin goes out about three times a week to see after the cattle.

One of the most visible changes he has seen come over the country is brush. When he was a boy he often helped dig out old stumps and roots for firewood because timber was scarce. He could climb up on the old walls at Belle Plain and see the roundhouse at Baird. "Today," he declares, "you can't see fifty feet."

One of his brightest memories is of milking Longhorn cows. He says it used to take eight to ten cows to give enough milk for the average family. An aunt's family used to milk Longhorns regularly, and at best they never got more than a quart per cow.

But the boys had a lot of fun, first breaking the cows and then riding the calves. It took two people to milk a wild cow. The usual way was to snub her to a post or tie her head in a manger, then tie her hind feet together so she couldn't kick. It goes without saying that she didn't give much milk under that kind of stress. But to a bunch of boys it wasn't the milk that counted; it was the fun.

"Little Ways West" Turned Into
Long Journey For Sheep Buyer
Livestock Weekly, July 3, 1975

AL DUMAIN was known on ranches all over West Texas, but he in no way fitted the classic image of either cowman or sheepman. Primarily a lamb buyer representing midwestern farmers, he never showed any inclination to conform to the western image or to appear to be anything different from what he was: a businessman and a product of the Kansas City stockyards. He made no effort to take on either Texas speech or a West Texas cowboy look. He typically wore plain khakis and went around bareheaded, regardless of the ferocity of the sun. You accepted him as he was or left him alone. Those who accepted him usually profited by it.

≈

SAN ANGELO   Al Dumain got his first big sheep buying order because an Indiana man didn't know how far it was from Fort Worth to Valentine.

Dumain, now semi-retired at eighty-three, was for two to three decades one of the leading buyers of West Texas sheep. His biggest single order, which he kept for about twenty years, was from Producers Livestock Marketing Association in Indiana. He often bought 200,000–300,000 head a year for them.

How he got that order is one of his favorite stories. In the mid-

1930s he was operating on the Fort Worth Stockyards as a sheep buyer in partnership with Si Boyer. Indiana Producers for many years had been buying Montana lambs and yearlings for its farmer feeders, but the Montanas were getting too big to suit many of them. Head salesman Ray Neal decided to try Texas. He turned up in Fort Worth, looking for large numbers of yearling muttons. Dumain had some lined up with Worth Evans at Valentine, in far West Texas, out past the Davis Mountains. Neal wanted to see them if it wasn't too far.

"It's just a little ways out west," Dumain said. "I'll take you."

Neal was getting tired by the end of the first day, when they reached San Angelo to spend the night. He asked how much farther it was to Valentine. Dumain told him, "Just a little ways out west."

The journey took two days, the trade about fifteen minutes. But Neal needed more sheep. Dumain happened to know some for sale at Del Rio, "just a little ways down the river." They drove down there and bought the sheep. It still wasn't enough. Dumain got on the phone and located another string, just what was needed, back out at Marathon. "It's just a little ways west," he said.

Worn out, Neal shook his head. "You go buy them for me. I'm going back to Indiana."

Dumain kept that order until Indiana phased out of lamb feeding in the mid-1950s. By then, he says, the corn support level made it easier to grow corn for Uncle Sam than to put it through lambs.

Dumain grew up near Kansas City and at a young age went to work for a commission firm in the cattle yards. Sometimes if they finished early, they would send him to help on the sheep yards until the end of the day. He learned how to handle and judge sheep, and gradually the firm made him a part-time sheep salesman. After a couple of years he went into a partnership dealing in sheep.

In those early years, when runs were light, he would travel all over the country to buy sheep. He even got sheep out of the piney woods of the Southeast, all the way from Louisiana across to Florida. People ran sheep and other livestock loose in the woods. Occasionally ten or fifteen families would get together and round up everything— sheep, cattle and hogs. The sheep would be hand sheared on a table and the wool sorted out for the individual owners. Lambs were seldom castrated, so a lot of longtailed bucks three or four years old would turn up, wormy and weighing as little as seventy-five pounds. The wool was coarse and grew mainly on the backs and sides; bellies and necks were bare.

Dumain noticed that sheep receipts from most of the country were extremely seasonal, but Texas seemed to have sheep on the yards almost every day of the year. He began doing more and more business in Texas and finally moved to Fort Worth about 1930. Fort Worth had big sheep receipts in those days. In addition, Dumain made frequent trips west to buy direct or through commission men and speculators.

Eventually, particularly after getting the big Producers order, he found he was spending an average of six months of the year in the West Texas sheep country. He liked to buy his lambs west of San Angelo and particularly west of the Pecos, an area that produces relatively light numbers anymore. He also liked the Del Rio area. He would usually begin buying oldcrops—born the previous year—in the Uvalde-Del Rio area in the spring, then move up to San Angelo and out to the Davis Mountains as the lamb season progressed.

He averaged putting 50,000 miles a year on a car and trading for a new one annually. The long unpaved roads would shake them down. In the 1930s and 1940s he usually carried two or three spare tires in the trunk.

Producers liked to get lambs in large bunches so it could sort out uniform sets for small feeders. Many a time Dumain thought he had finished an order, only to get a phone call from Neal asking for eighteen more loads.

Dumain preferred to load his own lambs rather than trust that to someone else. Most of the shipments were by rail until well in the 1950s. In his opinion the railroads in general brought many of their problems upon themselves because of their independent attitude when they had a virtual monopoly. They often provided the very minimum in service.

It used to take six to seven days for a load of lambs to reach Indiana by rail from Texas. They would arrive so dehydrated and knocked out that it took at least a week to get them back on their feet. By contrast, trucks can haul sheep almost anywhere they need to go from Texas in twenty-four to thirty-six hours and unload them exactly where they are wanted.

Dumain used to carry a pinch bar in the trunk because the railroads would spot a string of cars at the loading pens and leave them. Moving them into place was up to the stockmen. The usual method was to pinch them along with the bar, a slow and back-bending process.

A lot of shipments had to be loaded in the night, especially along the Southern Pacific, to catch night freights moving east with California produce. Stockpens in general were poorly lighted, which was not always bad. Sheep tended to stop when they saw their shadows cast by artificial light. To expedite loading, Dumain often hung Coleman lanterns at the ends of the car; the lambs would move toward the lights and fill the car.

Usually he worked best with one helper of his own choosing. He found a lot of help which people sent along was in the way half the time.

One man from whom he would buy lots of lambs was the late Sid Slaughter. Slaughter usually bought thousands of West Texas lambs, keeping the ewes and reselling the muttons. Dumain remembers one time that Slaughter had 5,000 yearling muttons to load out of Sierra Blanca. Ray Willoughby bet him that he couldn't weigh and load them all in one day. Slaughter took the bet, kept three loading chutes busy at a time and finished at 5:00 P.M.

In Dumain's early days as a Texas sheep buyer, the standard arrangement was a ten percent cut, and sometimes a buyer took twenty because most of the lambs still carried a lot of the wrinkles that showed their Merino background. "Where a sheep buyer made the most enemies was in sorting sheep the way they should be sorted," he says.

He made a few, though he says he made a lot more friends. Once in a while he ran up against a rancher who felt obliged to settle their disagreement with his fists. "I'm not a fighter and never was," Dumain declares, "but I've been hit a few times." His usual defense was simply never to buy sheep at that place again.

He also ran into a "fill artist" every so often, one who filled his sheep with water to make them weigh more. He tried to avoid ever doing business with one of them a second time. "There were too many good people to trade with; I didn't need those others."

The wrinkled lambs so prevalent in his early buying years began disappearing in the 1930s as Rambouillet breeders smoothed out the wrinkles. Corriedales also started to take hold for crossbreeding as more ranchmen began to concentrate on a better feeding lamb. A scattering of blackfaces turned up, though their big increase started in the 1940s.

The drouth of the 1950s, besides breaking the sheep markets down to ruinous levels, also caused a severe drop in numbers from which the industry never recovered. Buyers were unable to get the numbers they had formerly bought, but the quality was far better. Dumain recalls that in the 1930s he often had trouble putting together sets of lambs that would average sixty pounds; more often they ran fifty to fifty-five. "Now," he says, "the dogies weigh more than that."

Dumain says he never made any really big money out of lambs. Most of his buying through the years was on order rather than on speculation. "It's hard to mix order buying with speculation. You'll be tempted to sell your own stock, and that's when you lose your order business." He used to speculate on ewes to some degree because this did not conflict with the lamb trade.

Although Dumain often worked out of San Angelo for months at a stretch, he never actually lived there. During the years he lived in Fort Worth, his wife was often troubled by a bad sinus condition. Occasionally they traveled to Las Vegas, Nevada, to visit relatives. The condition would let up. About twenty-five years ago they sold their Fort Worth home and bought one in Las Vegas. It was a small town of perhaps 18,000 people and had little or none of its present notoriety.

Because of his wife's health he stays home more now, but he still comes to Texas for a while during the lamb season. Awhile back he was here to sell 4,000 oldcrops for a longtime friend, Earl Byrd. They had wintered so well that packers took them all.

Four thousand looks like a lot of sheep today, but in Dumain's heyday that was a little string. Often he bought 5,000–10,000 head in one phone call. Once he bought 50,000–55,000 head in a single deal in a San Angelo hotel room.

His biggest regret is that he finds few people still alive with whom he traded thirty or forty years ago.

"I've traded with lots of men and later with their sons, and even the sons are gone."

Contrasting Natures Helped Make Owen Brothers' Partnership Work

Livestock Weekly, February 26, 1981

KELLY OWEN was one of those people who could walk into a hotel lobby and draw all eyes to him. He had a natural charisma that grew out of a boundless zeal for life. He loved nothing more than making deals— win, lose or draw. His brother, Bill, by contrast, was quiet, reflective, the hardworking type, not much for show or for getting far away from home. Their contrasting personalities made them a good team. Kelly went out and brought in the business, while Bill's conservatism served as a lid to keep Kelly's enthusiasm from bubbling over and putting out the fire. They were an asset to the livestock community in Central and West Texas.

≈

SAN SABA   Bill and Kelly Owen, brothers, were an ideal pair for a trading partnership. Bill tended to be conservative and preferred to stay close to home, taking care of details. Kelly was outgoing and enthusiastic, liked to travel and was great at stirring up trades that just had to be made.

Kelly kept Bill punched up, while Bill held the lid on.

That partnership started in 1934 and continued until Kelly's death in a plane crash in 1963. In the years since, Bill has done far less trading and has concentrated mostly on ranching, individually and in various family partnerships. It is not nearly so exciting, but he sleeps better. In the 1950s he and Kelly used to winter 20,000–25,000 oldcrop lambs each year. At seventy-six, Bill now has about 10,000, running less country and using less help. His cattle operations also have been trimmed in recent years.

His father, Ralph Owen, was born here about 1874, his mother about 1876. All the time Bill was a boy, he had to help haul drinking water. The family drilled eleven holes on the place and never found water. That memory left a mark. In later years he always made sure of the water supply on any place he and Kelly bought or leased.

The family ran a few cattle and sheep. His father made a living trucking until he went broke in 1923 and was never able to get back into that business. He farmed sixty to seventy acres of cotton and corn. "We never made more than a bale and a remnant," Bill recalls.

In his youth, Bill hauled cordwood to town, selling it to the school, the courthouse and individuals, a cord to a wagonload, one load a day, nine miles in and nine miles home. Deciding there had to be an easier way to make a living, he came to town in 1926 and went to work in a hardware store for $65 a month. That worked nicely until the store was sold and the new owner decided he was overpaid.

Bill joined Steve Ballew in opening a tin shop. Ballew was a good tinner, and Bill learned the trade to a point that he is still adept at it when his ranches need any work of that sort. The partners made a lot of money selling International Harvester farm implements, too, until the crash of 1929 caught Bill with his signature on too many credit endorsements. He managed to pay off about $1,000, all that was due against him, then was unable to borrow a penny for four or five years. "The mistake I made was in paying the bank," he declares.

Kelly was six years younger than Bill. He worked for an oil company as a sales rep, then rode a freight train to California in 1933 and picked grapes. He came back a year later, no richer but well-traveled. He and Bill began trading in partnership, buying anything they thought they could resell, including cattle, sheep, horses, hogs, mules, even junk iron.

The late Sam Laird operated the Corner Drug, an institution that comes near to being a shrine in the memories of San Saba natives. That store was Bill's and Kelly's "office."

The timing was good for cattle trading. The government cattle-killing program had ended, and prices began a slow and modest uptrend. Bill and Kelly bought old fat cows in the country for $40, took them to Fort Worth and doubled their investment. They were dealing in small numbers, however, and they spent several years building a "real good hold."

Kelly was noted for his willingness to trade on just about anything. Bill says part of his brother's success resulted from the fact that he would stay a little longer and listen a little more than most people, giving him trading opportunities other people overlooked.

Their first land purchase was the Chamberlain Ranch. When World War II began, Kelly sold his interest to Bill and went into the service. He spent most of the war stationed in San Antonio and, when he was off duty, trading on the yards. The late Maurice Cohen, another cattle buyer fondly remembered throughout the Hill Country, was a good friend of his.

While Kelly was gone, Bill ran some cattle and sheep and did some trading of his own. Upon Kelly's return in 1945 they began branching out and growing. Their big effort was on oldcrop lambs, bought for winter pasturage. They would bring in a trainload at a time and show them to prospective buyers. Whatever they didn't sell, they put on their own pastures.

They leased their first part of the Gibbons Ranch about 1945 or '46, getting the rest of it three or four years later, a total of 16,000 acres. The Owen family ranched it about twenty-five years. They also leased the Hall ranch immediately north of the Gibbons, about 3,500 acres more. They could stock the two ranches at about one steer calf and three lambs to ten acres. They could rough the calf through winter on about 100 pounds of cake and usually figure on 150 pounds of gain. The lambs would usually gain forty pounds without feed and go out fat in May.

The lambs the brothers bought in those days usually weighed about sixty pounds coming in. In later years the lambs would get much bigger and heavier as ranchers bred them up and also cut down their stocking rates. The heavier lambs did not leave so much room for maneuvering.

A big percentage of the lambs came out of the Fort Stockton-Alpine country. The brothers bought Jim Espy's Fort Davis lambs twice, 12,000 each time. When Espy built his home there he said he was going to put up a sign, "Built by the Owen Brothers." When Bill and Kelly each built nearly identical homes on either side of the San Saba-Lometa highway, they told the ranchman they were going to put up signs, "Built by Jim Espy."

Their South Dakota connection, which became a hallmark of their operation, began in 1952. They bought a 3,500-acre ranch from the late Miles Culwell of San Angelo. That ownership opened the way for them to lease 40,000 acres of Indian reservation grass in a horseshoe bend of the Missouri River. They stretched twelve miles of fence across the neck of the horseshoe and had a big pasture. They managed to keep the place intact for seven or eight years, until the government began to take it back to put Indians in the cattle business. The brothers then lost all of it in a period of three or four years. By that time, however, they had bought other land in the same area, keeping some, reselling some at a profit.

They shipped their first trainload of cattle—104 cars—to South Dakota in the spring of 1952. "That was a way too many," Bill recalls. "The back end of the train had a whip to it." Afterward, they never used more than fifty cars at a time.

They kept shipping cattle by rail about ten years, summering them on Dakota grass. One time they shipped a lot of their cows which they desperately wanted to keep at San Saba, but a long drouth made it imperative to move them. The Owens and their crew finished loading the cattle about dark and watched the train pull away. That night, it rained four inches.

It was Kelly who did most of the traveling to the Dakotas. He once threw a big barbecue for the Indians as a goodwill gesture, but he never got up the nerve for a repeat performance.

Kelly was "everybody's friend," Bill recalls. Even people who met him but once or twice would vividly remember him years later. "He was like that even as a kid," Bill says. "He never wanted to hurt anybody. It was against our rule to make anybody mad about anything."

Even when a livestock deal occasionally went sour, the brothers made it a cardinal rule never to take their troubles to the courthouse.

Though Kelly was always looking for something to trade on, Bill's conservatism would occasionally rub off onto him. Once in South Dakota an old man offered to sell the brothers 3,500 acres at $22 an acre. The price was right, but he insisted that the brothers take seventeen acres which had been cut off by a highway. Kelly decided $22 was too much for those orphan acres and held out until the old man took the place off of the market. A year or so later the old fellow sold the ranch to somebody else for $35.

In the mid-1950s, Kelly started flying to South Dakota. Bob Sieker piloted for him at first, but often Sieker was busy when Kelly needed to go. About 1955 or 1956, Kelly learned to fly and got a pilot's license.

Bill never shared his enthusiasm for flying and never rode with him. "I owned half interest in an airplane for years and never sat down in it," he says.

The only time in his life he ever went up was in the early 1920s, with a barnstorming pilot who took people on short flights at a $1.50 a throw. Bill stood on a wing and held onto a strut. It didn't scare him at the time, but he was just a kid then. He got more cautious as he became older. He always preferred to drive, though he admits that if he had to make a really long trip today he might consider taking a commercial plane.

Mrs. Owen has made three trips to Europe by air. He tells her three times is the charm, and she'd better not go again.

Kelly was flying his plane when it went down with him at Leddy, Oklahoma, in 1963, killing him and three passengers.

The brothers had been full partners; they did not even have separate personal bank accounts. This led to some formidable problems in settling the estate.

Bill still trades a little, but close to the belt. He buys lambs for wintering, not for trading. He keeps 800 to 900 black cows, breeding them to Hereford bulls. He weans and winters the calves, selling them as yearlings. He and Mrs. Owen have been leasing out their South Dakota country. They have sold the land to their children and are pasturing cattle for others.

He doesn't miss the trading so much. "It worked well when Kelly was alive. We were partners for thirty years and never had a cross word. Kelly made most of the trades. I stayed here and tried to keep some money in the bank."

He doesn't see much room in today's livestock business for the kind of trading he and Kelly used to do. The trader has followed the commission man into limbo in today's system of auction selling, order buying, and so forth, he believes. It was a little like riding a ferris wheel anyway, one time way up and next time way down.

In 1952 the brothers sent 10,000 yearling ewes to graze the old Sunflower Ordnance plant in Kansas. The ewes fattened but found no buyers. The Owens lost $100,000.

The following year they made a deal with Joe Mayer of Arden, Texas, to summer 6,000 of his ewes in return for the lamb crop. It was dry in Texas, but Mayer didn't want to sell his ewes. It turned desperately dry in Kansas, too, and the Owens kept itching to sell the ewes or ship them to Dakota. Mayer had the faith that has sustained West Texas ranchmen since the time the Comanches left. "It'll rain," he said. And at the very last possible moment, before total disaster, it did. He was able to take his ewes back to Texas, and the Owens wintered the lambs at a profit.

Joe Mayer was a son of Abe Mayer, noted San Angelo ranchman. The Owens made a deal once with Abe Mayer that, as things worked out, was about to lose them a small fortune. Mayer voluntarily cancelled the deal. He said if he went through with it Uncle Sam would get most of the profit anyway.

In the fall of 1953 the brothers bought 10,000 lambs on a drouth market. The lambs fattened during the winter and made a little more than $100,000 the next spring, canceling the loss on the yearling ewes they'd pastured in Kansas.

A 1,200-cow deal with the old Bar S Ranch at Barnhart showed a profit on the first 1,000 head, but the last 200 were caught by a plummeting market. They wound up losing more money than the whole deal had originally cost. "If we had bought ammunition and shot those 200 cows the day they were delivered, we'd have been money ahead," Bill says.

He has always regarded sheep as the better investment. Over the years, he declares, sheep have made three times more money for the dollars invested than cattle ever did.

Happy Smith's Cattle Train Left Him Standing by Railroad Tracks

Livestock Weekly, October 27, 1983

I CAN'T remember when I didn't know Happy Smith. He day-worked with my father several times, and he put on the first rodeo I can ever remember seeing, the one described in this article. One day in the fall of 1983 he called Dave Gotschall of West Texas Boys Ranch, asking him to come out and talk to him about his plan to leave a substantial bequest to the ranch. He asked that Dave bring me with him. We had a grand day-long visit with the old cowboy in his modest home on the west side of Odessa. Barely two months later, Happy was gone.

≈

ODESSA   H. W. "Happy" Smith can still remember in great detail the only time he ever rode a cattle train. That was in April, 1926, when he was working for rancher Elliott Cowden.

Cowden loaded 2,237 steers on forty-five cars at the T&P stock-pens in Odessa, bound for summer grass at Rosalia, Kansas. How does Smith remember the numbers so vividly? He says the steers were thin and weak, and he thinks he tailed up every one of the 2,237 at some point on the trip.

Asked if he rode the caboose, he declares, "Caboose hell! I was in the cattle cars trying to tail up them poor little steers. I walked the tops of them cars like a brakie."

By the time the train made its mandatory stop for feed, water and rest somewhere in Oklahoma, Smith needed it far worse than the cattle. He got a room in a little hotel near the stockpens and told the station agent to send for him when time came for the train to leave.

The agent forgot. When Smith woke up to the sound of the train and went running to the station, the passing caboose was moving too fast for him to grab ahold. The agent expressed his regrets but said the best he could do was to put Smith on a passenger train the next morning. It would overtake the freight farther down the line. When the train pulled in, Smith climbed aboard.

"And who do you think was on it? Mr. Cowden himself," Smith recalls. To his relief, Cowden understood the situation and made nothing of it. Smith got back on the cattle cars many miles down the track.

They reached Rosalia about 3:00 A.M. and started unloading the thin, hungry steers onto grass which reached to their bellies. When the job was done, Smith went for breakfast and some rest. Later he came back and found the steers hadn't moved. They had their heads down in that green grass and wouldn't even look up. Coming from the dry Odessa country, they thought they had landed in heaven.

Missing the train wasn't the only trouble. He had left Odessa in his shirtsleeves, in warm weather. He found the temperature dropping sharply as he went north. He had lost most of one finger from his left hand while racking pipe for an oil company, and the finger was still bandaged.

"I felt like the rest of that finger was going to freeze off before I could get out of Kansas," he says.

He never offered to ride another cattle train.

Later—he believes it was 1927—he went to Hollywood with Jack Hoxie, a western silent film star. Hoxie stopped in Odessa on a personal-appearance tour, and Smith took a couple of quarts of whisky in a suitcase to Hoxie's room in the then-new Elliott Hotel. Those were Prohibition times. Hoxie was pleased to get the whisky and hired him as a flunky to take care of his costumes, his Cadillac and to run whatever errands might come up.

As the tour continued Smith became aware that Hoxie had whipped a film director and was on his way down and out. He also saw him whip his advance booking agent.

In Hollywood, Smith worked as an extra in some western filming for Hoxie. The worst spill he took was doubling for Hoxie in a scene where he was supposed to jump a mule off of a high pier, then be rescued from the water by a pair of bulldogs. They poured "high-life," a chemical used to eliminate prairie dogs, on the mule to burn his hide and make him run. The fall didn't worry Smith as much as those two dumb bulldogs. "If they'd ever bitten me, I'd've drowned them," he says.

He did not work with other western stars but met several including Hoot Gibson ("He was a real cowboy"), Tom Mix, and Ken Maynard ("I didn't like him—he was mean to his horses").

Smith stayed with Hoxie from spring through fall, then came down with yellow jaundice and returned to Odessa. The movie bug did not bite him deeply; he never considered going back to Hollywood.

Smith, now going on seventy-six, was born in Odessa December 23, 1907. His father, R. W. Smith, had bought a ranch north of town in 1906. He and a neighbor hired a teacher and set up their own school district, but they took the children to Odessa for school when Happy was in the fourth grade. There he saw his first "funny paper" ("My daddy didn't allow such as that") and read his first comic strip, Happy Hooligan.

When the teacher asked him his name he popped off, "Happy Hooligan." She bent him over his desk and administered severe corporal punishment. The pain wore off, but the name never did.

His older brother, the late Cal Smith, was an Odessa ranchman and for many years one of the prime movers in the Sand Hills Hereford and Quarter Horse Show and Rodeo.

Happy broke off schooling and began working for wages at about thirteen. Many of the early years were spent working for the Cowden families.

He believes he helped drive the last trail herd through downtown Odessa, 1,500 big steers from Elliott Cowden's ranch north of town. They were driven through to the stockpens on the T&P tracks a few blocks east of downtown.

"Them women would come running out of the houses with a broom or a mop whipping the cattle, and they'd've whipped us if they could've. The cattle went through their yards and gardens. You talk about trouble . . . they were all mad at us."

He remembers a lot of stories about people in the Odessa-Midland-Crane country. He remembers J. T. McElroy, El Paso packinghouse operator who owned the McElroy Ranch near Crane. McElroy would periodically ride the train from El Paso to Odessa, rent a buggy and team from Charlie Beardsley's stable and drive the thirty miles south to the ranch.

On one such trip he stopped at the Dawson wells, a point just inside his north boundary, to water and rest his team. A couple of McElroy cowboys who did not know him were there, practicing up for a rodeo or something, roping anything that would run. One rode up to him and asked, "Would you like to see me fairground that cow?"

McElroy said he had rather not, and asked who the cattle belonged to.

"Some old rich so-and-so out of El Paso. He never comes out here, so he'll never know it."

McElroy went on to headquarters. When the cowboys came in, he had their checks written.

"That old rich so-and-so from El Paso doesn't like you roping his cattle," he said.

Far from rich was the late Billy Peays, a longtime wagonboss in the Midland country, who sometimes ranched for himself in a small way. Working on the McElroy Ranch one time, he was seen to study something on the ground, then get off of his horse and pick it up. Later, when the herd was thrown together, he was asked what he had found. He showed a rusty old bolt with two washers on it. The bolt was beyond salvation, he said, but the washers were still good.

"If you ever get a place of your own," Peays added, "you'll learn to pick up things like that."

Sam Preston was coming in from his ranch south of Midland one time when he saw a drunk coming down the lane toward him. A non-drinker himself, Preston pulled across the bar ditch and up against the fence to get out of the way. The drunk ran into him in spite of all that.

When the drunk asked whose fault it was, Preston declared dryly, "Mine. I had plenty of time to've taken that fence down and gotten out of your sight."

Smith always liked rodeos and helped put on some north of Odessa in the early 1930s, in a big dry lakebed on the Gist ranch. The arena was formed by parking the cars as sort of a fence. The only real fencing was some lumber which Smith leased from a lumberyard to put up corrals for broncs and roping stock. He would wire the boards to the posts rather than drive nails. That way they could all be turned back to the lumberyard later.

"I got throwed off out there about as far as a man ever got throwed off and lived," he declares.

Smith alternated cowboying and working in the oilfields, whichever presented a job opportunity at any given time. Oilfield work paid better, though there were times when it did not pay at all. Some oilfield companies were notoriously broke.

Once, hauling oilfield supplies from McCamey to Andrews, he had to have his truck pulled through the deep sands by a team of mules. Finally exhausted, he pulled off to the side of the road north of Odessa and went to sleep. There the backtracking boss found him and declared, "Don't you know you're four hours late?"

Smith said, "And four months ahead of my paycheck."

He never did trust the new rotary drilling rigs. "There was too much going on, and a man could get killed. A lot of them did." He quit oilfield work and went mostly to trading cattle and horses about 1942.

He owned a little place near the shipping point of Duero, west of Odessa, and leased some adjoining country. He was finally offered a chance to buy it at $300 an acre, but he remembered seeing it sell for fifty cents and turned it down. He decided it was time to retire from the cattle and horse business anyway.

The cows he sold for $500 he saw selling later for $350. "Cattle went to the bottom, and land went to the top."

The people who bought the land drilled for water. "They didn't get but four gallons a minute. I could have told them, but they didn't ask me. I just stood back and watched them spend their money."

He was married in 1939 to Kathleen Davis of Eastland County. She died of a heart attack in January, 1983. They never had any children of their own, but they raised five boys they considered needy, buying them clothes and sending them to school. All five turned out well, Smith says proudly. He has long been a contributor to West Texas Boys Ranch and similar charities.

He has seen a lot of changes in the Odessa country, some good and some not. He worries about the direction of humanity. "We're running backwards as fast as we can go."

A wagon road used to pass in front of the Smith ranch house when he was a boy. Neighbors would visit and help each other. People on their way to town would stop and ask if the Smiths needed anything they could bring for them.

"Next thing you know, here came the automobiles. It wasn't any time till people would just wave; they wouldn't stop. It wasn't long after that till they wouldn't even wave.

"I don't even know my neighbors here. They are working all the time."

Saddlemaker is Former Smuggler: He Carried Bibles into Russia

Livestock Weekly, February 13, 1986

How rapidly things can change! At the time this was written, in 1986, Bibles were still contraband behind the Iron Curtain. Today it is reported that church membership is growing more rapidly in Russia than anywhere else in the world. Obviously, religion had survived underground during the dark generations of repression, waiting to explode under the light of freedom.

≈

SAN ANGELO   Saddlemaker John Piland finds his current occupation carries far less stress than one which occupied eight years of his time from 1974 to 1982.

An ordained Southern Baptist minister, he was a "God smuggler," carrying Bibles into Iron Curtain countries in defiance of Communist law. From bases in Holland and Germany, he made thirty-four trips into Eastern Bloc countries including East Germany, Poland, Rumania, Hungary and Czechoslovakia, a couple of times into Russia itself.

Mrs. Piland accompanied him and shared the risks on twenty-two of these trips. They were never caught, but the stress built to a point that he eventually suffered a heart attack. They returned to their native Texas in 1982 to seek a quieter life. He had been a saddlemaker in earlier years, so he returned to that trade.

The Pilands knew each other in their youth, growing up on farms about ten miles apart near Honey Grove in northeast Texas. Piland first began making saddles thirty-five years ago for his late brother Henry in the Dallas area. He worked for several leather-working and saddlemaking firms in that region and for some time was production manager in a large saddle factory.

He was in that trade in the Fort Worth-Dallas area until 1971, when he received a call to the ministry in Europe.

He helped organize an American servicemen's church in Holland. There he met a Dutch missionary who eventually got him involved in what the Dutch called "God smuggling."

His first trip into Russia was to deliver fifty Bibles and a number of concordances and new testaments as well as film strips of Bible stories to an illegal church in Leningrad. He carried them in suitcases, covered by a layer of clothing. Entry was made on a tour conducted by the Russian tourist agency. Getting across the border was touchy, but making contact with the recipient minister was touchier.

"I was not running any heroic risk myself," he declares, "but the person I was delivering to would have drawn at least five years, possibly ten, at hard labor if we had been caught.

"I never enjoyed anything in my life as much as I did meeting that Russian family."

One advantage of traveling in Russia, he continues, is that it makes a person that much more appreciative of American freedoms.

Many of the trips into the Eastern Bloc were to deliver Bibles and other religious materials in Russian to go-betweens in the satellite countries who later would complete their delivery into Russia.

Most often, Piland says, he and Mrs. Piland traveled in the guise of tourists. "She was a good cover for me," he comments, "because we looked like a regular tourist couple."

A frequent cover was the use of a camper, which on one occasion hid 2,000 Bibles furnished by the United Bible Society in Stuttgart, Germany.

The Russian Bibles were photocopies of one which the Communist government put into limited circulation among its relatively small number of showplace churches, kept to convince westerners that it allowed religious freedom.

The Russian government has maintained tight controls on Bible distribution, Piland says, restricting them to approved ministers and churches and making it difficult for individual citizens to acquire one. It was to put them into the hands of the people that the Bible Society came into being and that Europe's God smugglers set upon their mission.

He contends that a strong religious feeling persists among the Russian people despite the best efforts of the Communist government to suppress it. The faithful run frightful risks to keep the faith alive and pass it on to the young.

It has been illegal to teach Christian religion to youths under eighteen, on the theory that if they have not acquired faith by then they probably never will, he says. The government has taken children away from "unfit" parents found guilty of teaching illicit religion.

The government controls its approved churches and forbids other forms of worship. People can be jailed on charges of illegal assembly for meeting in homes for unauthorized religious activity.

A pastor who strays beyond official bounds can be declared unemployed, and being unemployed is against the law. Many ministers do other work to earn a livelihood, but they may lose these jobs if they are caught going beyond legal limitations. This puts them into a classic "Catch-22" situation. They are in violation if unemployed, but they may be shut off from employment if they displease the authorities.

Despite all these attempts at suppression, church membership is growing faster in Russia than anywhere else in the world, Piland declares.

He says he always felt under tension from the time he started planning a trip until he had completed it and crossed a frontier back into a free country. At times, when approaching the border of an Iron Curtain country, he would become nauseated from the stress.

Always, however, he became easy when he actually reached the line. "God always gave me peace," he declares. "I would be as calm at the border as if I had been just an ordinary tourist. God always traveled along with us."

The nearest he ever came to being caught was in Rumania, about a year before he came back to the U. S. He and Mrs. Piland had delivered about half their cargo of Bibles from a camper in the interior of that country and were to deliver the last half in a town almost on the border.

The first delivery went smoothly. As a rule, the satellite countries were usually less risky than Russia itself, especially Poland, where Piland says the church's influence remained extremely strong and the Communist party maintained its power over a resentful people only through military strength and the Russian threat.

Plans came unraveled on the final delivery. The original arrangement had been that the Pilands would take a hotel room and make their contact, carrying the Bibles to the minister's home in suitcases.

But because of some unforeseen local event, no hotel rooms were to be had. Plan B was to check into a campground, rent a Rumanian automobile that would be less conspicuous than their camper and make the deliveries in that. But no rental cars were available either.

All that was left was to park on a curb some distance from the minister's house and make the deliveries in suitcases, as inconspicuously as possible.

The minister's daughter and son came with a bicycle to carry the suitcases. Unfortunately there were not enough suitcases to move all the Bibles and a contraband tape recorder in one trip. Mrs. Piland went to the minister's home with the youngsters while Piland stayed by the camper and the remaining goods.

The youngsters came back for a second load.

Unfortunately a policeman had seen enough from a distance to arouse his suspicions. The boy and girl had barely gotten away when he angrily confronted Piland and demanded to know his business.

Piland had grown used to lying in the Lord's service and maintained that he was simply a tourist, stymied by the lack of available hotel rooms. The policeman did not believe him, and the situation became tense.

The boy and girl were still in plain sight, headed home with the bicycle and the suitcases.

"All of a sudden the Lord spoke to me," Piland says, "not in words that I could hear with my ears, but in a feeling of peace that came over me. He was saying 'Don't worry, I've got everything under control.'"

The boy and girl were not yet out of sight, but somehow the policeman failed to see them. He arrested Piland and took him to the stationhouse, where he was grilled at some length. A senior officer finally became weary of the contest and advised Piland to get across the border as quickly as he could. As soon as Mrs. Piland returned, he took the advice.

That kind of stress finally led to his heart attack.

"We took that as a cue that our work was finished," he says.

The Pilands returned to El Paso, where he and son Tim planned to go into the wholesale saddle business but found the economy not very encouraging. For three years he worked in a San Angelo saddlery.

He and Tim began their own saddlemaking business in San Angelo about 1985. Tim, thirty-four, started helping his father when he was still a boy, cutting leather straps to earn money to buy his mother a birthday present. By the time he was twelve he was making youth saddles; full size saddles were too heavy for him to lift.

Mrs. Piland has gone back to school. She is a government major at Angelo State University.

That, like saddlemaking, is a much more peaceful endeavor than smuggling Bibles past the Iron Curtain.

The Way It Was

Ira Bird Still Lives Where Father
Saw Big Buffalo Herd in Early 1860s

Livestock Weekly, November 27, 1969

IRA BIRD lived far into his nineties. He told me a story about his Ranger father, who as a teenager rode into the Yellow Wolf Valley of present Coke County while on an Indian-scouting expedition and was awestruck by the sight of a buffalo herd so large it seemed to blacken the range. The memory of it haunted him for more than twenty years, until finally he brought his family to that valley. He stayed there the rest of his life.

≈

SANCO   At eighty-eight, Ira A. Bird was by a considerable margin the oldest consignor to the recent Concho Hereford Association bull sale in San Angelo. He fed, combed and brushed his two bulls and led them through the ring himself. Though he has turned most of his land and cattle over to his family, he retains a few cattle himself "to keep from getting rusty."

Bird was around to see most of the settling up and later the gradual exodus of people from this region near the Colorado River. He was six when his father brought the family here in 1887. It was mostly open range country then, but within very few years it was settled thickly and much of the land put to the plow. In the last twenty to thirty years Bird has watched a reversal of this process, the people pulling out, the small farms consolidating and going back to range-land.

Bird's father, Miller Bird, first saw this area as a teenaged boy doing Texas Ranger service during the early part of the Civil War, helping the meager home forces keep Indians turned back from the settlements while most of the older men were away at war. He fought in the unfortunate Dove Creek battle west of present-day San Angelo in 1865, when Rangers and Confederate soldiers mistakenly set upon a group of friendly Kickapoo Indians and got badly whipped. Miller Bird never forgot the day he rode up on Yellow Wolf Creek and saw a buffalo herd so huge that later he said the land was black with them. When he pointed the family wagon west from Hamilton County more than twenty years later, he headed back to the spot he had carried so long in his memory.

It was there that Ira Bird grew up.

"When we came to this country," he recalls, "you could have loaded a wagon with buffalo heads and horns. The buffalo hunters must have killed a lot of them in this part of the world." He has often wished he had saved some of them, but they were so commonplace that no one at the time gave them much thought.

Within a short time after the Bird family settled on Yellow Wolf, the country had ten times as many people as it has today, Bird believes. Lots of people took up a quarter section for nothing but a filing fee.

The elder Bird, ever a frontiersman in spirit, began to feel crowded and got an itch to move up to Oregon. Mrs. Bird told him if he went, he went alone, so here the family stayed.

In the beginning a lot of tough people lived here. Most farmers lacked money to fence their land, so it was left open. Bird's father had a steer yearling that ran with the neighbors' cattle. One day one of the neighbors came around peddling beef, and Bird bought a quarter from him. He never saw his yearling again, and he always figured he had bought his own beef. As solid settlers came in and planted roots, the rough element felt the pressure and pulled stakes. It didn't take many years to clean house.

The little town of Sanco was started soon after the Bird family arrived. Bird remembers that his father hauled most of the box lumber used in building the first eighteen by twenty-six-foot schoolhouse there.

"That was all the school I ever went to," he says. He attended there until he was sixteen or seventeen years old, took an examination and was given a teaching certificate. At seventeen he was teaching in the Horse Mountain school four miles north of Sanco. One of his pupils, Homer Lowe, was half a head taller and a year or two older than Bird himself. But Bird got on his good side by playing mumbletypeg with him. The younger kids all patterned after Lowe, so Bird never had any problems.

He married at eighteen. In those days school ran only about six months of the year, so Bird farmed the rest of the time. About 1901 a scourge of grasshoppers cleaned pastures and most of the fields here, so he went with two brothers to the South Plains north of Big Spring. They got hold of three sections of school land on and near the head of Tobacco Creek, about eight miles east of present-day Lamesa.

In those days Colonel C. C. Slaughter was still holding great amounts of ranch country against the onslaught of settlers. The state land was leasing for three cents an acre. Soon after 1900 this land started being thrown open for settlement at $1 an acre, three percent interest, forty years to pay. Slaughter and his cowboys were determined to hang onto as much of it as they could, and feelings between them and settlers such as the Birds were not very cordial.

The cowboys packed the county clerk's waiting room the day that particular land was put up. Bird and his brothers took their places in the room. His recollection of that event is that there was a lot of pushing, shoving, slugging and cussing, and he was on the receiving end of quite a bit of it. He got some land but not what he wanted. The cowboys got the best of it, most of which went to Slaughter.

In time Bird sold his meager holdings there for very little and returned to Coke County.

He bought his first registered cattle in 1916. Ironically, they came indirectly from the Slaughter herd. He has always had some since, though the cattle he has today are not descendants of those originals. His were the first registered Herefords in this community, though

John and Phil Lee had long had some near San Angelo, John Gist and Henry Halff had them around Midland and the Lewis family around Blackwell.

They were a far cry from the twenty-eight East Texas cattle the family had brought here trailing their Studebaker wagon in 1887. Looking back, he can see that the family was very poor in those early days. But they didn't know it then because everybody around them was in the same shape.

Though he has always had cattle and ridden horses, he has never regarded himself as a cowboy. About 1953 he had some blood circulation problems. Returning home from the hospital, he saddled his horse, then found he couldn't get on him. He hasn't ridden since. Nevertheless, he still drives his own car and pickup, though when he gets to a city like Abilene or San Angelo he turns the wheel over to someone else.

One big change he has seen has been the encroachment of brush. He recalls that in his boyhood there was mesquite in the low places in Coke County but not all over. When he was on the high plains he could ride ten miles and never find anything big enough for a switch. He once chased a wolf three miles across open country that is heavy in mesquite today. He shot the wolf at the Slaughter fence. In those days the Slaughter people paid $15 bounty, but Bird didn't collect it because he was of the settler group.

Shooting of Karnes Sheriff Started Biggest Manhunt In Texas History

Livestock Weekly, June 8, 1972

THIS article grew out of a great deal of research I did while working on one of my last paperback original western novels, *Manhunters*. The story of Gregorio Cortez is fascinating for what it says about racial relations in South Texas into the early years of this century. It indicates that though we still have some distance to go, we have indeed come a long way. I also used the novel to point out that racial bias is not a one-sided phenomenon; it cuts both ways.

≈

KARNES CITY   On June 12, 1901, the Karnes County sheriff died after a sudden exchange of gunfire with a Mexican cowboy, setting in motion the biggest single manhunt in the history of Texas. The fugitive, one Gregorio Cortez, became a desperate villain to the Anglo people of South Texas but a folk hero to the Mexican people on both sides of the border.

His story arouses controversy even yet. In 1958 a Mexican-American educator, Dr. Americo Paredes, published a book which showed him largely in a favorable light and drew a lot of fire from long-memoried people in South Texas. The following year the late William Warren Sterling, former Texas adjutant general, published a Texas Ranger history that included a chapter on Cortez and described him as an experienced and desperate horse thief. Even Sterling paid tribute to Cortez for his endurance and cunning, however, and questioned whether Cortez was personally responsible for all the deeds laid at his door.

Both authors indicated that the whole event might have resulted from a tragic comedy of errors and the faulty translation of a few Spanish words by a man the sheriff had along as an interpreter. Sheriff Brack Morris had gone to a shack used by Romaldo Cortez,

Gregorio's brother, to ask questions about a mare Gregorio had traded. He found both brothers sitting on the front porch resting after the noon meal. He evidently decided to arrest Gregorio. Cortez later testified that he said he couldn't be arrested for nothing. The interpreter may have confused the word "nada," which means "nothing," for "nadie," which means "nobody." He told the sheriff Cortez had said nobody could arrest him. The sheriff then drew his pistol.

The unarmed Romaldo, fearing his brother was about to be shot, rushed at the sheriff and was fatally wounded. While this was going on, Gregorio pulled a pistol and shot the sheriff. The interpreter quickly decided he was of no help to anybody and took out through the mesquites in a hard run. A rescue party later found the sheriff dead, two hundred yards from where he had been shot.

Though born south of the border, Gregorio had spent years well to the north in Texas. Instead of fleeing south to Mexico, as many expected, he went north to hide out among friends and relatives. He spent a night at the farm home of the Robledo family near Gonzales. Some of them, at least, were unaware of what had happened. By some form of persuasion never recorded, officers found out from Gregorio's wife where he might go first. A small posse led by Sheriff Dick Glover of Gonzales County made a lightning raid on the Robledo house, figuring to catch Gregorio inside. But he was outside, in the dark.

Each side later claimed the other fired first. Glover was shot out of his saddle and died almost instantly. The farm's owner, Henry Schnabel, a member of the posse, was killed moments afterward. Cortez later said he fired into the posse after the shooting began and might or might not have killed Glover. Various people in the house were at first accused of killing Schnabel, but in time it became widely believed that he was killed by other members of the posse during their wild firing. At any rate, two highly respected sheriffs and one landowner were dead.

Cortez, barefoot, laid low in the brush. After the shooting was over he slipped back into the house under the noses of the searchers and retrieved his shoes, then made his escape. The possemen had wounded a Mexican woman. They hanged a young boy to the point of unconsciousness trying to make him tell where Cortez had gone, something he didn't know in the first place. He was the first of several who would be hanged in the same manner over the next several days.

The *San Antonio Express* noted that three had been hanged, one to death and two to unconsciousness. "They have emphatically refused to give any information, [which] shows that they have no regard for death nor punishment." What it really showed was that they didn't know anything to tell, but it would have made a man highly unpopular to have said so at the time.

Over the next ten days literally hundreds of men from all over South Texas joined in the search for Cortez. Hardly a lawman in the southern half of the state was not somehow involved.

It was an exceedingly bad time for Mexican people in the area. The feeling between them and the Anglos had been barely better than a state of open warfare in the first place. That many innocents suffered grievously is a matter of record. It was widely believed that a whole "gang" was involved with Cortez. It was open season on any of them, because the official descriptions given over the wires showed him to be from five-eight to six feet tall, one saying he walked erect, another saying he walked with a stoop.

A wire from the town of Gonzales protested to the *San Antonio Express* that people there were accused of killing several Mexicans and hanging one. "This report is not true," it said. "Only two Mexicans have been killed, one near Ottine for resisting arrest and another for similar offense." Near San Diego one Mexican was captured and another killed by a posse which then found that neither was Cortez. "But," said the *Express*, "they were probably all horse thieves."

Cortez was reported seen, captured and/or killed at many points, often the same day, leading a newspaper to comment dryly that he had "passed over the pike" a lot of times to be still on the move.

With hundreds of people scouring the country for him, he walked all the way up to Gonzales, where Glover and Schnabel died, and then headed southwestward in the general direction of Laredo, finally convinced that Mexico was the only safe place for him. He rode down a couple of stolen horses before he took the brown mare that itself became legendary in South Texas for its endurance and heart.

Contrary to general opinion at the time, he traveled alone and largely without outside aid after he left the shootout at the Robledo place. He was seen at times and not recognized, seen and recognized at other times but lost in the heavy brush thickets. At one point, starved for water, he found a waterhole well-guarded by possemen. He rode out a way, gathered up a good-sized string of cattle and drove them up to the water, posing as a cowboy just doing his job. The possemen never bothered him.

He occasionally bummed food and water from Mexican people, most of whom knew who he was but wouldn't tell. Always behind him was an experienced tracker, Emanuel Tom, relentlessly pressing, keeping him moving. At one point Cortez became so tired and discouraged that he lay down to wait for capture. But he had messed up his trail so well that Tom and the posse lost time. Cortez rested up, took fresh heart and went on.

He was near Laredo and only a few miles from the border when he was finally caught. He was betrayed by one of his own people to whom he had gone for food and a place to rest. The betrayer sought a $1,000 reward but never collected more than $200; the rest was split among several Anglo officers.

Cortez was taken peacefully June 22 by a Ranger and a customs officer. But if they hadn't taken him, others probably would have. A posse of Mexican-American officers from Laredo arrived on the scene moments after the capture. And the tireless tracker Emanuel Tom got there just twenty minutes after Cortez was caught. He had personally followed the fugitive more than 300 miles.

Cortez had finally had to leave the brown mare in a state of exhaustion. It was later revealed that possemen had ridden at least half a dozen horses to death in the long chase.

Cortez was taken to San Antonio rather than to Karnes City because of fear he might be lynched. A huge crowd gathered at the passenger station to watch his arrival. But he had been smuggled into town unceremoniously on a freight train that had even stopped at Cotulla to unload cattle.

He was given a swift trial and sentenced to death, but his courage and the likeable character he displayed in jail earned him many powerful friends once the first heat of anger had passed. The conviction was reversed. Eventually the only charge which stuck was one for theft of the brown mare, which incidentally had been renamed Fanny Cortez and shown at the international fair in San Antonio.

After twelve years in prison he was pardoned by Governor O.B. Colquitt in 1913. Cortez promised to stay out of the area where he had his trouble. He went to Mexico and took up with the losing side, the Huerta forces, in the revolution. He returned to Texas to recover from wounds and died in Anson at the home of a friend in 1916, at age forty-one.

Almost before the smoke cleared away, Mexican border singers were making up "corridos" or folksongs about him. Dr. Paredes in later years made a collection of the many variations of the Cortez corridos and the legend which blew him up into a combination of Robin Hood, Pancho Villa and Superman, killing so many Texas sheriffs that they fell like the leaves from the trees.

Graveyard Is Only Relic Left
of Fort Davis on Clear Fork

Livestock Weekly, June 15, 1972

THOUGH I did not get around to writing the novel until some years later, I was gathering background for *Stand Proud* when I visited the site of old Fort Davis on the Clear Fork, subject of the Newcomb diaries. Quite a bit is said about the civilian fort in Sallie Reynolds Matthews' classic frontier reminiscence, *Interwoven*. Walking over the ground on a dull, windy day, seeing the encroachment of a wide gully upon the old 1860s graveyard, I could share the sense of melancholy that permeated the Newcombs' accounts. It was not a happy place.

≈

BRECKENRIDGE   In the latter part of the Civil War, Indian pressure became unbearable on farms and ranches of outlying settlements in what was then far western Texas. Families pulled back into little enclaves for mutual protection, a practice known then as "forting up." When men ventured out to farm or hunt cattle, they usually did so in groups.

Most of these civilian "forts" such as Fort Hubbard and Fort Owlhead had short lives of a year or two, left no records and little or no physical trace.

Two old family diaries and a brush-hidden graveyard under a stand of ancient liveoak trees are all that remain of Fort Davis on the Clear

198

Fork of the Brazos River, barely inside the Stephens County line. Established in October 1864 and deserted less than two years later, it was named for Confederate President Jefferson Davis. Nobody seemed to care that there was another Fort Davis farther west out in the mountains.

A revealing day-to-day record of events in that hardship community was left in diaries kept by schoolteacher Samuel P. Newcomb and his wife, Susan, who had been a Reynolds. The accounts, still in family hands today, reveal no glamour, no glory. On the contrary they stress poverty, fear and sometimes actual hunger.

A physical description of the fort is given in one of S. P. Newcomb's early entries. It was 300 by 375 feet, divided into sixteen lots seventy-five feet square with a twenty-five foot alley running east and west. He wrote: "There is now some over twenty good houses finished in the fort. I say good houses for they are the very good of the kind. They are pickett houses (the spelling is Newcomb's) covered with dirt and the cracks stopped with dirt. They are a very quick house built and very comfortable so far as warmth is concerned, but not very nice as you may suppose."

The following August 25, 1865, he was not so enthusiastic: "Last night after all had got to bed and all was still, I was awakened by the half of one of Sergeant Irwin's house tops falling in with a tremenderous crash. But luckily no one was hurt. The dirt top houses can be dangerous unless they are made very strong and of good timber."

Newcomb and his wife gave considerable attention to the Indian problem, voicing strong suspicion that the Union was encouraging Indian depredations against the Confederate frontier.

Death was always near, not only because of Indians but because of the primitive nature of the settlers' lives. Newcomb spent January 1, 1865, helping bury a twelve-month-old child dead of exposure. He was in a dark mood. "Many of us that are now breathing the breath of life in perfect health will be mouldering in our graves long before the last day of this year rolls around."

He was to live longer than he appeared to think at that time, but not too long. He was caught in a rain at Fort Griffin a few years later, took pneumonia and died, still quite young.

On January 20 he mentioned three men named Mercer, Jackson and Irvin who "had left this country with a drove of beef steers about three months ago for Mexico," expected to be back in six weeks. It was thought they had been intercepted and pressed into Confederate service. "They left here before the last grand indian rade and therefore knew nothing of the people 'forting up' untill they heared of it in Mexico."

On February 2 he expressed a fear that Indians and Kansas Jayhawkers would "come down on us in the Spring in numbers heretofore unknown, and make an attempt to break up this frontier. It is true that they can do us a great deal of harm in the way of driving off our stock which I do not see any possible chance to prevent, but if we will work upon our forts, perhaps we can make them safe enough to save our scalps which is dearer to most men than all their property."

As spring came on, plans were made to build a heavy picket fence around the fort to aid in its protection. Each man was allotted the duty of cutting and hauling in pickets to build forty-four-and-a-half feet of fence. All were not diligent, as indicated by Newcomb's entry of March 12, telling about an Indian scare when a man named McCarty was chased three miles into the fort by four or five Indians:

> The news spread over the fort in an instant and then all was in confusion. Some women were running about gathering up their children. Some were in tearful distress about husbands that were out steer hunting, horse hunting, etc. Others were so badly frightened that they ran from place to place like they had lost all reason. . . .

"I think this will stir some in this place up to their picketing."

The scare abated, for the very next day Newcomb opened a school. "This day I commenced a school in this place for a term of fourteen weeks. I have only nineteen schollars at present and most of them very rude and wild unacquainted with school discipline."

An indignant entry March 22 indicated that the Confederate government was not always beloved: "They say a man from the eastern part of this State by the name of Scot with 45 hands is up in this country gathering beef steers and giving the people nothing in return except a quartermaster's receipt. The people of this country have been badly treated at several different times in a manner similar to the above or worse. As the people of the frontier have not been taken into the Confederate Service, the people of other parts of the country appear to think they can come up here with their threats to report the frontier man to the Confederate Service and force him into any measure they please. The frontier men are not so easy excited now as they were at first, as they have lost some of their beef steers which is their only dependance, the only product in this country."

Both Newcombs' diaries frequently mentioned one John Selman, who had come home from Confederate service and joined the home militia. On April 29 four soldiers arrived from Fort Belknap to arrest Selman for desertion. The war ended shortly, however, and Selman came back.

This was the same John Selman who as an old man in El Paso killed John Wesley Hardin in 1895. A rough customer even as a young man, Selman drifted into outlawry around Fort Griffin in the 1870s and continued a spectacular but little-publicized career of lawlessness in New Mexico during and after the Lincoln County War.

The old frontiersmen were not always so infallible and dauntless as they appear in movies. On May 21 Newcomb wrote of an Indian fight which "took place a few days since between about 40 militiamen and 25 Comanches. The white men succeeded in killing and scalping three Indians, but by the time they had accomplished this there had been two white men accidentally wounded by their fellow soldiers."

Life in the tight confines of the little fort must have been wearing on people's nerves. On July 8: "We had a small but very disgraceful fight in this place to day between Mrs. Musgraves and Mrs. Clark, the result of children difficulties."

Buffalo in large numbers sometimes grazed within easy shooting distance of the fort, and stragglers on several occasions wandered in among the buildings. They were usually attacked by every dog in the place and killed on the spot.

The cattle industry was in its infancy, and such later terms as "cowboy" and "roundup" do not appear in the Newcomb diaries. On January 6, 1866, Newcomb gave this description of a cow hunt:

> The cow-hunter of this country starts out upon his one or two weeks with his wallet of provision and camping blanket tied to his saddle, and his cow whip, which is from ten to sixteen feet long, and then his gun lashed to the bow of this saddle to protect himself from the Indians. Thus equipped he travels over a large scope of country, driving in his stock to mark and brand the calves, and where night overtakes him if there is plenty of water and grass he camps, hobbles his horse, eats his supper of bread, dried beef and cold water, then lies down upon his blanket with his saddle for a pillow and sleeps as soundly as a king in his palace on a bed of down.

Mrs. Newcomb was sometimes inclined to humor:

> Mr. Linch says that he thinks the Indians are going to keep the ranch for him this year, he says if they are he would like for them to let him know before he puts himself to any trouble to repair the ranch.
>
> The Indians borrowed Taylor Mauldings horse and he came over to buy another.

The fort's small unfenced cemetery remains today a few hundred yards north of the Clear Fork in the middle of a brushy pasture south of Woodson. The ravages of time and weather have made it impossible to get an accurate count of the graves; they number a dozen or more. Only two still have legible tombstones, one from 1865, one 1866.

Time and elements may eventually destroy the site. A large and growing gully has reached within a few feet of the cemetery. Each time a new chunk of earth sloughs off into the gully, the end is a little nearer.

Crane Is No Cowtown, But Provides
a Very Helpful Mineral Supplement

Livestock Weekly, August 17, 1972

THOUGH I have lived in San Angelo considerably more than forty years, *home* in a sense is still Crane, the West Texas oilpatch town where I went to school. The first flush of its boomtown days was fading when we moved there, but I can still remember much about the way it looked, its tents and tarpaper shacks, its little shotgun houses, its only paved street the highway that went through the middle of town. I called upon those memories to help me write *Honor at Daybreak*, a fictional account of a late 1920s boomtown in many ways much like Crane.

≈

CRANE   It would be difficult to regard Crane as a ranching town, although sheep and cattle ranches surround it. The town's lifeblood has always been oil. But it would also be difficult to visualize a thriving ranch business around Crane without the oil industry, for that mineral supplement has helped pull many a shaky ranching operation through hard times.

And hard times have been frequent here in this low-rainfall, sandy, mesquite and greasewood area where livestock have to be a little lonesome to do well.

Crane last weekend threw a big old-settlers' reunion to celebrate a dual occasion: the county's forty-fifth year and its billionth barrel of oil.

Eighty-seven residents petitioned for organization August 11, 1927, and got it September 3 of that year. Several thousand people were here Saturday for the celebration.

The county had been created on paper as far back as 1887 by the state legislature, but until the first oil was discovered in 1926 there just weren't enough people inside its boundaries; for administrative purposes it was tied to Ector County's apron strings. From 1907 to 1917 the population ranged from seven to fourteen, and in 1918 it boomed to twenty-seven.

Among the ranch operations in the early 1920s were those of J. T. McElroy and the Cowdens, McGees, Clarks, Tubbs and Barnsleys.

The first wildcat rig located in the sands late in 1925. By April the driller, B. F. Weekley, was all but broke and unable to pay his crew. He already owed one of his employees $500 for labor and for boarding the rest of the crew; in desperation he offered him an offset eighty acres in payment, but the man refused. On April 19, 1926, the crew put in a long day, stopped for supper, then went back to the rig for one more round before dark. The well came in big. The offset eighty soon sold for $80,000. In later years it would have been worth far, far more than that.

That was a time of oil booms in West Texas; many another boomtown already had come into being, like Ranger, Best, Pyote and McCamey. Some would survive; many would not. Real estate developers soon acquired a townsite on the edge of the McElroy Ranch and began selling lots. Crane was first a tent city, then gradually most of the tents gave way to tarpaper and sheet-iron shacks and simple "shotgun" houses thrown up of raw lumber. Few people built with any view toward permanence; the life expectancy of these early boomtowns was roughly comparable to that of a baby lamb born on top of a coyote den.

The first grave in Crane was that of a cafe cook who became embroiled in an argument with another cook; he came staggering out of the cafe with an ice-pick hilt-deep in his chest, fell on the wooden sidewalk and died in front of several startled onlookers. They wrapped him in a blanket, carried him over the sandhills to a convenient spot where no building site had been laid out, and there they buried him.

A tiny frame shotgun house might rent as high as $100 a month. Oil was as cheap as ten cents a barrel, but water was $1 to $2 a barrel, hauled from water wells out in the burgeoning new oilfields. Recycling was an economic necessity; the rinse from a family's laundry might become the bath water for each family member, using it in turn; then it might be used for mopping the floor and the remnant carried out and poured on a few thirsty flowers and shrubs in the tiny yard.

The relatively high-paying oilfield work drew some rough characters, either to work or to live off of the workers. Crane's small red-light district was just northwest of the main part of town. The early boom came during prohibition, so the bootleggers had a thriving trade.

A few years ago, when the red-light district had long since passed into history and the three surviving brown shotgun houses had long been vacant, Tex Brightman bought them to clear the lot. An old-timer told him he ought to be jailed for destroying important landmarks. Beneath the three old houses Brightman found a truckload of bootleg whisky bottles, casually thrown there during the town's early years.

The rough customers have perhaps always been given too much attention and have overshadowed the fact that a great many oilfield workers were peaceful and religious, even bordering on the Puritanical. From the first, they put up church buildings much more substantial than the houses they lived in. On at least one occasion indignant local citizens called on the Rangers to help put a stop to some couples living together without benefit of clergy. The Rangers conducted a small group wedding, shotgun style. One prospective groom called up the telephone operator and invited her to run over and attend his wedding. She protested that she had nothing suitable to wear. He assured her she was in better shape than he was; he was wearing handcuffs.

Much of the early work was done by big teams of mules and horses, many belonging to J. J. Willis of Odessa, because the sandy land was hard for trucks and cars to negotiate. Until regular roadways finally were laid out to Odessa, some of the McElroy pastures were spiderwebbed by treacherous two-rut roads whose sandpits could ensnare a vehicle like flypaper catching a fly. For years, these early roads were dotted by rusting hulks of old automobiles whose engines had been burned up in a futile effort to dislodge them from the sand.

Shovels were standard equipment for any traveler. Sometimes a good blanket was sacrificed, being laid under the wheels to furnish a little traction.

The oilfields were both a boon and a bane to the ranchmen. Leases and royalty payments helped them weather some bad drouths. On the other hand, livestock mortality in and around the oilfields could be rather high. Cattle died from drinking oil and mired down in slush pits. People as well as livestock died from poison gas until the gas was properly flared. A few oilfielders found that stolen beef tasted better than bought beef. When the Depression hit Crane, many people moved away but didn't take their dogs with them; roving packs of starving dogs took a heavy toll of livestock before they were killed off.

But taken as a whole, relationships between ranch people and oilfield workers were good. Many—even a majority—of the men in the oilpatch had come originally from ranches and farms, or were just one generation removed from them.

Today there may be about as many horses stabled in and around the Crane roping arena as there are on all the working ranches combined. The young men—and some no longer so young—of the town and the oilfields still maintain a keen interest in calf roping.

Though signs are beginning to point to change, the Crane County ranchman's tax bill has been kept low by the high evaluations placed on the oil industry. Crane has one of the best school systems in the state for a town of its size. During the 1950s drouth the county and school district waived all livestock taxes; they felt they didn't need the money as badly as the ranchers did. Even today, few cattle and sheep are being assessed, and these only because owners voluntarily render them for reasons of their own.

But landowners in some other Texas oilfield areas are beginning to feel a sharp pinch as oil production declines. Their counties and school districts carry an ever-increasing commitment even as the oilfield tax base shrinks. As a result, land and livestock taxes have to assume a rapidly increasing percentage of the burden.

That hasn't hit Crane County yet. Many Crane people say these fields have production potential extending far into the future. They concede that widespread waterflooding is being used now in the shallower fields, and waterflooding usually is the beginning of the end. But when the shallow fields are gone, Crane still has extensive oil pay on three deeper levels.

A recent survey showed about 6,000 wells pumping oil in the county. The 1970 census listed 4,172 people, about 500 fewer than in 1960 but a far cry from the 159 qualified voters when the county was formally organized in 1927.

What probably caused as much pain as the loss of 500 people during the decade was the decline in the official rainfall. Ten years earlier the average rainfall was given as fourteen inches, certainly low enough. But by 1970 it had shrunk to twelve-plus.

Water, incidentally, has been a consistent victim in the drive for oil production. Despite the Texas Railroad Commission's well-publicized efforts in recent years, salt-water pollution continues to spread, gradually wiping out one good water well after another. Much of this trouble comes from old oil wells and dry holes abandoned years ago by oil companies long since disappeared. Some of those early wells were plugged by nothing more substantial than a mesquite stump.

Another point: over much of the county the oil companies were granted extensive water rights years ago, before the pollution and depletion problem was recognized. The companies have a legal right to continue pumping unlimited amounts of fresh water for the waterflooding of old oilfields.

Oil Riches Ruined Some Ranchmen,
Says Company Land Man C. C. Pope

Livestock Weekly, February 1, 1973

THOUGH we never printed much about the oil industry in the *Livestock Weekly*, oil and gas were an integral part of ranch operations in much of West Texas. It was said that the most rewarding type of shade for cattle or sheep was an oilfield pump jack and that oil was the best mineral supplement for livestock. Because I grew up on a ranch at the edge of a large oilfield in Crane and Upton counties, I related very well to C. C. Pope's account of his experiences as an oil company land man in early boom days. Not until my novel *Honor at Daybreak* in 1991, however, did I ever use my own oilpatch memories in a book.

≈

CLARENCE C. POPE during his long career saw the ranchman and landowner from a different vantage point than most people. Pope was always giving them money—or trying to.

Pope, now retired in San Angelo, was an oil company "scout" in the first years of the big Permian Basin booms, and from 1930 until his retirement in 1960 was a company land man. It was his responsibilty to arrange oil leases. That meant a lot of horse trading with ranchers who thought they ought to get a little more, and company officials who thought the deal ought to be made cheaper.

Looking back over those long years and the hundreds of land deals in which he participated, he says he can remember many times when he did the rancher a favor, perhaps even saving him from ruin. He can also remember instances in which the money instead of being a blessing turned into a curse, and ruined the people who got it.

His job put him into something of an adversary relationship with the rancher, but almost always a friendly one. He says in thirty years he was never ordered off of a place.

"Most people were glad to see me come," he says. "My experiences with ranchers were pleasant. They were hard to deal with—real horse traders—but once a trade was made, everything was alright."

He always found that lambing time was the biggest fly in the ointment for an oil company working on West Texas ranches. On a sheep outfit, a seismograph crew could simply figure on shutting down for a couple of months in the spring. Dynamite blasts and newly born lambs wouldn't mix any better than oil and water. Even a truck driving across a pasture could cause problems if the sheep were used to being fed from a truck; the ewes would chase after it, leaving the lambs behind.

He recalls an instance in Yoakum County when another oil company land man was trying to persuade a farm couple to accept a $5-per-acre lease. Torn by indecision, the farmer suggested they all get down on their knees and pray over it together, the land man included. They prayed, the couple accepted the money, and the company struck oil on the place.

Less happy was an experience Pope had in Coke County trying to persuade an elderly ranchman to accept a $10,000 offer for renewal on a place where the lease was about to expire. A severe drouth was underway; the man needed the money. But he held out for more. The company, under terms of the expiring lease, rushed to drill a well it really didn't want to drill at all. The well came in dry, and the rancher was never able to lease the land again at any price.

Pope says drilling a well was always a risk both for the company and the landowner. Often a ranchman felt more secure when the company never drilled, for he could continue leasing his land indefinitely. Once he had a dry hole or two, he might never be able to lease it again.

On one of his early trips as an oil scout on primitive ranch roads in Crockett County, his Model T was running hot, and he drove up to a ranchhouse to get some water for the radiator. He was met at the door by a gray-bearded old ranchman who turned out to be the noted J. M. Shannon. Shannon genially asked him in, drew him a map to the wildcat well he was searching for and helped him get water for his radiator. In the process the old gentleman asked if it might be possible for him to get an oil lease on some of his land for twenty-five cents an acre.

At that time it was a long way to any known oil production, and to Pope's knowledge Shannon was able to lease very little land during his lifetime. But after his death a considerable oilfield was developed. Today that land endows a large hospital in San Angelo.

Pope has recently published his memoirs in a book logically entitled *An Oil Scout in the Permian Basin*.

He always treasured his six years as an oil scout in West Texas and eastern New Mexico (1924–1930) as being the freest and most interesting period of his life. It was a scout's duty to stay on the move and keep his company informed on all oil exploration in his assigned territory. Pope's territory for Sun Oil Company was the whole Permian Basin.

He would leave San Angelo on a Monday morning, heading west in a Model T equipped with shovel, chains and two spare tires. There wasn't a mile of paved road west of downtown San Angelo at the time he started. When he was lucky, he traveled on good graded roads. He was still fortunate when he had a decent two-rut ranch road. Much of his mileage was made out across the ranch country on tracks left by the oilfield equipment trucks. If mesquite thorns punctured his tires, he stopped and patched them on the spot. If the car broke down, he had a set of tools to fix it himself.

He says he was lucky; he never spent a night camped by the side of the road because of a breakdown.

For four days each week he would work out of old established towns like Fort Stockton, or such new oil towns as McCamey or Iraan. He saw all the boomtowns in their infancy. Some survived. Some like Best and Pyote faded away.

He remembers a particularly rough one known as Grube. When discovery of the Yates field led to the establishment of Iraan, it also led to the birth of Grube, just across a wooden bridge. The Pecos River was all that separated the two towns. It also happened to be the county line. Iraan was in Pecos County and was well policed. Grube, however, was in Crockett County and so inaccessible to Ozona, the county seat, that it was allowed to run wide open. And wide open it was, for a time. The Pecos County peace officers could only sit on the wooden bridge and watch.

But one day the Texas Rangers came, and a county line meant nothing to them. They walked over the bridge and started cleaning up. Pretty soon Grube was only a memory.

Because of the vastness of the area, oil scouts formed a sort of fraternal order. During the week each man telegraphed his company officers any hot information he thought was of immediate interest. On Fridays all the scouts would meet and pool the week's information for the general benefit of the industry. Except for a couple of majors which had their own large scout staffs, the oil companies encouraged this mutual cooperation.

On rare "tight" wells, secrecy was the order, but otherwise information was freely given. A scout for one company was welcome to check the logbook on a rig owned by a rival company or wildcatter. He made it a point to carry chewing tobacco for the drillers, who couldn't afford to smoke on the rig because of the fire hazard. If he met them in town, he bought them a meal. In return, they told him everything they knew.

Even on a "tight" well, an observant scout could make some close guesses by simple observation, by counting the stands of pipe in the derrick, by looking at the drilling line. "Tight" wells were resented in the trade, but on the other hand they were a challenge.

Fortunes might ride on the accuracy of a scout's report. If a well in a new area showed promise, oil companies would want to start leasing land around it before confirmation ran up the price. If prospects looked dim, a company wanted to be cautious in investing.

Pope recalls one deep test well that nearly all the scouts were touting as extremely promising, causing considerable lease speculation. But one scout—not Pope—sagely kept his company out of the trap. He had seen salt crystals on the drilling line. Surely enough, the well turned out to be mostly water.

Although Pope was on hand during the development of the huge Permian Basin oilfields and personally participated in the expending of millions of dollars to landowners, as a salaried company man he made it a policy not to speculate personally and create any conflict of interest. Beyond a little royalty, and his salary, he did not participate financially. He says it was probably better that way.

"Most of the people I knew who suddenly came into big riches just weren't able to handle it. One way or another it ruined most of them, or at least ruined their sons and daughters, and their grandchildren."

He always thought the most fortunate people were those who came into enough money to make them comfortable, or to pay them out of a hole some drouth had left them in, but not enough to make them rich.

He knew oil men who struck it rich, then turned around and lost it drilling for more oil. At that, he always considered them more fortunate than the ones who spent theirs on wine, women and song, for those often lost themselves as well as their money.

Sherwood Land Rush Depended More Upon Muscle Than Legs

Livestock Weekly, April 1, 1976

A NUMBER of West Texas counties had land rushes just at the turn of the century as school lands were thrown open for settlement. Unlike the great rush in Oklahoma, the Texas variety was confined to county courthouses and courthouse squares. The one described here was typical in many ways. I heard similar stories about another at Eldorado, in Schleicher County, from an old gentleman who had been county clerk there at the time. The material for the Sherwood article was gleaned from contemporary newspaper accounts. I interpolated some of this into a sequence in my novel, *Stand Proud*.

≈

SHERWOOD Sherwood's great land rush of 1903 was so exciting that it was rerun. But unlike television repeats, it didn't come out the same way the second time.

The old Sherwood (Irion County) courthouse still stands, seldom used except for occasional social functions. The official affairs of Irion County were moved across Spring Creek to Mertzon in 1936. But there was a time, before the railroad came, when Sherwood was an active, hustling town.

It was especially active March 7, 1903. On that day forty-six sections of school land were taken out of grass lease and thrown open for filing under the state homestead law. Somewhat the same thing was happening in several other West Texas counties at about the same time.

In Oklahoma, land seekers lined up and made a famous race on horseback or in wagons to try to drive the first claim stake upon an actual piece of land. In West Texas the races were confined to the courthouse square; the target was the county clerk's office. The first to come, theoretically, would be the first served.

Usually the victory went to the strong, not the fleet.

The big Irion opening was to be at 7:30 A.M. on a Saturday morning. Clerk W. W. Carson explained ahead of time that his door would remain locked, and that he would receive filings through a window which opened onto the courthouse yard.

To be certain of their place in line, two local citizens took their stations at about 9 A.M. on Friday, prepared to camp and wait almost twenty-four hours. So no one would push them aside, W. E. Branch and Harris Francis tied themselves against the clerk's window with ropes and straps. There they remained through the night while the town filled up with land seekers arriving on horseback, by wagon or hack, and even afoot.

A little past midnight, knowing things would be crowded later, clerk Carson decided it was time to slip into his office. A man named H. H. Mitchell, bearing a handful of applications, followed him closely and pushed through the door right behind him. Once inside, he pointed out that it was now legally the appointed day and tried to make Carson accept the applications. Carson refused. When Mitchell declined to accept the situation, Carson picked up a heavy seal and swung it. He missed Mitchell and knocked a lighted lamp to the floor, starting a small blaze. In the ensuing scuffle Mitchell's applications all wound up in the fire and were burned. The defeated Mitchell retired from the fray.

The thick smell of oil smoke forced Carson to open a window and try to air out the office. Frank Allison of Eldorado promptly climbed through the window and made the same demand that had led to the difficulty with Mitchell. When Carson declined to accept his papers, Allison threw them into the office and considered them filed. Carson took another view. The papers remained on the floor all that day and over the weekend, well trampled and never acknowledged.

Meanwhile, Branch and Francis stayed strapped to their window, secure in the belief that they would be first.

But they did not reckon on the determination of a set of cowboys from the Six Ranch, aided and abetted by some friends. Shortly before 7:30 A.M., these gentlemen formed a flying wedge, rushed the head of the line, unceremoniously unstrapped Branch and Francis and carried them away from the scene of action.

Their position in the line was taken up by cowboys chosen for muscle and will.

The waiting line turned into a skirmish line, men wrestling and struggling either to keep the place they already had or to take a better one from somebody else. Several times the displaced ones formed ranks into the sort of flying wedge that had defeated them, but the "Six boys" held their ground against all counterattacks.

The local law stood by among the spectators. The sheriff had decided that he and his men would take no hand except to prevent murder. Clerk Carson also stayed clear of the fray. His only rule was that he would serve those who appeared at his window. How they got there was not his concern.

When the appointed time came and he opened for business, the Six hands were in front. By the time they were through they had filed on thirty-eight of the forty-six sections. The "Sherwood Gang," badly beaten down, came in for the leavings, belatedly also filing on a total of thirty-eight sections.

A group arrived from Eldorado a little late. The fun was over. They hurried to the window and threw their applications in, but these wound up on the floor with Frank Allison's.

It was estimated that about 150 men were in and out of the line and the scuffle at one time or another. Some were considerably more out than in.

Normally that would have ended it, but a technical error was discovered. The leases had not expired until midnight on Saturday, rather than midnight on Friday.

A rematch was called for. Clerk Carson refused to open the office on Sunday, so the whole thing had to be done over again Monday.

This gave all sides time to recruit extra muscle. The Six cowboys were reported to have imported help out of San Angelo at a cost of about $150, no small sum in those days. Dawn found the cowboys at the clerk's window, just where Branch and Francis had been on Saturday. A number had tied or strapped themselves to the wall.

But this time the tables turned. The Sherwood bunch had done a superior job of recruiting. Half an hour before the window was to open, a wedge of big husky fellows hit the cowboys like a freight train. A local cheering section lined the yard, most of them rooting for Saturday's losers.

Superior numbers and weight soon told against the cowboys. One by one they were carried out of the line, placed face down on the ground and sat upon by somebody heavy enough to be sure the wind didn't blow them away.

When Carson opened his window, he saw a bruised and battered set of faces, completely different from the ones who had first presented themselves on Saturday. After the Sherwood group was through filing, the cowboys were let up and told they were welcome to whatever land was left. Little was.

Contemporary newspaper accounts describe the two rushes as bruising but not mean, and even in the worst of the wrestling match there was more laughter than profanity. A lot of clothes were torn up, but no bones were broken.

Declared a San Angelo man, L. C. Fisher: "I have been in a West Texas land rush, and I wouldn't get into another one like it for $2,000 in gold. I have had an elegant sufficiency."

The filings from both days' rush were sent to Austin, and the state land commissioner recognized those from the second day's run. The "Six boys" had won the first skirmish, but they lost the war.

Lubbock Blacks Follow Trail Of
Lost Cavalrymen On Plains

Livestock Weekly, August 10, 1978

IN WRITING my novel, *The Wolf and the Buffalo*, I borrowed from the history of the Nolan Expedition of 1877, one of the most remarkable ordeal-and-survival stories in Texas history. In real life, a group of black buffalo soldiers under Captain Nicholas Nolan pursued breakaway Comanche warriors out into the desert west of present Tahoka and became lost in the sands. They suffered grievously from thirst and hunger. In 1978, a group of young black men in Lubbock decided to pay tribute by reenacting that event. This article grew out of their experience, which became an exhausting endurance contest in its own right.

≈

MORTON   About 101 years ago a troop of Tenth Cavalry black soldiers and two white officers on the trail of Comanche raiders became lost on the rolling prairies and in the shinnery sandhills west of present Tahoka. Their eighty-six hours without water in the blazing torment of a July sun have gone down as one of the great ordeal stories of the Southwest.

A group of young black men from Lubbock has reenacted that tragic event to a degree by riding and walking much of three days along the same general course, wearing replicas of the original cavalry uniforms. Their aim was to dramatize the black contribution to West Texas history.

Though they had a water truck and bedding along to provide some comforts the real soldiers never had, they found that even their simulated expedition was far more severe than expected. They came to a new appreciation for the frontier cavalry.

The real-life saga has gone down in history as "Nolan's Lost Nigger Expedition" of 1877, a name not particularly relished by today's black consciousness groups.

Though Colonel Ranald Mackenzie's great raid on the Indian winter camp in Palo Duro Canyon had driven most Comanches to the reservation late in 1874, stray parties of unreconstructed warriors continued to slip away on raiding trips. One such party dealt misery to buffalo hunters through the winter of 1876–1877 in the Double Mountain country. They climaxed their adventures with a daring and successful night-time horse stealing raid on Rath's hunter supply camp in the spring.

Captain Nicholas Nolan and Lieutenant Charles Cooper left Fort Concho (San Angelo) July 10 with about forty black cavalrymen to try to find the Indians. They joined forces with a vengeful band of buffalo hunters who had dubbed themselves "The Forlorn Hope" and had fought a pitched battle with Comanches in Yellow House Canyon near present Lubbock. With the hunters was a "reformed" *Comanchero* trader named Jose Tafoya or Tafolla, acting as guide and tracker.

Along came Comanche war chief Quanah Parker, carrying a pass from Mackenzie himself at Fort Sill, permitting him to venture out onto the plains and try to persuade the runaways to rejoin the fold. Though more inclined to shoot him than salute him, Nolan was obliged to let him proceed.

Later, when the soldiers and hunters were undergoing their terrible ordeal, there was strong evidence that Parker and the raiders watched from afar, enjoying their predicament.

A camp was set up at Double Lakes, near present Tahoka. Tafoya sent word to Nolan from present Rich Lake, near Brownfield, that he had found Indian tracks. Nolan hurriedly put his troops on the march, not even taking time to be sure their canteens were full. They quick-timed to alkaline Rich Lake, then appropriately known as Dry Lake. Most of the soldiers had drunk up their water and found none fit to refill their canteens. They dry-camped that first night, July 26, somewhere near present Meadow in southeastern Hockley County, many already suffering.

Evidently well aware of pursuit, the Indians left a zigzag trail that kept the soldiers away from any hidden watering places and wore out both men and horses.

By early afternoon of the second day the troopers and the buffalo hunters who had accompanied them were evidently well across the line into present Roosevelt County, New Mexico. Horses exhausted and men not much better, Nolan called a rest stop in the sandhills.

It was obvious the men were lost. Nolan blamed Tafoya in particular because the scout had been so intent on the Indians' tracks that he forgot about landmarks. There would have been few if any. It became evident that the number-one priority was no longer the Indians; it was to save the men's lives. One after another fell victim to sunstroke or heat prostration.

Nolan gave Tafoya his own horse and sent him looking for Silver Lake or Yellow House Springs, to the east. He ordered some of the stronger troopers with canteens to follow the guide at their own pace and to bring back water for the others. They did follow Tafoya to water, all right, but they did not return to the others.

The main body turned back, moving in a generally easterly direction where the hunters believed Silver Lake to be. Men dropped out, prostrated by heat and thirst. The straggling command that night flopped in exhaustion on a little round hill less than a mile west of the New Mexico-Texas state line and west of Morton. That small prominence, which would go unnoticed in hillier country, has been known ever since as Nigger Hill.

The men spent a horrible night on that dry, open hilltop, many delirious. By this time they could no longer eat the rations they carried because their mouths and throats were dry and swollen.

Bad as the previous two days had been, the march away from the hill was worse. The men strung out, staggering blindly across the intermixed hard prairie and shinnery sand. At a point somewhere north of present Morton, the group split. Nolan quarreled with the buffalo hunters, who were convinced it was not far to Silver Lake or Yellow House Springs. He had no faith in them and opted instead to return to Double Lakes.

It turned out the hunters were right. The strongest of them reached water toward the end of that day. The soldiers—those who survived—still had two desperate days and nights to go.

The command virtually disintegrated. The men were drinking their own urine and that of their horses, sweetening it with sugar so they could force it down. When a horse would stagger and fall, the men would cut its throat and fight over the blood.

All horses dead or abandoned, the two officers mounted the two surviving mules while the men dragged along afoot. In the wee hours of the morning of July 30 they came onto a clearly-beaten trail which they hoped would lead them to the lakes. Firing their guns as a signal for the others behind them to keep hope, they pressed on. Five miles down the trail, about 5:00 A.M., they came to the lakes of salvation.

The first arrivals flung themselves into the water, recuperated to some extent, filled canteens and started up their backtrail to rescue the friends they had left scattered behind them.

For four black soldiers, help was too late.

It was a story with all the elements for a historic epic—acts of bravery and self-sacrifice, acts of cowardice and desertion. Most of all, it was a story of endurance.

In a sense the mission was a failure because Nolan and his men never caught up to the Indians. However, Quanah Parker took the warriors back to the reservation, and it was the last time a war party of any real size ventured out onto the Texas plains.

The reenactment was carried out by a Lubbock group which calls itself the Roots Historical Committee. More than twenty started the first day near Brownfield on horseback. Some never intended to make the whole trip. Others had the intention but found the weather hot and the road long.

By the second day they were down to nine of what group leader Eric Strong called "the pure in heart." Heatstroke and fatigue had eliminated two more by noon. The remaining seven—including one Hispanic who represented Jose Tafoya—walked the rest of the way, much as the real soldiers did.

Ironically, the area over which Nolan's men staggered and starved is broken up today into irrigated farms with wells pumping vast amounts of cool, clear water. Because of the fences and farms, the Lubbock men followed the roads and only approximated the actual route. They carried no water but drank fruit juices and Gatorade.

On their second day they met a rousing reception at Morton from county and city officials and townspeople, who feted them royally with steak.

The final morning they started walking about 3:30 A.M. and reached Nigger Hill while the air was still cool about 9:00 A.M. There, on a stockfarm belonging to C. C. Ashbrook, they found a small crowd waiting to cheer their arrival. Blistered and weary, the marchers conducted memorial services for the men who never made it home from the real Nolan expedition.

The trip, though only a simulation, was more of an ordeal than the Lubbock men had expected. But Strong said afterward that it was worth it all. He found that a great many people in the area—black and white—knew nothing about the Nolan story or about the part Tenth Cavalry troopers had in opening the region for settlement.

He felt that the trip dramatized to a lot of black people that they too have a historic heritage on the Texas plains.

When Is An Unlikely Story Folklore Rather Than Outright Fabrication?

Livestock Weekly, April 10, 1980

MORE than a dozen years ago I was asked to make a banquet talk to the Texas Folklore Society. I was vaguely aware of the organization but for one reason or another had never attended one of its annual meetings. I was so taken by the group, however, that I have not missed a meeting since. I have come to realize that formal history doesn't tell half the story. Often we can learn more about a people through their folklore than through their footnoted history. Folklore may not always be depended upon for pure facts, but it is long on truth. Yes, there *is* a difference.

≈

SAN ANTONIO   Folklore has been defined in at least one instance as something you want to believe but can't prove. J. Frank Dobie has been credited with saying that if a certain event didn't happen the way he described it, it should have.

Folklore has always been important to Texas. A lot of people outside of the state claim that Texas is mostly folklore, and very little truth.

In any case, Texas has had a folklore society for a little more than seventy years. Its members have met annually most of that time, except for breaks during the two world wars. It was in session here last week for the sixty-fourth time to let modern-day folklorists carry on a tradition pioneered by such people as Dobie, the Lomaxes, Walter Prescott Webb, Mody C. Boatright and many others less known to the outside world but revered by those people who don't let the lack of a footnote stand in the way of a good yarn.

There was, for example, James M. Day, English professor in the University of Texas at El Paso, debunking to a degree the debunkers of Pecos Bill. There are those who say the Pecos Bill cowboy character is a comparatively recent fabrication of professional writers and has no basis in what is termed the "folklore" tradition . . . that is to say he was invented for profit rather than by a deliberate nonprofit liar.

Not so, said Day, who claimed Pecos Bill was gradually amalgamated out of old Pecos River country stories. Evidently in an earlier day a number of characters bore the nicknames of Pecos Bill and Pecos Joe. Their exploits, real and embroidered or made up of whole cloth, were passed around the Texas range country until they fused together and lost whatever literal truth they may have had in the beginning. They were eventually written up by folklorists Tex O'Reilly and Mody Boatright and in more recent times given cartoon shape by Walt Disney.

History has a way of neglecting those people who do not in some conspicuous way shape destinies of nations or states. Not so with folklore. It has time for everybody, so long as their story is interesting. Lou Rodenberger, a specialist in energy communications for the Texas Agricultural Extension Service, talked about the old-time country schoolteachers of the early 1900s, whose one- and two-room schoolhouses often remained the focus of community affairs until at least the late 1940s. As examples she pointed to her own parents, Carl and Mabel Halsell, both retired from teaching and living near Cross Plains.

Mrs. Rodenberger has studied the memoirs, written and oral, of country schoolteachers from one end of the U. S. to the other and has found them very much alike, virtually interchangeable except for the names. She said today's teacher has largely been swallowed up by mass education and lost in anonymity, but the country schoolteacher of an earlier time was often an all-purpose community leader, called upon not only to teach the youngsters but to furnish social and spiritual leadership in the community.

Folklore can be a physical thing, highly tangible. Sylvia Ann Grider of College Station described the folk art of using petrified wood as a facing for houses instead of brick or more conventional stone. This usually occurs in areas where such petrified wood is so common that it has become an obstacle to field cultivation and has been removed. Most people don't like to discard it ignobly in a rock pile at the turnrow, so they have long had a tendency to make decorative uses of it.

One area where this has been done almost to excess is along Highway 21 in the Brazos Valley near Bryan-College Station. Examples are found in Cook's Point, Bryan, Caldwell, Giddings, Winchester and other nearby towns.

A lot of livestock men know William N. Stokes, Jr. of Lake Dallas for his longtime leadership in the Federal Intermediate Credit Bank of Houston and his importance in the agricultural loan field. They may not know that he is and long has been an avid collector of and speaker on folklore. He told several humorous courthouse yarns, including one about the Batesville lawyer who had agreed to take a piece of land as his fee for getting a defendant acquitted. He lived up to his part of the bargain and successfully got a "not guilty" verdict. That same day the client brought in a deed, duly signed. But shortly his ex-client sued for recovery on the grounds that the deed had been obtained under duress.

The lawyer indignantly denied any duress. He simply declared that that low-down s.o.b. (our initials, not his) had reneged on his agreement. "I just laid my pistol up against his head and cocked back the hammer and told him that if he didn't sign I'd blow his brains out, and he signed then and there of his own free will."

Martha Emmons of Waco, a legend herself among Texas folklorists, described some of the early leaders in that field who helped make folklore a respectable subject on campuses across the land. Of Dobie, whose name is probably most recognizable to the public, she said he was a "potent, inspiring listener. That was why he could gather so many good stories, because he never missed a word."

She remembered one of the first yarns she heard from Boatright, who told about a missing cutting horse found in the middle of an antbed, "cutting out the bull ants." And she remembered a Texas town so overloaded with ghost stories that "the whole town is haunted, and all the roads leading to it."

June Welch of the University of Dallas recalled one boyhood

meeting with a great uncle, Lucien Thompson Owens, ex-Confederate soldier, Ranger and sheriff of Decatur. He found the old gentleman dark and unsmiling, a terror to a tiny boy fed on legends.

Welch told a family story about the time Owens was called by friends to Sunset when it was being terrorized by two brothers and their gang. Though it was outside of his jurisdiction, he went anyway. He braced the brothers, shot one, grabbed the other and used him for cover while he made his way back to the railroad station. There he held the outlaw at gunpoint and the gang at bay while he telegraphed friend Dan Waggoner for help. Waggoner, famous pioneer rancher, armed a bunch of cowboys and rushed with them to Sunset on a flatcar, lifting the siege.

Welch told of an uncle who rode the train to Decatur to ask Owens' permission to marry his daughter. A couple of rowdies made nuisances of themselves on the car. When the train pulled in, Owens stood in the station. He always made it his business to see who got off the trains. One of the rowdies distracted him while the other slipped around and hit him from behind with a big rock. Staggered, Owens nevertheless pistol-whipped both. He hoisted one onto his shoulder and dragged the other all the way to the jail.

"And that," said the uncle with awe, "was the man I had come to ask if I could marry his daughter."

Paul Patterson, retired Crane teacher, storyteller and onetime cowboy, went to Australia last fall, fulfilling an ambition nursed since he had gotten to know Aussie soldiers in North Africa in World War II and found them fighters not only by profession but by hobby.

He said he found the Texas cowboy and the Australian "stock boy" incredibly similar in virtually every respect except the lingo they use. The contrast in their expressions is spectacular, he found, but the thoughts behind them are very much alike.

"They were all of a single mind in the way they think and act and eat," kindred spirits whether they look to the North Star or the Southern Cross, he said.

225

Indian Battle on Dove Creek Was
Costly Mistake to Texans

Livestock Weekly, April 10, 1980

EVERY war has its stories of costly errors of judgment, usually uncovered after a strong attempt to keep them from the public eye. The Civil War certainly had its share. One of these was the battle of Dove Creek, west of present San Angelo, in which a combination of Rangers, Confederate troops and citizen militia mistakenly attacked a large band of friendly Kickapoo Indians migrating south to Mexico to avoid entanglement in the war. I used this battle as an early pivotal event in my novel, *Stand Proud*. My principal character as a very young man suffers a wound in this fight because of other men's folly, and he vows never again to let anyone else give orders regarding his life. From that point on, he stubbornly makes all his own decisions, some of them painfully wrong.

≈

SAN ANGELO   The books which tell about the great Indian fights usually overlook the battle of Dove Creek, fought about twenty-five miles west of here January 8, 1865.

They shouldn't, because in terms of the number of combatants involved on both sides it was one of the major engagements of western history. But it has remained obscure for several reasons. One probably is that it happened in the final year of the Civil War, when most people's attention was focused on battlegrounds far to the east. Secondly, it was fought by mistake. Third, the white men took a terrible whipping, suffering heavy casualties at the hands of Indians who up to that point had been friendly.

A number of the participants left written accounts which differ in particulars but agree on most major points. One point on which all agree is that the battle never should have taken place. It left a legacy in blood to be paid by innocent settlers along the Texas border into the next decade.

During the Civil War years when so much of Texas' strength had been sapped in the battle for the Confederacy, Indian pressures along the frontier had become severe. A Ranger force was scattered thinly down a long "picket line" from the Red River to the Rio Grande, augmented by citizen militia. Ranger scouting parties ventured far out into Indian country, looking for sign of possible raiding parties in an effort to head them off before they could do mischief.

In December 1864, a scouting company under Captain Jack Cureton came across a huge abandoned campsite near the ruins of old Fort Phantom Hill on the Clear Fork of the Brazos. Cureton judged the Indians to have been Kiowas. That was the first in a series of costly errors.

Colonel J. B. "Buck" Barry, an old-time Indian fighter and Mexican War veteran in command of the Ranger forces operating out of Fort Belknap, pulled in all the Rangers he could afford and called on the citizen militia out of Brown, Comanche, Erath and Parker counties. Various accounts differ on the number of men involved in the pursuit and battle, but the *Handbook of Texas* places it at 370.

While awaiting reinforcement, Captain Cureton continued to trail the Indians, moving south in great force. The Rangers found a campsite near old Fort Chadbourne, and another, very fresh, on the North Concho River near present Water Valley. The Indian trail was so wide and so beaten out that it could be followed at night. The horse herd, Cureton knew, was tremendous.

He and other Rangers were puzzled by the fact that the tepee poles were bent over at the top, not Kiowa or Comanche style at all. An opinion began to form that these were Kickapoos, who had always been friendly.

The Rangers had found the Indians camped in the fork between Dove Creek and one of its tributaries before the "flop-eared" militia finally arrived under command of Captain S. S. Totten. There was, according to the account of George W. DeLong, a considerable body of opinion among the Rangers that these Indians should be left alone.

But in those times, when Indian raids were suffered at frequent intervals along the frontier and occasionally deep in the settlements, any armed Indian was considered a probable dangerous enemy. The objections were overruled and the attack begun awhile after daylight. Totten's militia were to hit the upper end and the center. Captain John Fossett and the Rangers were to hit the lower end and cut off the Indians' huge horse herd.

Judge I. D. Ferguson was a young Ranger in the latter group and wrote a full account in 1911, not long before he died. He stated that the Indians had a horse and mule herd, numbering 6,000–7,000 head, held by about fifteen herders along the creek.

Ferguson had a feeling of dark foreboding as the rush began, but he quickly lost it in the excitement. The Indian herders were soon killed, and he was chagrined because he hadn't gotten one himself. Ferguson and seventy-five or so men were sent on around to the south side to be sure no Indians escaped. That was a moment of supreme overconfidence.

The militia, because their horses had been tired out by the long ride to catch up to the Rangers, charged into the Indian camp afoot. The camp was placed amid heavy brush and briars, through which the Indians had hacked narrow trails. This restricted both the view and the movements of the attacking group.

After the first surprise, the Indians quickly rallied a strong defense that in a short time turned to the offensive. The great charge stalled out, turned into a slow retreat and finally into a general rout. Indian warriors managed to drive a wedge between the militia and the Rangers and were frequently surrounding small groups of them.

Ferguson's horse was bleeding and slowing down. He watched helplessly as a friend fell farther and farther behind on another wounded horse and finally was swallowed up and slaughtered by the pursuing Indians. Soon Ferguson found himself in the same predicament, losing ground. Despairing, he reached a point where fear left him and he was resigned to death. But a group of Rangers saw his desperate situation, charged the Indians and rescued him.

The battle continued for hours, seesawing back and forth but always winding up in the Indians' favor. They had good Enfield rifles, recently acquired in trade further north, whereas the attackers had a motley collection of rifles, shotguns, muskets and pistols.

The Rangers tried hard to get away with the Indian horse herd they had captured, but they were unable to hold it, and it fell back into Indian hands. Four Tonkawa scouts who had accompanied the Rangers ran away with most of the militia horses and the Ranger horses that weren't being ridden when the battle started. With the horses went all the supplies, all the food.

The Indians retired from the fight sometime in the afternoon, though they left sharpshooters to harass the Rangers and to cover the quick removal of the camp. They needn't have worried. The battle had gone so badly that the Texans wanted no more of it; they just wanted to treat their wounded, bury their dead and retreat toward home.

By the report of Colonel Barry, they had lost twenty-three men killed in the battle, and several others were mortally wounded. These would be buried wherever they happened to die in the slow, agonizing retreat eastward along the Concho River. A volley of rifle fire would sound over each new grave. Ferguson left one of his best friends in one of those unmarked places, lost now for more than 100 years.

To add to the men's misery, a heavy snow fell during the night after the battle. Ferguson wrote: "The cry of the wounded men and the groans of wounded horses, and the white snowflakes falling through firelight furnished a weird picture of distress rarely ever seen in Texas."

Long pecan poles were cut and makeshift litters prepared to carry the wounded. One end of each pole was tied to a stirrup on one side of a horse, the other end to a stirrup on the same side of another horse trailing behind. The wounded were placed on blankets tied across pairs of these poles and between the two horses. The retreat was slow, painful and hungry in the deep snow.

For three days, until they finally caught up to the Tonkawas and their own horse herd, they had nothing to eat except a few stray Indian horses they had butchered.

A few miles short of the John Chisum ranch at the junction of the

Concho and the Colorado, they found men driving several beeves out to meet them. They feasted, finally. At the Chisum ranch a mortally wounded lieutenant named Giddens dictated a farewell letter to his wife, then died. Like others before him he was given a rifle-fire salute, then left alone on the Concho River, sacrificed to a battle that should never have been fought.

The Indians had indeed been friendly Kickapoos, not Kiowas or Comanches. After the Dove Creek battle they were never friendly again. Under Chief No-Ko-Wat they continued their move across the Rio Grande. They became implacable enemies of the Texans and for several years launched vengeful and often bloody raids across the river, quickly retreating to sanctuary deep in their Mexican fastnesses.

Not until one of the greatest Yankee Indian fighters of them all, Ranald Mackenzie, led U. S. troops across that river and bearded them in their own den did they let up on their punishment of Texas for what the Confederates did that day on Dove Creek.

Rodeo Life

Like Ol' Man River, Freckles Brown Keeps Rolling On, And On And On

Livestock Weekly, April 1, 1971

PROBABLY no rodeo cowboy has ever been more respected and loved by his peers than the Unsinkable Freckles Brown, a Presbyterian deacon who continued riding broncs and bulls far beyond the normal retirement age. His most famous exploit came at the National Finals Rodeo in 1967, when he was forty-six. Against all odds, he successfully rode the previously unridden bull Tornado of the Jim Shoulders rodeo string. It was called the greatest bull ride in rodeo history. He rode his last bull at age fifty-three. In 1987, at sixty-six, he finally lost the toughest contest of his life after a courageous four-year bout against cancer, which also took his friend and contemporary, Casey Tibbs. Both names are still spoken with reverence in the rodeo community.

≈

SOPER, OKLAHOMA   Among the bulls which came up in the draw at the recent San Angelo rodeo was a big dun Brahman which goes by the name of V61. In about 300 times out of the chute, he had never been ridden. But betting around the coliseum was that he would be ridden in San Angelo, for the man who drew him was the Unsinkable Freckles Brown.

At fifty, Brown is sometimes called the Satchel Paige of rodeo because he continues to compete fulltime at an age twenty to twenty-five years beyond the average in the sport. He rode his first contest bull at Willcox, Arizona, in 1937, four years before all-around champion cowboy Larry Mahan was even born.

Ten times he has been carried out of an arena because of a broken leg. He doesn't remember how many ribs he has had broken. Twice he has suffered a broken neck.

In fact, he broke his neck in October 1962, but won the bull-riding championship for that year anyway because he was so far ahead in the standings that no else could catch up with him. The doctors took a piece of bone from his hip to replace shattered bones in his neck, and one told him he would never ride even a gentle horse again. Nine months later, Brown was back on the broncs and bulls.

Brown won't predict when he might retire; nobody has ever shown him yet that he should. "If I ever get to dreading the stock, I'll quit," he says. So far he has never dreaded either bronc or bull; on the contrary he still enjoys them and always looks forward to the next rodeo.

Brown considers himself a fulltime contestant, though he has a small ranch near Soper that he bought out of his rodeo winnings.

He was born January 18, 1921, on a farm which his father had homesteaded on the Platte River between Fort Laramie and Lingle, Wyoming. Besides farming, his father broke horses for wages on a ranch near Cody. During the hard Depression years he broke and trained horses on various ranches in that part of the country. Like a sailor renting a rowboat on Sunday, Freckles sometimes rode broncs for sport at picnics and similar gatherings. He was sixteen the first time he got on a bull. By the time World War II came along, he was rodeoing a lot.

The army sent him to Fort Sill, where he took basic training in horse-drawn artillery and spent two years shoeing horses and mules. In the latter part of the war he was sent to Washington to learn Chinese (he says he never did learn it very well) and went on to China as a member of the cloak-and-dagger OSS, training Chinese paratroopers. He got home in the fall of 1945 and went to rodeoing in the spring of 1946. He has been at it ever since, except for time out healing from injuries.

He originally considered himself basically a bronc rider. "I don't know just why I started riding bulls," he says, "maybe just because they were there." For years he rode broncs and bulls impartially. In fact, for a long time he also worked a fourth event, bulldogging.

He never roped professionally. "I can rope a cow in the pasture, but not to beat anybody," he says. "On those ranches in the North Country, as quick as they found out you could ride a bronc you never got another gentle horse so that you could learn to rope."

In July 1962, he got to doing some figuring. He was sitting third in the RCA bull-riding standings and saw he had a fighting chance at the championship if he would make more rodeos and concentrate on the bulls. Many of the rodeos had only one go-round in bull riding. He could ride his bull, hop a plane and make another rodeo, whereas if he were also in the bronc riding he had to stick around and be tied to one show.

"I won more money just riding bulls than I had been making trying to ride bulls and broncs."

He has almost but not quite quit riding broncs. If he has to stay at a show anyway, and if he sees that the bronc-riding competition is not too fearsome, he still enters the bronc events.

His ranch here is a cow-calf operation, partly in coastal bermuda. He fertilizes but is in a fifty-inch rainfall area and doesn't irrigate, though he has riparian rights to river water. He cuts about 6,000 bales of hay a year from a twenty-three-acre hay meadow and keeps his mixed-breed cows on native grass.

He finds having this place keeps him in good physical shape. "Every time I come home there is six times more to do than I can get around to." After that broken neck in 1962, he spent part of his recuperation time clearing timber; he figures dragging those logs around helped strengthen him and get him back into the arena sooner. Brown watches his physical condition. He does not smoke, drinks little, and does pushups and pullups every day. He does not do roadwork, but when he goes from one place to another, he does it in a trot.

Last fall he and Ronnie Bowman of Durant, Oklahoma, conducted a bull-riding school for eighteen boys. They had about sixty bulls. Though the school itself didn't make any money, they cleared a profit on the bulls, selling ten or twelve to rodeo contractors at a good price and sending the rest to packers.

Brown says the average would-be rodeo hand today doesn't have the background opportunities he had; most ranches no longer keep the rough stock they used to.

It is hard for the rodeo strings to find enough good replacement broncs. A few people raise bucking horses by "breeding an old rank mare to some owl-headed stud," but this is hardly a profitable business. Only two of ten such colts will develop out well enough for rodeo, and the other eight are good for nothing but soap.

Brown says the average rodeo bronc has a good life and a long one. Many last far into their twenties. They are well fed, carefully handled and don't do a fraction as much work as a ranch horse.

Pitching comes natural to bulls, especially those carrying some Brahman blood, though any string of prospective rodeo stock takes a lot of weeding.

Of V61, which Brown drew for the first time in San Angelo, he says, "I don't believe I was ever on one like him, one that jumped that high in the air and dropped his head that way. He was one rank son of a buck."

For most of the required eight seconds, it looked as if Brown was going to take him. He rode him longer and farther than any rider ever had before. But a couple of seconds before the buzzer, Brown came down. "I was doing everything just about the way I wanted to do it, but I didn't quite ride him."

He says he doesn't brood over getting thrown. He figures a bull or bronc rider has to stay on fifty percent of the stock to earn enough money to remain on the circuit and make a living. He has to ride ninety percent of them to stay in the top four or five spots in the RCA standings. But that implies that even so, he is going to be thrown ten percent of the time.

"There is always another rodeo next week," says Freckles Brown, "and I am looking forward to it."

Toots Mansfield Hasn't Retired;
He Just Doesn't Travel As Much

Livestock Weekly, November 16, 1972

SOFT-SPOKEN Toots Mansfield has been a hero to other rodeo cowboys for more than fifty years. He was among the first to look upon rodeo seriously as a profession and to train his body and mind for it, doing roadwork at a time when that seemed the sole province of professional boxers. He was and still is a gentle man and a *gentleman*.

≈

BIG SPRING   Don't consider Toots Mansfield retired just because he doesn't show up at the ropings much anymore. When he does go, he goes to compete; and when he competes, he competes to win.

At fifty-eight, the man who was seven times world's champion calf roper devotes most of his time to a small ranch operation east of Big Spring and plans on competing at several steer and team ropings every year. This year, however, a kidney stone hit him while he was on his way back from the Cheyenne rodeo. That required surgery, which led to some more surgery. He had to give up three Texas steer ropings he had counted on this season: Post, Happy and San Angelo.

The last time he had any surgery was thirty years ago. "I had my appendix out and was roping again in two weeks," he says. He's finding recuperation takes longer now.

Though he doesn't plan to give up roping any time in the foreseeable future, he has about decided to retire from conducting roping schools. He was the originator of this now-popular form of industrial education back in the mid-1950s. In more recent years several top ropers have conducted similar sessions, and bronc-riding schools have become even bigger than roping schools. This year Mansfield teamed with Olin Young and Jim Prather to conduct a roping school on the OS ranch near Post.

He figures he has trained 250 to 300 boys since he started about eighteen years ago. He seldom encounters a totally green one anymore. Nearly all bring a certain amount of experience and skill to the school. That is making rodeo competition extremely tough.

The money in rodeo is much bigger these days than in his peak years. RCA records indicate that his biggest year was 1948, when he won $17,812 and his sixth championship. By contrast, Dean Oliver won a record $38,118 in calf roping in 1969. Phil Lyne took last year's title with $28,220.

To the best of Mansfield's recollection, his first championship in 1939 was won with about $5,000 to $5,500.

The first time he cleaned up at Cheyenne, he won first day money and the average and got $930. He says fourth day money alone would pay about that much now.

"I think I came up in the best era," he says. "The money wasn't as big, but it was easier to win and it went farther. Competition was always tough, but not as tough as it is now."

He says if he were starting out today, given the same youth, the same skill and athletic ability he had before, he doubts he could ever repeat his feat: seven championships and thirteen consecutive years in the top bracket of the standings.

In his early years he would go to Cheyenne and compete against thirty-five to forty ropers. This year Cheyenne had about 220 calf ropers. He figures when the competition gets this keen, the results come down largely to the luck of the draw. There are so many skilled cowboys so well mounted that the deciding factor is likely to be the calves they get.

He sees the great mobility of rodeo contestants today as a reason why some are able to gross so much money. "We never thought much about driving all night to get from one rodeo to another, but it never occurred to us to get into an airplane," he comments.

He made perhaps twenty to twenty-five rodeos a year in his peak winning period. A roper today has to make nearer fifty to have even a shot at the championship.

Toots Mansfield grew up on his father's ranch near Bandera. He had two brothers, Bob and Ray, who both roped, though neither ever did it as a profession. Ray helped Toots get started. In the early and mid-1930s, calf and goat ropings were a regular part of many country picnics and barbecues. The Mansfield boys thought they were doing very well to make four or five of these in a summer.

After he graduated from high school in 1933, Toots began rodeoing seriously. By the 1935–1936 season he was making a living out of the Texas rodeos. He had teamed up with Juan Salinas of Encinal, another great roper of the time, Juan entering him in the shows and furnishing him the use of his horse, Honey Boy, a son of Cotton-Eyed Joe.

The first time Toots ever went out of state for any serious rodeoing was 1938, when he and Salinas went to California to make the spring shows. He did well enough that he came in second in national standings that year and took his first championship a year later.

He kept up the pace throughout the 1940s and well into the 1950s. During the '40s he earned a name as a great match roper. His rare consistency would often let him rope ten or twelve calves without missing a loop and without varying the time by more than a couple of seconds.

Part of his success was because of his roping skill, but much of it was due to what he did after he hit the ground. He discovered very early in his barbecue jackpot days that putting a loop around a calf's neck was the easy part; flanking and tying in a hurry was something else. As a youngster he practiced untold hours of flanking and tying, using the family milk-pen calves.

During his peak he also stayed in training like an athlete, doing roadwork and exercises. This is not uncommon among rodeo hands today, but it was in the 1930s and 1940s.

He always paid credit to his good horses, such as Smokey, his famous gray, and Quaker, a black for which he paid $2,500 when the horse was already thirteen years old. Quaker paid for himself within about three months. He also had a good steer horse he called Old Roan, on which he won $15,000 in a single day at a winner-take-all steer roping in Clovis in 1947.

He began tapering off after placing third in the calf roping standings in 1955. "I was running out of horses," he says. "All my good old horses played out at about the same time."

Moreover, he was tired of the grind. "When you're twenty-three, twenty-four years old, everything is fun and you don't mind driving all day and night. But by the time you're old enough to know something, you find all that traveling and dragging a family around isn't funny anymore."

In the early 1940s he used Rankin as a base for his rodeo travels, leasing a little ranch country there. Later he lived in Big Spring, Mrs. Mansfield's hometown. Her father was the late Marion Edwards, her grandfather pioneer ranchman W. P. Edwards. Toots' traveling companion at times was his brother-in-law, Sonny Edwards, who also roped. Toots also traveled some with Walton Poage of Rankin, each using the other's horses on occasion. During his Rankin years he was in a nest of real top ropers who lived in that area: Poage, Harry Howard, Bill Nix, Allan Holder, John D. Holleyman and George, Earl and Bill Teague.

The last three years he has been living on the old Arrington ranch south of Coahoma, which he is leasing from Mrs. Edwards. He also has a nearby farm which he bought several years ago. He leases out the cotton and maize acreage but cleared about 175 acres more of the farm and planted it to grazing crops, which he uses to supplement the rangeland. Last summer he kept all his cattle on fields and allowed the ranch to rest and grow a good crop of grass; rain was plentiful.

His present cow herd is made up partly of Hereford-Jersey cross cows which he originally bought as roping calves for $75 each and later kept over to breed. He says he realizes they are not prestigious, but they are easy breeders, excellent milkers and raise a calf that dollars out with just about anybody else's. He has some half-Brahman cows, which are also good mothers, and a smaller number of good Hereford cows which he bought. Lately he has been breeding back to Charolais bulls, buying these as yearlings, growing them out, using them a year or so and reselling for more than he paid for them.

He also always keeps some calves around whether he actually uses them or not. "I feel naked without a few roping calves," he says.

Faith And Hard Work Put Rope Back Into Roy Cooper's Hands

Livestock Weekly, March 20, 1980

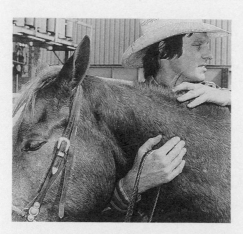

MEMBERS of the roping fraternity will tell you that Roy Cooper in his prime was a phenomenon. Even today, he remains a threat anywhere he shows up with a rope in his hand. Long before I ever met Roy, I knew his father, Tuffy Cooper of Monument, New Mexico, who was a formidable contestant himself in his day. Rodeo runs in the family. Roy's cousin Jimmie Cooper, of Monument, no longer competes as much as he did a few years ago, but he has been a powerhouse too. A few years ago a rodeo photographer caught an amazing series of pictures of Jimmie rescuing a bronc rider who had been thrown but had hung his foot in the stirrup and was in danger of being dragged to death. Cooper rushed out, grabbed the horse around the neck and through sheer bulldogger strength brought the animal to a stop until others could free the downed cowboy.

≈

DURANT, OKLAHOMA   Last summer a lot of people were saying Roy Cooper might never rope again. Practicing roping calves in Ernie Taylor's indoor arena at Hugo, he accidentally caught his wrist in a coil of rope and broke it in several places.

It would have been a tragedy, for he was considered one of the most phenomenal young ropers to come along in years. Known to fellow rodeo contestants as "Cooper the Looper," he had come out of junior and collegiate rodeo to be Professional Rodeo Cowboys Association (PRCA) Rookie of the Year and world's champion calf roper both in the same year, 1976. He had followed up with two more consecutive championships. He was on his way to a possible fourth championship when the June 6th accident knocked him out of contention.

Both he and good friend Ernie Taylor cried when first examination in the doctor's office showed the career-spoiling potential of the accident. At twenty-three, Roy Cooper should have had years of prize winning ahead of him. But the examination showed breaks in the navicular bone and two other main bones. Even if the bones knitted, blood circulation might not recover to a point that the wrist would ever be right again.

Unwilling to give up without what rodeo regulations call "an honest effort," he went to Dr. Peter Carter, Dallas hand surgeon, and Dr. Pat Evans, doctor for the Dallas Cowboys. After surgery began a long and painful period of therapy, hope and growing determination. Wearing the cast, he could not at first even bring his fingers together and touch his thumb. That came, after a while.

Walt Garrison of the Dallas Cowboys gave him a small wrist exercising device containing a steel ball. This began to build strength.

It wasn't enough, though. When the first cast came off after eight weeks, Ernie Taylor was with him in the doctor's office. They both cried again, for it looked worse than they had thought.

By this time young Cooper had begun drawing on the religious faith he had been brought up with. "I began asking God's help in letting me rope again," he says. Gradually he felt that his prayers were being answered, for strength was growing.

One part of his therapy was water skiing. The first time he tried to get up on the skis, he couldn't grip the rope with his right hand. In a week's time he was holding on and bringing himself to his feet with his right hand alone.

He had access to a whirlpool every day on the campus of his alma mater, Southeastern Oklahoma State University in Durant. He would immerse his wrist first in hot water, then in ice water to get the circulation going.

His wife Lisa was always understanding and helpful through the blackest of the days, and nights. "She saw how badly I wanted to rope," he says.

Unable to sleep, he would sometimes arise at 3:00 or 4:00 A.M., go outside and practice roping at a calf head mounted on a hay bale. She would get up and go out with him.

He laid out of rodeo through all of June, July and August, but he was practicing. He taught himself to rope left-handed and eventually was catching seven out of ten. But he knew he wasn't fast enough, and he was unlikely ever to become fast enough using his left hand. He had to get that right hand back into shape if he was to win again.

In September he decided to try a rodeo and went to Pendleton. After missing his first calf he was ready to give up and go home. Dee Pickett, Rookie of the Year, told him, "Roy, I've seen you miss when you had a good arm." He stayed, caught his second calf and took second place in the day money.

Feeling better, he went to the Mesquite, Texas, rodeo and tied a calf in 8.9 seconds. In Omaha the first week of October he tied two calves in 8.9 and 10.1 and picked up $2,500. That was the tonic that he needed. "I thought I was as good as new."

He wasn't, of course, but he had made up his mind by then that he would be, and sooner rather than later.

"I decided God had let me rope again, and if He let me rope again He meant for me to win again."

He had won $19,223 for the year before the accident. On the recovery road he won enough more to give him a total of $23,974, which took him to the National Finals in Oklahoma City. There he won the average and $15,000, six months after an injury that had appeared likely to retire him from competition forever.

Roped on Rodeo

Family Weekly, May 27, 1984

THOUGH rodeo remains exotic to most people outside of the West, it is as familiar and comfortable as an old pair of boots in ranching country. A national newspaper Sunday supplement asked me to compare rodeo today (in 1984, at least) to rodeo as it was in its early generations. The money today is far better, but one thing remains unchanged: a man can get hurt.

≈

DURING my boyhood on the McElroy Ranch, a highlight of any year was the Fourth of July rodeo. Never a good cowhand, I remained a dedicated spectator, but many ranch cowboys competed, including my calf-roping brother Myrle. Even then, rodeo was a different sport from the first event held in Pecos on July 4, 1883.

On that occasion, cowboys from four Pecos River ranches competed for $40 in prize money and tried to settle an argument over which outfit had the saltiest ropers and riders. Tray Windham won, taking just twenty-two seconds to tie his steer in the middle of Oak Street.

Last December, in Oklahoma City's National Finals Rodeo, about ninety top rodeo cowboys and fifteen of the fastest-riding cowgirls competed for $806,500 to determine the 1983 world championships. Roy Cooper of Durant, Oklahoma, became champion all-around cowboy by virtue of having won $153,391 in competition during the year, $20,952 of it in the ten-day finals themselves. In the 100 years between those two contests, rodeo moved gradually from ranch-team competitions and country steer ropings to the big rail-transported Wild West shows of Buffalo Bill, Pawnee Bill and the 101 Ranch, all more exhibition than contest. The early years also saw lesser-known traveling bronc shows of Texas horsemen such as Booger Red

Privett and Pecos Pate Boone visiting towns much too small for a cowboy of Buffalo Bill's stature.

Growing up in a hotbed of great contest ropers, we McElroy Ranch "buttons" often warmed ourselves in their reflected glory by running practice calves into the chutes for John D. Holleyman, Walton Poage, the George Teague family, and occasionally, seven-time champion Toots Mansfield. They rodeoed for fun, and for honor.

The average contestant of an earlier time was likely to be a cowhand who, in town for a holiday from some ranch at the forks of the creek, was looking for a little fun and hoping to collect enough prize money to buy a new pair of high-heeled boots. No one, except perhaps Mansfield, seriously considered rodeo as a livelihood, because few cowboys made more than a handful of rodeos during a year.

The old-time cowboy infrequently spent his hard-won money for a hotel room, and he might have shared space with several others who sneaked bedrolls upstairs while the desk clerk snoozed at his post. Riding a packed French forty-and-eight boxcar in a World War II troop train, I was reminded of a crowded Pecos hotel room at rodeo time.

One legendary roper, Bob Crosby of Roswell, New Mexico, became as famous among ranch folk of the 1930s and 1940s as any movie star. I was taken to meet him at a Midland rodeo and stood in awe of my first real celebrity.

Crosby never let fame complicate his lifestyle. A rodeo committee once planned a grand reception for him at the town's best hotel before a roping match. The committee waited and waited and waited. Crosby had arrived unannounced and quietly set up camp at the fairgrounds. Committee members found him boiling his coffee over a campfire, his horses staked beneath the trees.

Today's professional may sometimes sleep in an airport waiting room, but seldom in a bedroll on the ground. As a youngster, T. C. "Buck" Steiner, now eighty-three years old, traveled two years with Hoyt Campbell's bronc show. His roof at night was the open sky, which leaked, of course. The rodeo stock were walked from town to town, grazing other people's grass and sometimes their crops. In their wake, angry citizens vowed vengeance should the rodeo people ever pass that way again.

If the show drew a good crowd, the cowboys might buy chicken. If it did not, they settled for feathers. Many a time, Steiner recalls, breakfast consisted of cold biscuits dipped in gravy made of leftover grease from the previous night's thin supper.

The first rodeo I remember was a jumped-up local affair in a dry lakebed north of Odessa, Texas, in about 1930. Automobiles parked in a horseshoe formation served as an arena fence. That didn't prevent a bronc from pitching between two cars and racing off across the prairie. Such rodeos were fun but usually lost money for everybody concerned.

Indeed, inadequate pay for contestants caused one of rodeo's biggest changes: organization of the cowboys. In the sport's early decades, suitcase promoters put up lump-sum prize fees. Sometimes a promoter left town hurriedly during the final performance, "forgetting" to pay the cowboys at all. As late as the 1950s, one such promoter in a Central Texas town victimized cowboy movie star Tex Ritter and all the contestants.

Years of dissatisfaction led to a successful cowboy strike in 1936 at the Boston Garden Rodeo. Among the strike notice's sixty-one signers was one of our own McElroy Ranch cowboys, Manerd Gaylor, who sometimes let me ride his sorrel roping horse, Socks. Out of this came the Cowboys' Turtle Association, forerunner of today's Professional Rodeo Cowboys Association.

The Turtles fought and won a better deal for the rodeo cowboy, not only in prize money but in fairer judging and the standardization of events. This led to better shows for the spectators and an increase in attendance.

The Turtles, and later the PRCA, policed not only the promoters but the cowboys. To erase the old public image of the rodeo cowboy as a brawling, whiskey-slugging ne'er-do-well given to skipping town ahead of his creditors, the organization set up rules of conduct and fearlessly blacklisted cowboys who violated them.

The old-time rowdiness, always exaggerated, receives little patience from most of today's professionals. They simply don't have time for it. Modern cowboys can't carouse all night and beat an athlete who trains like a Marine. In recent generations, rodeo has evolved into today's fast-moving, highly structured professional competitions between skilled and dedicated athletes. And the cowboys themselves have changed.

Buck Steiner began rodeoing with what he terms a "low third-grade education." He declares, "Sometimes there wasn't a cowboy in the bunch who could read road signs well enough to get us to the next town."

Steiner, who produced rodeos for some forty years, adds that many of today's best professional rodeo hands worked through high school and college rodeo. They enjoy the sport but treat it as a business.

In 1983, Roy Cooper competed in more than 132 rodeos between the season's January opener in Odessa, Texas, and December's National Finals. Computers operated by the PRCA helped him map an itinerary for the largest possible number of shows and allowed him to submit his entries so he didn't have to arrive until time to ride. Now a pro occasionally charters a plane to help him reach two rodeos slated for the same day.

Courage, however, is an attribute that all rodeo cowboys share. Many a bronc rider comes out of the chute with braces on his knees or a cast on his hand. Charles Sampson, the competitor from California who won 1982's bull-riding championship, wore a special helmet in last December's finals to protect facial bones previously shattered in a head-to-head encounter with a bull.

And age is an implacable enemy of the rodeo cowboy as it is of other athletes, though some choose to ignore it. Bill Nix of Rankin, Texas, developed heart trouble in the 1950s but shrugged off his doctor's advice to quit roping. When professional advice turned to heartfelt personal pleading, the sympathetic Nix told a kinsman: "I've done the only humane thing a responsible man could. I've changed doctors."

It's natural for fans of every sport to conjecture about the greatest competitors of all time. They speculate on how Dempsey or Louis in their prime would have fared against Ali. Rodeo fans fantasize calf-roping matches between Jake McClure of the 1930s, Toots Mansfield of the '40s, Dean Oliver of the '60s, and today's phenomenal Roy Cooper. They match yesterday's bronc riders Pete Knight or Casey Tibbs against today's Monty Henson or Brad Gjermundson.

It is an interesting—but futile—exercise. If it were possible to bring the old-time champions forward in time with the skills they had at their peak, many observers (including my brother Myrle) say today's champions would probably beat them. This is because the sport's techniques have been honed to a finer and finer edge. Mansfield polished what he learned from Juan Salinas and other top hands of McClure's generation. He passed on what he knew to Oliver's, which improved on it and passed it on to Cooper's. Today's champions are the product of all those generations.

Mansfield pioneered the concept of a roping school in Big Spring, Texas, some thirty years ago. Now rodeo schools are common for every contest event. The classroom is an arena, the text live broncs, bulls and roping stock. Almost every champion of recent years has shared knowledge with young hopefuls.

Many of today's rodeo schools feature one subject the old-timers never thought of: mental preparation. Team-roping champion Leo Camarillo demonstrates concentration by going down a line of strangers and asking their names, then retracing his steps and repeating the names from memory.

Though most fans find rodeo more exciting today than ever, some say it may have become too professional, too structured, with one show too much like another. Such fans reminisce fondly about the slower-moving and amateurish rodeos in which competitors were mostly local, known to spectators by their names. When Flop Roberts roped a calf or Red Whatley rode a bronc at a Midland rodeo in the 1930s, we cheered harder because we knew them. Those rodeos sometimes clunked along, but they were fun: no life-or-death struggle for a title, no breakneck rush to reach another rodeo two hundred miles away before dark.

Three years ago, a new-old type of rodeo started at Wichita Falls, Texas—a throwback to those old-time local rodeos. It is a team contest between working cowboys from rolling plains ranches such as the Pitchfork, 6666 and Waggoner.

An enthusiastic public response to this Texas Ranch Roundup spawned a dozen similar ranch rodeos across the western part of the state. These shy away from professional rodeo fare like steer wrestling and bull riding, turning instead to such real-work events as branding, cattle penning, cutting-horse competition, and a once-popular event seldom seen in professional rodeo anymore, wild-cow milking.

These shows offer more fun than money. Tray Windham, who won the first Pecos rodeo a century ago, would understand that.

Writing About the West

S. Omar Barker Just Missed Being Born In Texas—By About Five Years

Livestock Weekly, July 25, 1968

I READ S. Omar Barker's western stories and poems from the time I was a boy and never dreamed he would someday become a personal friend and even something of a mentor. After I began to publish pulp magazine stories with some regularity in the late 1940s, I started receiving occasional letters of encouragement from him. One evening the telephone rang. It was Omar. He said, "Elsa and I are stopping in San Angelo on our way home to Las Vegas (New Mexico). Would you mind if we come out and visit for a little while?" *Mind?* I would have walked barefoot halfway to Las Vegas just for the chance to meet him. We had a wonderful visit that lasted far into the night, during which he gave me some useful pointers about fiction-writing techniques. Through the Western Writers of America, we enlarged upon that friendship, my wife Ann and I visiting Omar and Elsa in their home several times as well as sharing some wonderful times with them at WWA conventions. They were both an inspiration, and we miss them.

≈

LAS VEGAS, NEW MEXICO   S. Omar Barker has been called the "poet lariat" of New Mexico. His humorous verses have been published in everything from *Captain Billy's Whiz Bang* to the *Saturday Evening Post* and *Wall Street Journal*. Like this one:

> The coyote of the western ranges
> Survives despite all modern changes.
> He taunts the world with yapping drollery—
> And does not practice birth controllery.

Barker, who grew up as a cowboy and farm hand in the mountains near Beulah, northwest of Las Vegas, makes no claim to having been any great cowboy himself. But he takes pride in knowing the cow and the cowboy well. Now seventy-four, he came along early enough to know the old-timers when they were still in their prime. He made a career of writing about them, for he estimates that he has published some 1,500 short stories and has sold about 2,500 pieces of poetry.

But he's not the only writer in the family. His wife Elsa has had a considerable writing career in her own right. She started out by typing her husband's stories, then began writing her own and for many years was a mainstay contributor to *Ranch Romances*, one of the greatest and longest-lasting of the pulp magazines.

The pulp magazines are gone, but the Barkers have not retired. Omar a couple of years ago published a novel based on the New Mexico mountains of his boyhood. Elsa is in charge of the English department at Las Vegas Junior High School. Omar's humorous verses still show up in a wide variety of publications and most recently in *The Cattleman's Steak Book*, a carriage trade cookbook which may or may not have helped boost the cattle market. This fall Doubleday is due to publish a collection of about 160 Barker verses under the title *Rawhide Rhymes*, featuring drawings by western artist Nick Eggenhofer and a foreword by Fred Gipson of *Old Yeller* fame.

Barker always says he missed being born a Texan by about five years. That's how long it was after his father moved from Albany, Texas, to Beulah, New Mexico, until Omar was born the youngest of eleven. His father was a small operator, never owning more than 150 cows in his life. The Barker boys grew up as familiar with the hoe, plowhandle and fishing pole as with a horse. They all became woodsmen.

Omar figures he's probably one of the few writers who sold material to Sunday school papers and *Captain Billy's Whiz Bang* at the same time. Tame as *Captain Billy* may appear today, in its time it seemed as scandalous as *Playboy*. Omar was selling material while still in high school as early as 1910 or 1911. He taught in Tularosa in 1913 to 1914, immediately upon finishing high school, and then was principal in Santa Rosa in a school where many of the students were older than he was. Not until he got back from army service in World War I did he get to start college. He studied at Highlands in Las Vegas and taught English in high school.

Barker sold his first western fiction to *Top Notch Magazine* about 1920. By 1925 he was able to cut loose from other work and write fulltime, taking no other jobs except as temporary fill-ins. One fill-in was as publicity director of the Las Vegas Cowboy Reunion. Conn W. Jackson was president of the reunion the time Barker brought out a book of verse. When the reunion directors met, Jackson laid down the law: "Boys, you're all going to buy two copies of Omar's book before we start the business of this meeting." Barker sold twenty-four copies and was on his way.

One other fill-in job was a session in the New Mexico state legislature, an experience he remembers with mixed emotions. In 1924 his father attended the state Democratic convention and came home carrying a list of state candidates. To Omar's dismay one of the names was his.

"I'm a Republican now," he says (he's been a Republican since Roosevelt days), "but I believe I was the first Democrat elected in San Miguel County in about forty years."

To win, he had to make most of his political speeches in Spanish. Most legislative business was conducted in two languages, so he became fluent in Spanish. One dose of politics was all he wanted. He retired at the end of the term.

Barker was in on the heyday of the pulp magazines, which began in the 1920s, his stories bringing one to three cents a word. His best year, unlikely as it might seem, was 1929, when his writing earned

$10,000. Pre-inflation, pre-income tax, that was a good $25,000 or $30,000 today. Eventually his fiction started hitting *Saturday Evening Post*, which paid top rates in the country.

He and Elsa were married in 1927. She started writing professionally about 1930, selling her first story to *Ranch Romances*, one of Omar's bread-and-butter markets. Her novelettes and serials became a fixture in that magazine and remained so until it went off the market in the late 1950s. Where Omar's trademark was humorous western stories, Elsa's was western mysteries flavored by romance. She sold an estimated 150 short stories, thirty novelettes, thirty novels, twenty serials, and had a number of novels printed in Europe. She still writes occasional articles.

They helped each other, but they never actually collaborated on stories. When one got high-centered on a story, the other often could think up a new angle to get the yarn rolling again.

They lived in the mountains near Sapello until 1957, within half a mile of Barker's birthplace. Finally, because he was having some health problems at the time and realizing how much deep winter snow might stand between him and a doctor at some needful time, they moved down to Las Vegas.

Widely noted for spontaneous wit, Omar Barker is in demand as a lecturer and after-dinner speaker. He has a lot of fun over his initials, claiming that years ago he tried to register his brand as the Lazy SOB, but some other lazy s.o.b. had beaten him to it. He settled for Lazy SB.

Until he finally brought out his 1966 novel, *Little World Apart*, he had specialized in short works. For years friends kept urging him to write a full-length book. His stock answer was this, "I've been working on one: call it *The S.O.B.'s of San Miguel County*. Every time I think I've about finished I run into another one."

Though humor is his long suit, Barker has written a lot of serious material, both in prose and poetry. Possibly his best known single work is a poem entitled "The Cowboy's Christmas Prayer," which has been printed widely, read several times on network television and recorded by Jimmy Dean. He has contributed to over 100 publications during his career, and his works have been published in sixty-five or seventy anthologies.

He takes spells of letter writing, and his friends usually save the letters because they are invariably sprinkled with little verses like this one:

> The horny toad, ill graced but harmless,
> Is thought by some to be quite charmless.
> At least he helps eat garden ants up—
> And does not try to crawl your pants up!

Cowboy Glenn Vernam Overcame Handicap to Write Horse History

Livestock Weekly, July 31, 1969

NOT ALL western writers look western, but Glenn Vernam did. His bowed legs, his boots and Levis and his tall-crowned hat said *cowboy* from as far away as you could see him. Many who knew him or knew his fictional stories about western courage never knew his personal story of determination, of the lengths to which he went to finish what he considered his life's work in a tight race with potential blindness.

≈

JOSEPH, OREGON   Glenn Vernam, Oregon cowboy-author, has written many fiction pieces for publication during his career, but none matched his own story of dogged determination and courage in the face of threatened blindness.

Near the finishing stage of his life's work, a definitive history of the man and horse together, cataracts robbed him of sight in one eye and were rapidly stealing sight from the other. Knowing he might not have much time and determined to finish, Vernam taped a magnifying glass to one end of a cardboard tube, like the core of a toilet paper roll, to concentrate what little vision remained. Looking down that tube, he laboriously drew 240 pictures to illustrate the development of horse gear from the ancients to the cowboy.

He was well qualified for the latter because he has been a cowboy most of his life and looks it. He still wears an old-fashioned roll-edge hat of a type seldom seen anymore, and keeps it totally innocent of any crease. His legs have been stiffened by his seventy-three years but still are bowed to fit a horse.

The family moved from southwestern Nebraska to western Colorado in a wagon when he was twelve, settling on the north fork of the Gunnison around Hotchkiss and Crawford. His father was a rancher-farmer. Vernam gave up school early, seeing little need of it for a cowboy; he went to work for ranch wages at fourteen. Starting on the Gunnison, he worked over parts of western Colorado and northern New Mexico, rode the caboose of a cattle train to Omaha in 1913 and then came west again to the Fort Collins area of Colorado. Over the years he drifted also into Wyoming and Montana. He did a little freighting and packing, but mostly he punched cows. In his own words, he was an incurable tumbleweed.

After marrying in Cody, Wyoming, he decided it was time to become more responsible, so he took out a homestead near Deaver in Wyoming's Bighorn Basin. That he describes as a short course in starvation, though he and his wife stayed seven years. When at last they went under, they moved up to Idaho and eventually to Oregon.

Sometime in the late 1920s, still cowpunching, Vernam became short of patience over some of the western stories he read and decided he could do as well. He bought a secondhand typewriter at $3 a month. He wrote his first piece in the fall and sold one the following April, a little article on cowboy lingo for *Triple X Western*.

He kept quiet about what he was doing because he didn't want the cowboys razzing him. But when the first story was published, he says, "I carried the magazine sticking out of my pocket for two months so people would have to ask me what it was."

Writing was not so lucrative that he could quit ranch work and devote himself to it, though for a time when the first story sold he drew up plans for a mansion not yet built. He wrote for western magazines and for such popular youth publications as *Boys' Life* and *Open Road for Boys*. He was still working on ranches as late as 1950.

The biggest job of his life started with a little idea, a simple article on evolution of the western saddle. As he began to gather material, he was amazed at how much he didn't know. One discovery led to another, and before long he was up to his hips in a major research job. The short article was forgotten. He visited or corresponded with museums, old-time saddlemakers and the like. He learned things about stirrups, trees, and so forth that he had never dreamed of. And his work on saddles led to discoveries about bridles, harness and other accoutrements.

He found himself going far beyond the cowboy to medieval times, and then to the ancients. The story of horse gear led to a major study of the horse itself, its domestication and the many uses to which man has put it through the ages.

In all, Vernam spent a dozen years collecting material. He had such a mass of notes that he spent two more years putting them into usable form.

During this time, his eyesight was failing. But there still remained the awesome job of illustrating the work. Because of his research, he knew he was the man to do it; he was the only one who had the background. But it would be a race against blindness. A doctor warned him that a cataract operation might fail and leave him without sight. Determined that fourteen years of work not be spoiled for lack of pictures, he devised the cardboard tube and magnifying glass and went to work. He drew when he felt like it, and also when he didn't feel like it. He worked long and hard, and he won his race.

The result was 225,000 words of text and 240 drawings, which Harper and Row published in 1964 as *Man On Horseback*. The publishers trimmed the text to about 160,000 words and selected 170 of the pictures. Though there are lots of horse books on the shelves today, there is probably not one so definitive on its subject.

Like most of his fiction, his battle against blindness had a more or less happy ending. He underwent operations and a long period of recovery that eventually brought back much of his sight, though he wears thick glasses and has little peripheral vision.

Vernam had enough material left over from the big book that he put together another he calls *The Three Pillars of the Cow Country*, though no publisher has yet bought it. It's about the mutual development of the range cow, the cowboy and the cowhorse.

He has a novel, *Indian Hater*, just now being released by Doubleday, his first long work in many years.

He says he and Mrs. Vernam are sustained now by a garden, a milk cow and his writing. They live about ten miles out of Joseph (population 900). "It's not very noisy there," he comments, except on rare occasions when his three daughters and one son, thirteen grandchildren and fourteen great-grand-children all arrive at one time. He finds plenty of fish in the creek and can see deer and elk on the hills. He can't get television or read the tiny type in the daily paper, seldom looks at the clock or worries about the calendar.

Walter Gann Revisits Homeplace
Where Much Texas History Was Made

Livestock Weekly, May 29, 1971

I HAD read Walter Gann's book, *Tread of the Longhorns*, many years before I happened to meet him one day in the lobby of San Angelo's Cactus Hotel. Later we rode together over into Concho and Coleman counties, where he showed me many historic landmarks he had known in his youth. Most of these, including the small pioneer towns of Stacy and Leaday, now lie drowned beneath the deep waters of a man-made lake. A few historic structures were saved, however, moved to higher ground before the dam's gates were closed.

≈

LEADAY   Walter Gann, whose 1949 book, *Tread of the Long-horns*, is a respected history of the Texas range industry, was back in his native Coleman County last week for a visit to old bronc-stomping grounds. Now eighty-three, he has been a cowboy, big-steer man, sheriff, writer, and for thirty years special agent for the Union Pacific Railroad.

Gann's father, Oliver, came to the southern part of Coleman County in 1878. His own father, ranching in Bexar County, had bought 1,200 acres of unfenced range for him. Oliver Gann brought a little bunch of cattle and horses to Elm Creek, missed his own place by less than a mile and camped for some time on the Day Ranch before he discovered his mistake. For many years the place where he had settled by error was known as the Gann waterhole.

On his land were stone corrals and ruins of a stone house where pioneer rancher Rich Coffey and others had forted up in the so-called Flat Top settlement in Indian times during and right after the Civil War. It had later been a stagecoach stand.

Oliver Gann was one-legged. At eighteen, he was riding the saddle mule while driving a six-mule team hitched to a wagon. The lead mules boogered at an oncoming rider and forced the saddle mule over the wagontongue. Oliver Gann was a good rider, nevertheless. He had a strap affixed to the right side of his saddle; he would flip his wooden leg up out of the way and secure the stump under that strap.

A neighbor, Jim Currie, was missing his left leg. It happened that their foot sizes were the same, so when either man bought a pair of boots or shoes, he would give the unneeded one to the other.

The elder Gann leased land in various places in the area, keeping a herd of mother cows at home and speculating on steers elsewhere. He often sent big steers to grass in Indian Territory, which gave son Walter a good deal of travel and broad experience.

When Mrs. Mabel Day Lea, Coleman County's biggest landholder of the time, started closing out the Day Ranch cattle operations she hired Oliver Gann to supervise the operation. It took several years. During that time, the Ganns had a home in Coleman.

On one occasion, after a hard day spent loading cattle onto railroad cars, the cowboys set out to celebrate. A passenger train came through Coleman each night about 11:00 P.M., and people who had nothing better to do would go down and watch. This particular night the cowboys were on the platform and making considerable noise. The telegraph operator tried vainly to quiet them and in his anger made the mistake of attributing canine ancestry to one of them.

This cowboy went to the Gann house, got a Winchester rifle, called out the operator and shot him on the platform. He escaped, taking the rifle with him. He was later caught when he contacted a girlfriend who had moved up onto the plains; he was sent up for life, but later pardoned.

Walter Gann went with his father's herds wherever his help was needed. In 1903, when he was fifteen, he was with a cowboy named Dixon Baird taking care of 1,500 steers his father was grazing in the Creek Nation, Indian Territory. One afternoon three cowboys came by on the dodge. They quietly but firmly detained Baird and Gann at the line camp until after dark, eating supper and feeding their horses on Gann's father's grain. Upon leaving, one of them flipped the boy a silver dollar.

Bright and early next morning three marshals showed up, tracking the men. Later Baird and Gann heard shots from a long way off. The lawmen came back with the three cowboys . . . one lying dead across his horse, one wounded, one handcuffed to his saddle. They had robbed a bank somewhere around Muskogee.

Gann says being a youngster, he had no better judgment than to spend that silver dollar the first chance he got. He has wished a thousand times he had kept it.

The Gann ranch headquarters was polling place for one Coleman County precinct. It was strictly Democrat country in those times, and modern notions about civil rights hadn't yet made a ripple. One neighbor became angry at something the Democrats had done and threatened to jump the traces. Another neighbor, who had a black horsebreaker named Ab working for him, told him, "Well, go ahead and vote Republican if you want to. I hadn't intended to let Ab vote, but if you go Republican, I'll send him to kill your vote." The neighbor stayed with the Democrats.

In 1907 Walter Gann drifted out to Pecos County with the idea of taking a job until he got acquainted with the country, then taking up school land. Arthur G. Anderson was one of the biggest sheepmen in that country but was also a big cattle owner. Gann worked under John Trent, the cattle manager, helping drive two herds of about 1,800 steers each to grass in the Seminole area. They were thin, hungry and mean to run. Gann did not remain in Pecos County.

A Coleman friend had gone to Poughkeepsie, New York, to attend business college, and he talked Gann into going there too. Gann studied bookkeeping awhile but says he got little use from it; he tried working in a bank in Santa Anna but didn't like it and quit after about a month. He drifted up to Montana to work cattle during the summer of 1909, intending that time to stay the winter. The second cold norther sent him south.

He began trading steers in the Coleman and Concho country, as his father had done. He married in 1912. His father died in 1913 at sixty-three, and Gann closed out his father's ranching operations.

In the drouth of 1917 he and some other young stockmen pooled about 1,500 head of distressed cattle and put them on grass leased from the Cage Ranch in Erath County. Gann also bought 1,800 Angora mutton goats. After he closed out this barely profitable deal, he, Sam Woodward and J. E. Boog-Scott bought 1,000 big steers on the Kansas City market and put them out on grass in western Kansas. The winter of 1918–1919 was a disaster and wiped out many operations, including theirs.

Gann stayed in that area. He was elected sheriff of Logan County, Kansas, in 1922, still handling cattle on the side for himself and others. In 1925 he became a special agent for the Union Pacific, a job he was to hold for thirty years, operating out of Denver. It was detective work, but he says it was largely legwork and little excitement, much of it concerned with theft investigation and running down lost shipments and baggage.

Gann had long had an urge to write. When Hal Evarts, Sr., famous action story writer of the 1920s, came to western Kansas on a prairie chicken hunt, Gann outlined a story he wanted Evarts to write. Evarts suggested (as professional writers invariably do) that Gann write it himself. He did, though it was 1949 before it was published. It was a novel, *Trail Boss*, starting in Concho County, Texas, and ending in Montana. Gann followed it with his historical study of the cattle industry, and dozens of pieces for various historical magazines.

After retiring from the railroad, he moved to South Laguna, California, where he was once elected president of the California Authors' League.

Gann says he keeps planning to move back to Texas, but he hasn't gotten around to it.

Retired New Mexico State Game Warden Sees Ranchers' Side On Predators

Livestock Weekly, July 15, 1971

ELLIOTT BARKER was an older brother of the late S. Omar Barker. Elliott was remarkable, still leading long horseback trail rides and camping trips into the Sangre de Cristo Mountains into his eighties. He protested the loss of his driver's license in his nineties, when an examining officer discovered that he had to lift his right leg with his hands to move it from one foot pedal to another. Though a wildlife conservationist, he saw the rancher's side in the ever-contentious question of predatory animal control. Many self-styled ecologists today declare that no cost is too high, no sacrifice too great, so long as someone else has to make it.

≈

SANTA FE, NEW MEXICO   Elliott S. Barker, who was New Mexico state game warden for twenty-two years, says he always had sympathy and respect for the rancher's problems. He grew up on a small ranch above Las Vegas, New Mexico, and twice went broke trying to ranch for himself.

He says there is always some natural conflict of interest between game management people and ranchers, but he had a high degree of success in effecting satisfactory compromises. "If you understand each other's problems, you can always work things out."

Barker understood the rancher's problems only too well. He was three years old in the fall of 1889 when his family moved from Shackelford County, Texas, to a 160-acre homestead in the Sangre de Cristo Mountains near Sapello (the natives pronounce it Sappy-o), bringing fifty-nine cattle, twelve mares and colts, a yoke of oxen, two teams of horses and three wagons.

In time his father acquired an extra 160 acres and ran his seventy-five to 100 cattle on the public lands. The family grew potatoes and vegetables, cut timothy hay, clover and oats for the cattle, built a twenty-two-foot waterwheel and a small sawmill. The elder Barker built a reservoir. When it was full, it provided a head of water sufficient to power the sawmill about two hours. Then everything waited a couple or three hours until the water built up again.

The Barker boys grew up to be outdoorsmen, hunting, fishing, cutting timber. In 1908, when the U.S. Forest Service was in its infancy, Elliott Barker made a two-day pack trip across the mountains to Santa Fe to take a civil service examination. It was to be months before he heard whether he got the job, so he went back to farming, helping tend the family cattle, and to his work as a professional guide for hunters and fishermen out of the cities.

He had many notable experiences working with these people, but one which stands out in his memory is the hunter who accidentally tied a hard knot at the top of his lace-up sleeping bag and then developed a bad case of diarrhea.

He got the job, going to Cuba, New Mexico, as an assistant forest ranger January 2, 1909. The government was just beginning to impose grazing allotments on federal lands. A local political leader had mounted a strong opposition and resisted the counting of live-stock. The dispute came to a point that he drew a gun on Barker and Barker's senior officer, and the politician had to back down, losing face in the community.

The rangers posted Forest Service notices printed on cloth, which was expected to withstand weather and wear better than paper or cardboard posters. They did; many a sheepherder in the forests used them for dishrags. Once Barker came across a little girl wearing one for a skirt.

One day he arrested the sixteen-year-old daughter of a local rancher after he caught her fishing through the ice with a horsetail snare, out of season and without a license, four distinct violations. He thought she was too young and pretty to go to jail, so he had the judge put her on probation . . . to him. He says she still is; they celebrated their sixtieth wedding anniversary May 17.

Barker has achieved a reputation as a good public speaker. He says he learned that art trying to court his wife-to-be on a New Mexico party line.

World War I brought a demand for greatly expanded grazing on the national forests. A full ranger by then, Barker unsuccessfully opposed this policy. The end of the war found the forests overgrazed to the point of serious damage. Ranchers had borrowed money to expand herds and flocks and had kept their ewe lambs and heifer calves. The postwar depression caught a great many deeply in debt for this expansion, and they were wiped out. One of the biggest ranchers in Barker's forest shot himself.

Barker had some cattle of his own by then—bought at wartime prices. He decided to go into ranching fulltime and left the Forest Service. Almost before the ink was dry on his resignation, the bottom dropped out of the cattle market, and his cows were worth thirty cents on the dollar. All he could do was grit his teeth and hang on.

To supplement his sagging ranch income he farmed, hunted bobcats, trapped coyotes, guided lion hunters, "cruised" timber and at one point hired out to organize a fight against a massive forest fire. Gradually he got ahead, and the ranch prospered. It looked as if he was going to make it. Then in 1929 his calves dropped from $40 to $12, and he sold some fat steers at a heavy loss. Broke again, he saw no prospect of coming out.

On April 1, 1930, he went to work for the 360,000-acre Vermejo Park Ranch as game manager. That ranch, a combination cattle operation-game preserve, had made the first move toward restoring elk to New Mexico in 1911. When Barker went there the elk were thriving but the deer were going downhill. He quickly determined that mountain lions were badly out of balance and set to work thinning them out. He spent a year on that ranch and, along with his normal game enhancement work, he took sixteen mountain lions, forty-six coyotes and thirty-nine bobcats.

Through his career as a forest ranger and later as state game warden, he always took the position that predatory animals were not to be exterminated but must be controlled, kept down to balance with their natural food supply. He found that an area without enough predators would become overstocked by deer, while one with too many predators would not only lose most of its deer but would suffer heavy losses in domestic livestock.

He has never forgotten a fifteen-day period in which a single grizzly bear killed fifteen out of 100 cattle he had in partnership with his father. That loss took all the profit out of more than a year of work for two men.

"There is a sentiment flooding this country now that we should not kill any predator . . . or any other wild animal," he worries. "That sentiment is wrong."

He notes that no spokesman crying out against killing of predatory animals has ever offered to reimburse a stockman for lost cattle or sheep. "They want the rancher to keep and feed the predatory animal when he's sometimes having a hard time keeping shoes on his children's feet," Barker declares, adding that most New Mexico livestock belong to small owners.

He became state game warden April 1, 1931, and immediately had to butt heads with a governor who wanted him to appoint political friends and to assess all his employees two percent of their salaries to go into the party's state organization fund. Backed by the game commission, Barker refused on both counts and won. Later, both parties in New Mexico repudiated the two percent assessment. It would be reckless to claim that either has repudiated political appointments.

During his years in office he prosecuted game violations without regard to the culprit's position. He prosecuted a lieutenant governor, a governor's son-in-law, a Democratic state chairman, a state legislator, a chief of the state police, and even a member of the state game commission for which he worked.

He considered it his main job to build up New Mexico's wild game. In his twenty-two years, thanks to predator control and strict enforcement of hunting laws, he saw the state's deer increase from an estimated 60,000 to 200,000. He initiated transplants of game back into areas which had once been their natural habitat, including elk, sage chickens, beaver and bighorn sheep, the latter from Alberta, Canada. One of his district wardens, Paul Russell of Magdalena, developed antelope trapping techniques which were used in transplanting 2,800 head and starting sixty new herds between 1937 and 1953. That was the year Barker retired at age sixty-six.

He was eighty-four last December 25. On the Barkers' sixtieth anniversary, May 17, Governor Bruce King declared Elliott S. Barker Day in New Mexico.

Since retirement he has undertaken numerous special jobs on problems of game management, has guided and lectured, and has written three books about his experiences, the principal emphasis on wild animals, trout fishing and the outdoors. His latest, *Western Life and Adventures 1880 to 1970,* has been published only a short time. Earlier ones are *Beatty's Cabin* and *When the Hounds Bark Treed.* He has done many articles for popular national hunting and fishing publications.

Looking back, Barker says seventy-five percent of all the conflict he ever encountered between ranchmen and wild-game interests resulted from the disregard that some hunters and fishermen have for private property and other people—littering, leaving gates open, camping at watering places and chasing livestock away, not to mention the inexplicable mistaking of a two-point cow or a no-point horse for a twelve-point buck.

At Eighty-eight, Pate Boone Publishes Wild West Show Reminiscences

Livestock Weekly, July 15, 1976

I KNEW Pate Boone as an aging dealer in western-type antiques before I had any inkling of his adventuresome past as a cowboy and a Wild West performer. A mutual friend told me Boone had done his memoirs, then lost them. That he had the energy and determination to do them over again was indicative of the stern will that had driven him all his life. He was past ninety the last time I saw him, and he had never yielded an inch.

≈

CHRISTOVAL   Pate Boone has been many things in his time: cowboy, bronc rider, sharpshooter, Wild West show entrepreneur, blacksmith, antique dealer. He didn't expect also to become a writer. But at eighty-eight he has published a book about his life. Moreover, he had to "write" the book twice. He lost it the first time.

Boone, who should have retired more than twenty years ago but didn't have time and still doesn't, operates an antique store and blacksmith shop in downtown Christoval, about eighteen miles south of San Angelo. He still makes old-fashioned "gal leg" spurs and bits, plus hunting and butcher knives. He usually has more orders than he can fill.

For many years he wanted to publish his reminiscences. The first time he started writing in longhand, gave that up and dictated the story onto hours and hours of tape. The book was going to be published by academic people. But the project bogged down and the tapes were never retrieved from the mysterious mazes of academia.

Frustrated but determined, Boone started anew at well past eighty-five. This time he told the stories over a period of months to Mrs. Rena Dee Gaines of Christoval. She took them down in shorthand and then typed them.

He is a storyteller rather than a writer. The stories were published as he related them, without much polishing or professional editing. They are in a highly descriptive, conversational English that tells a great story but breaks enough rules to put a fifth-grade grammar teacher into second-degree shock.

The overall result may be better than if they had been strained through an academic committee. They might have gained some in organization, but they would have lost in spontaneity and natural-ness.

He's selling most of the books himself at $7.23. That odd figure isn't Pate's. It's the state tax.

His grandfather, said to be a grandson of Daniel Boone, disappeared just after the Civil War. Pate's father, J. C. Boone, migrated to East Texas from North Carolina at sixteen, married young, became a sharecropper and part-time blacksmith, and almost starved to death. The family finally landed at Olney, Texas, with a wagon, team and fifty cents. The fifty cents was spent on a jug of molasses, which Pate's older brother Bob promptly dropped and broke while trying to lift it into the wagon. The father took a job digging a well for cornmeal and bacon. In a few days he traded his wagon and team for a faltering blacksmith shop in the little community of Round Timber west of Olney in Baylor County.

The elder Boone drifted a lot, trying to find a place which he liked and presented some opportunity. He left Round Timber for Clyde, then settled on a farm near Trent. He leased some ranchland west of Odessa and sent the older boys, Bob and Pate, with a wagon and a herd of cattle to stock it.

On the way the boys got into a mean sandstorm blowing out of the south, somewhere west of Stanton. They camped on the north side of a tank dam for protection and tried to cook a meal but were drowned out by what they thought was a rainstorm. It turned out that the wind simply blew the water out of the tank.

Later the father got the itch to try homesteading in New Mexico. Among other things, he bought a string of wild horses. By then Pate was fourteen and Bob eighteen. They branded those horses with the family's Anchor B and proceeded to break them.

In July 1899, Bob got lost in the Capitan Mountains of New Mexico, wandered for two days without water and came within a little of starving to death. He finally found some water at the bottom of a deep crevice too narrow to crawl into. He cut holes in the brim of his Stetson, tied saddle strings through the holes and lowered the rock-weighted hat down the crevice to haul up water.

The following year Pate got lost east of the Pecos River and repeated his brother's stunt with a variation. He lowered a boot into an abandoned well he found, using the big spur as a weight. He managed to water himself and his horse but finally lost the boot in the well and had to ride out half barefoot. That escapade earned him a nickname he used in his Wild West show days: Pecos Pate Boone.

The boys eased into show biz sideways. When their father decided he had had enough of New Mexico and moved back to Trent, he gave the brothers all the Anchor B wild broncs they could gather as their pay for moving the family back to Texas. They gathered twenty-eight with the intention of selling them in Trent. But nobody wanted wild horses.

The boys built a round corral and started breaking them. This drew a crowd, particularly on weekends. Bob suggested they start charging admission, so they bought a ten-foot canvas and put it up.

Both boys were already good riders and crack shots, but they began practicing showy ways of doing both to help please an audience. They took their broncs first to Merkel, charging twenty-five cents admission, then back home to Trent, then to Abilene. Sensing that they had a good thing started, they began picking up some good bronc riders, among them Rapp Green, Bill Kennedy and Willis Barbee.

They advertised that they would try out any and all local broncs brought to them, often for a hat collection. They offered prize money to local cowboys who could ride certain bad ones out of the Boone string. They didn't have to pay off.

Before long the brothers were professional showmen, traveling across Texas, New Mexico, Oklahoma and into the Midwest. Sometimes they worked together; other times they had two separate shows. At one point Pate had a string of his own railroad cars, moving the show by rail. They usually chose the smaller towns, particularly in winter—towns that the big eastern professional shows never played, towns starved for entertainment.

Pate's first wife was named Ed. Her parents were dead set on having a baby boy, and when they didn't they gave the girl a boy's name. When she and Pate decided to get married they set out on horseback to find a preacher she knew. He was in his yard hoeing weeds. He called to his wife to bring out his Bible. He married them while they sat on their horses and he stood in the newly cut weeds. Before long Ed Boone was riding broncs in the show.

The big flu epidemic of 1918 brought one of Pate's biggest crises. A federal order shut down all public gatherings and entertainments. It caught the show in Kansas. Pate and most of the hands went to work in nearby oilfields. Pate's five-year-old son Tom caught the flu and nearly died. As he was beginning to recover, Pate's wife took it. The boy recovered, but his mother died.

Pate sold his railroad cars. When the federal order was rescinded in 1919 he took the show out again in wagons. He gathered a troupe of cowboys and circus acts and did very well after the war. He met and married a widow named Inda Vernon Cohn. She became a great show woman.

One of Pate's proudest memories is the special free performance he gave for that famous showman Pawnee Bill Lillie, who arrived one day just as the show was winding up.

"I wouldn't be surprised," Pate says, "if I have ridden more broncs than any man living. I would ride several in every show. When one of the boys was sick, I would ride his as well as my own."

The paid show was usually preceded by a free act, performed outside. Most often it was Pate doing his marksmanship stunts, having someone toss small objects into the air for him to shoot down. He would start with tin cans and finish on .22 shells.

He credits his marksmanship to steady hands—he never smoked or drank—and to keen eyesight. He can still, at eighty-eight, read a newspaper without glasses.

He always liked to end a show with a good act. Usually he did it by riding a bronc and firing a pistol into the air. It was loaded with blanks.

The show folded in 1924. Boone's children had to go to school, and Inda Boone was in badly failing health. The doctor recommended Arizona, but they never got that far. Boone began following the oil booms as a blacksmith, living in such towns as Wortham and Best, Texas, and eventually Hobbs, New Mexico, where he spent eighteen years. He moved to Christoval twenty-two years ago, seeking a better climate for his wife's health. Almost on the point of death when she arrived there, she lived another twelve years.

He has little patience with today's rodeos. See one and you've seen them all, he declares. They never change. "In our show we were always trying to think up something different, something the people had never seen."

These days he thinks a lot about the hereafter. He says if he could choose his own kind of Heaven it would be Boone's Mexico Ranch Wild West Show with all his old cowboy and cowgirl friends, most of whom have gone on long before. They would put on a great show, and he would close it out by riding a well-remembered bronc named Crazy Snake, shooting .45 blanks into the air.

Vic Pierce Publishes Memoirs of Ozona and Crockett County

Livestock Weekly, March 27, 1980

VIC PIERCE was one of those trend-setting ranchers others watch, then try to emulate. He had a soft voice, but whatever he said was worth straining to hear. One of Texas' leading sheepmen, he amassed a lot of ranchland and in time came into considerable wealth through oil and gas production on his properties. He told me a revealing story once which explained much about today's cold-blooded corporate mentality. He discovered that a major oil company had been under-reporting by a significant amount the production for which he was due royalties. When he threatened to sue, a company lawyer told him, in effect, "Look, we've made you a wealthy man. What if we *did* underpay you? You've got more than you need anyway, and income tax would take most of the rest if we paid you." The ploy did not work. Vic Pierce was smarter than that.

≈

OZONA   V. I. "Vic" Pierce has combined several careers during his eighty-six years. Brought up in the ranch business, he has been primarily a ranchman all his adult life, as well as a breeder of registered Rambouillet sheep and Hereford cattle. He has also been a banker. That list doesn't include a brief career as a bicycle repairman in his boyhood, or later service as a "water witch."

He has added one more item to the list: author. Pierce has published his memoirs, *Yesteryear in Ozona and Crockett County*, and has donated the book and all proceeds to the Crockett County Historical Society for continued development of a museum in Ozona.

The project came about largely by happenstance. Ten or twelve years ago a speaker failed to show up for a meeting of the local historical society, so the group called on Pierce to relate some of his memories of early days when Ozona was still young. His remarks were tape-recorded and put on paper, augmented later by additional interviews. The book project then got sidetracked for several years.

Last year Pierce was again prevailed upon to write some historical items for the *Ozona Stockman*. Out of these and the earlier taped talks came the book, full of anecdotes about the Pierce family and other West Texas people remembered from his boyhood and early ranching years.

He recalls how his father, Joe Pierce, Sr., left his Pennsylvania Quaker home at fifteen just after the Civil War and landed in San Antonio with a dime left in his pocket. He hired on with a freighting outfit and hauled supplies to West Texas military posts until an Indian put a bullet through his leg and killed the mule he was riding. He turned then to sheep raising on the James River near Junction at a time when that area was dominated by an outlaw element which made life perilous for settlers, especially sheepmen.

Vic Pierce was born in Junction and was just barely old enough to remember when his family moved west to Ozona in wagons. Cowboys were shooting up the town the night they arrived. The only person hurt was one of the cowboys, who bet he could shoot a bug off of the toe of his boot. He lost the bet.

The family lived in town during the school year and went to the ranch during the summertime, a common practice then and now. Pierce remembers that male teachers patrolled the streets on weeknights to be sure the kids were at home studying.

He remembers that a saloon-gambler element had the upper hand in Ozona at the time. They got their comeuppance through the election of Jeff Moore as sheriff. Moore, later a president of the Texas

Sheep and Goat Raisers Association, gave the rowdy element an ultimatum to leave town. Most of them did. One holdout operated a rough place at the south edge of town, surrounded by a high brush corral. The day he took office, Moore rode horseback into the enclosure with a box of matches, setting off the corral and the grass roof of the frame saloon. In a few minutes the proprietor had no reason for remaining in Ozona, and he did not.

As a boy Pierce got to know John Blocker, remembered as one of the most knowledgeable early cowmen in Texas. Blocker and a banker partner pastured several thousand cattle in Crockett County one drouthy year, and young Vic Pierce rode with the elderly Blocker in his buggy to open the gates for him. When Blocker and Jennings rounded up their cattle for removal, a couple of ranchmen (Pierce thoughtfully withholds their names) bought from them any ungathered remnants that remained in Crockett County. Blocker sold out cheap because his Seminole-black cowboys were top hands and were unlikely to leave very many. The night after the herd left the county, somebody popped a blanket and stampeded the cattle. About 200 of them strayed back to Crockett County where under terms of the contract they were regarded as remnants. They then belonged to the two ranchmen who in all likelihood had stampeded them.

Pierce says the coming of the automobile brought the most sweeping changes in lifestyles that he can remember. His father bought one of the first in Ozona but did not learn to drive. He left that up to son Vic, still in his early teens. Young Vic drove his father down into Mexico to buy livestock and up into the Osage country of Oklahoma, where he summered cattle. He drove for others in Ozona when his father did not need him.

He recalls a cattle drive into San Angelo and the girls from San Angelo's red-light district who came out on horseback to meet the herds and distribute their calling cards. He and another youngster slipped into a West Concho dancehall but left through a window when shooting started. The window was not open at the time.

His father remained highly dubious when ranchmen began fencing pastures and turning sheep loose, abandoning the ancient practice of herding. Joe, Sr., did not believe sheep had sense enough to go to water by themselves and would surely die. He was amazed when son Joe, Jr., not only turned his sheep loose but marked as good a percentage lamb drop as his father did under herd. The elder Pierce decided sheep had gotten smarter than the ones he had started with.

Pierce launched his sons into the ranching business the hard way. He leased them land and sold them sheep, but he didn't give them much; he let them make their own way and pay him.

He also educated them to know that what goes up will inevitably come down, a lesson reinforced in the early '20s when livestock and wool prices were on a boom. Vic Pierce had a wool clip in San Angelo. The warehouseman said he had a 67-1/2 cent offer but could get another dime within a week. Pierce decided to hold.

Walking down the street, he saw a beautiful Hudson Speedster on sale for $2,800, almost exactly the amount that extra dime would bring. He borrowed against his clip and bought the car. But instead of going up a dime, wool suddenly dropped to nothing. A year later Pierce shipped the wool clip to Boston unsold and finally realized a net of six cents a pound, not even enough to pay for the car. He was sick of the automobile by then anyway, especially after a local mechanic "adjusted" the timing. He finally sold the car for $300.

"I made a lot better trade when I sold it than I did when I bought it," he remarked.

He was a director of a San Angelo bank when the 1929 Depression began. After another bank closed, a run started on his. He hurried to San Angelo from Ozona in the dark of night, running over a milk cow on the way, using a farmer's lantern in place of his smashed headlights. While bank president Roy Hudspeth was in Fort Worth and Dallas raising cash to meet the run, Pierce and other directors scrounged cash locally and fast-talked as many depositors as possible into leaving their money. One way and another they managed to stay afloat until Hudspeth got back with two suitcases full of cash and restored enough depositor confidence to stop the run.

In the midst of the melee a livestock trucker stopped by to deposit a check. He never quite realized what was going on. As he left he told Pierce, "I'll swear, you fellows do a big business here on Saturday."

Among his other accomplishments, Pierce found out he was a pretty good "water witch." He witched wells successfully for other people, but he never could do it for himself. His own always turned out to be dry holes.

He celebrated his eighty-sixth birthday digging a water line. He said it was one of the best birthdays he could remember for the simple reason that he was thankful he was still able to work.

Fiction Writers Are Liars and Thieves

Banquet address to the Texas Folklore Society
at Lubbock, April 1, 1988

ON ONE occasion I was asked to talk about the sources of some of my novels and the way I sometimes interpolate real history and real people into fiction. I have given versions of this talk at least two or three dozen times since. My apologies to any fiction writers who do not consider themselves professional thieves, even though I know we all are.

≈

SOMEONE has said that fiction by definition is a lie. By extension this means that fiction writers are liars. In that context I will admit to it, and go a step further. I will say that fiction writers are thieves.

We steal stories wherever we find them, disguise them, paint them up like car thieves in a chop shop, then present them as our own. We watch people and steal their characteristics, give them to our fictional characters and call ourselves creative.

The beauty of it is that it is not against the law. Readers seem to see no harm in it. They'll even pay us well for doing it . . . now and then.

So I stand before you tonight confessing my sins, and even telling you a little about how I've done it.

Dr. C. L. Sonnichsen once said that if you steal from one source you are a plagiarist. If you steal from ten sources you are a researcher. If you steal from fifty sources, you are a scholar. My crime is much greater than that.

For instance, in *The Time It Never Rained*, Charlie Flagg is the middle-aged rancher who serves as the main character. He struggles through the long seven-year drouth of the 1950s, gradually losing a little here, a little there until he has lost most of what he owns, except for his dignity and his self-respect.

Many people have asked me if I modeled Charlie after their fathers. My mother believes he is modeled after *my* father. They are *all* right. I used so many things from so many people that Charlie Flagg is a little of all of them, but in total he is none of them.

Page Mauldin is another major character in the story, Charlie's best friend. Charlie is a small rancher, owning a little land, leasing some more. He is as big as he wants to be, nowhere near rich, but comfortable. Mauldin, however, is driven by ambition to be the biggest rancher in West Texas, and he just about is. But he is leveraged to the hilt and has his operations scattered all over the country. His size and his debts make him a lot more vulnerable even than Charlie, and eventually he loses everything.

To a very substantial degree, I modeled Page Mauldin after a real person, one of the biggest ranch operators in West Texas in the 1940s and well into the 1950s. I knew him fairly well. Eventually, like Mauldin, he lost almost everything he had.

When the book came out, I was a little nervous that he would recognize himself in the story. I didn't see how he could possibly miss the connection if he read it. One day I ran into him at the San Angelo auction. He said, "I just read your book." I thought, "Oh God, here it comes."

He said, "You know, I sure did enjoy it. That old Charlie Flagg was just like me."

He never tumbled to the fact that he was Page Mauldin, not Charlie. And you can believe that I never told him any differently.

Fiction writers share one advantage with painters: if they don't like something where it is, they can move it.

In my mind, I set *The Time It Never Rained* in the area around Eldorado, south of San Angelo. It had many of the kinds of settings I needed, a good combination of ranchlands and farmlands. Now, Eldorado is a nice town, and I have had a lot of friends there, but it doesn't have all the features I needed for my story. As an example, the book opens in the courthouse, and I wanted a nice Victorian courthouse, not a plain square type like Eldorado's. So I just moved the 1880s courthouse from Paint Rock down to Eldorado, which I called Rio Seco in the story. The Eldorado wool warehouse didn't quite fit the needs of my story, either, but there is a big one down at Sonora that was just right, so I moved it.

There is a little scene in the book where Charlie pauses in the warehouse to look at a coyote that has been badly stuffed. His legs are all out of kilter, his eyes are bugged out. His body is shaped like a square bale of hay. At his feet is an ironic little sign: "Bitten by a Boston wool buyer." Actually, I saw that one time in a wool warehouse in Eden.

The story has a coyote hunt. Cowboys are supposed to be wild, but you've never seen wild riding until you've seen a bunch of sheepmen after a coyote. I've known some pretty good cowboys who would back off and check it to them.

The coyote chase in my book gets pretty wild, but it is no wilder than one at Barnhart that inspired it. I remember people talking about that one for a long time. It got some riders spilled. The airplane used in the hunt came down too low and bumped a wheel against the cab of the pickup. Luckily no one was hurt. However, my dad was on a coyote drive north of Crane one time when the pilot piled up his plane and was killed.

In the real hunt at Barnhart, they never got the coyote they were after. Late that night, long after everybody had given up and gone home, two frightened wetbacks ventured up to a neighboring ranchhouse, looking for food. They had seen that mass of horseback riders and pickups and the airplane bearing down on them. They thought they were being hunted by all the border patrolmen in the world.

They dug deep down in some brush and hid while the whole procession passed by, almost on top of them. No one saw them. They were still lying there an hour or so later, terrified, when they saw the coyote come up out of his hiding place just a little piece away and trot off triumphant. I used that in the story.

There is a scene in which Charlie finally is forced to sell the last of his beloved cows. He has called out a cow trader from Rio Seco to bid on them. I based that scene fairly heavily on watching my father dicker with an old Midland horse trader named Big Boy Whatley. Dad enjoyed the challenge of trading with Big Boy. If you washed out even with Big Boy, you were in the big leagues. One time Big Boy brought a young horse out to try to sell him to my father.

He had a great story to tell. The horse was broke gentle as a dog. He knew how to watch a cow, and you could rein him with one finger. Pitch? No sir, he had never pitched a jump in his life. Why, even the womenfolks could ride him.

A cowboy named Happy Smith decided to try the horse. We've had space shots that didn't get as far off the ground as that horse threw Happy.

Dad chewed Big Boy out a little. "You told me that horse wouldn't pitch, when you knew damned well he would."

Big Boy calmly said, "That's the way I sell horses."

I also based the trader character to some degree on a sheep buyer and commission man who used to live in San Angelo. He could get awfully enthusiastic when he was trying to sell something, but he couldn't find one good thing about something you were trying to sell to him.

One time he was on the telephone at the feedyard, trying to sell a string of sheep. He painted them up something grand. "Straight four-year-olds they are, but they got teeth like a yearlin'. Conformation? Why, they're big and smooth and thrifty, as good as ever walked. And wool?"

He got so carried away with himself that he laid down the telephone, spread his hands about a foot apart and declared, "I tell you, they got wool on them this long."

I have taken a lot of abuse for the final chapter of that book. It seems that most readers would rather have had the story wrap up with a good rain, and everybody happy. But life isn't often that generous. The rest of the book was patterned after life, and I thought it would be a betrayal to have it end with all the loose ends tied up neatly and all problems solved.

Those of you who have read the book know that it ends with a big rain, all right, but there is an ironic twist. It is a cold rain that catches Charlie's Angora goats fresh out of the shearing pens. Freshly-shorn Angoras are extremely sensitive to cold rain. They can chill down and die in a matter of minutes. There is a bitter joke in the ranch country that shearing time always precedes the last cold rain of spring and the first cold rain of the fall.

Anyway, the rain comes, and Charlie loses most of the goats that have made it possible for him to survive the long drouth with a little something left of his former holdings. It is an all-too-common incident for people in the goat business. Every one of them who has been at it for some years can tell you a story.

I modeled *my* story somewhat after a true article written in the 1930s by San Angelo agricultural columnist Sam Ashburn, about a loss suffered by his friend Tex Ward. That article was considered so graphic that it was once reprinted in a journalism textbook. Sam Ashburn had been dead for perhaps thirty years when I wrote the final version of *The Time It Never Rained*, but I visited his widow and asked her permission to do a little gentle plagiarism. She seemed very pleased that someone remembered Sam's work.

An old friend of mine named Leo Richardson, at Iraan, was one of the best sheepmen I ever knew. He told me a story once about the time he was trying to get a start in ranching for himself, working for cowboy wages, saving every dime he could and investing in goats. With three or four years' savings he finally built up a fair-sized bunch, only to lose almost all of them in one cold rain.

Leo was one of the many models for Charlie Flagg. When the book first came out, we happened to be in one of our periodic drouths in West Texas. Leo told me he had read all but the last chapter. He was saving that one to read when it finally rained, because he felt sure it would rain in the last chapter of the book.

I didn't have the heart to tell him how the book was going to come out.

The Good Old Boys provides another example of literary license—moving things around. In my mind I set the story around Paul Patterson's original home, old Upland in Upton County. I changed the name to Upton City to allow me a little freedom with the facts, which is every folklorist's prerogative, not to mention fiction writers.

A homestead was an important focal point of the story. For it, I used my grandparent's old homestead about twenty miles north of Midland and a good sixty miles from the scene of the story. I did it that way so I would always have a clear mental picture of the setting.

Hewey Calloway is the main character. The time is 1906—Aught Six, the old-timers would have called it. Hewey is a drifting cowboy thirty-eight years old, going into middle age and the automobile age and not happy about either one of them.

When I was a boy on the McElroy Ranch in the 1930s, drifting cowboys would come through every so often looking for work. By that time they usually seemed to be driving an old Ford or Chevy coupe instead of riding a horse, but otherwise they were pretty much the same as they would have been thirty years earlier, when my father was a boy. To some degree Hewey was patterned after them, along with a healthy dose of imagination.

I dedicated the book to a bunch of the original McElroy Ranch cowboys I had known. In one way or another, most of them had a little of Hewey Calloway in them. Or vice versa.

In the story, Hewey has just spent the winter feeding cows up in the snows of the Sangre de Cristo Mountains of New Mexico. Now that summer is coming on, he is on his way down into hot West Texas to visit his brother and his family. Now, that tells you that Hewey is not totally in charge.

Brother Walter had once been a drifter like Hewey, but he has married and settled down to raise a family on a small shoestring homestead. Walter's wife Eve has affection for Hewey as a brother, but she is appalled at his lifestyle and his lack of responsibility. She is always worried that he will lure her husband or her young sons off to that same way of life.

If my grandparents were still living, I suspect they would find a lot of themselves in the characters of Walter and Eve, a lot besides just the use of their homestead for a setting.

There is another character in the book who is a kindred spirit to Hewey. His name is Snort Yarnell. He is something of a rounder, a good cowboy who gives not a thought to the consequences of anything he does.

To a large degree I modeled Snort after a cowboy named Bellcord Rutherford, who worked on ranches in the Midland-Odessa country. Every old-timer in that country can tell you a dozen Bellcord stories. One of them concerns the way he got his nickname. I have heard several versions, but the most likely is that when he was a boy he wanted a rope, so he climbed up into the bell tower of the church and took the bell rope. Ever afterward, he was called Bellcord.

I also borrowed just a little from an old cowboy and famous roper of the '20s and '30s and '40s named Bob Crosby. Crosby was a big, rough but honest fellow who had no pretensions about him. It is hard to overstate the esteem in which he and others like him were held in those days in the ranching country. In their environment, they were the equivalent of movie stars or rock stars.

I remember once when I was eight or ten years old, and Bob Crosby was going to rope in the Midland rodeo. My Uncle Ben took us kids over to meet him and shake his hand. I couldn't have been more awed if I had met the president.

Bob Crosby kept his fame in perspective and did not let it alter his chosen lifestyle, which was spartan. There is a story that he was once to be a star attraction at some rodeo. The town leaders decided to throw a big to-do for him as soon as he hit town. They prepared a barbecue and a whole blow-out, which they would kick off as soon as he checked in to the local hotel.

They waited and waited, but Bob Crosby never showed up. The barbecue got cold and the beer got warm, and the committee got egg all over their faces. Time came for the rodeo, and Crosby never had checked in. Everybody went down to the fairgrounds to start the rodeo without him. They found him camped down there with his horses under the shade trees, waiting for the show. Hotel? What did he need with a hotel? He wasn't going to be in town but three days.

He used to tell a story about the time he hurt his leg somehow. It got infected and must have verged on gangrene, because the doctor said it had to come off. Crosby did not agree with that diagnosis. The Lord had issued him two legs at birth, and he intended to check two legs back in when his time came. So he went home and treated himself. He made up a poultice of horse manure, applied it to the wounded leg and wrapped the whole thing with an innertube. It had a negative impact on his social life. But he saved his leg. I had Snort Yarnell tell that story in the book, on himself.

There is another character in *The Good Old Boys*, an old drifter who comes along a few chapters into the story. Of all the characters I have ever used, he probably comes about the closest to being lifted right out of real life and put in a book just as he was, or at least as

I saw him. In the novel he is a senile old ex-trail driver on a wornout black horse. He comes by Walter and Eve's homestead for a handout; he is what used to be called a chuckline rider, which meant riding from one chuckwagon or line camp to another, taking a meal or two and then moving on.

He is not given to spoiling good water by immersing his body in it, so he has a fairly ripe aroma on the downwind side. Walter welcomes him with traditional West Texas hospitality, but Eve feeds him on the porch and tries to stay upwind.

When I was a boy in the 1930s, I saw an old man just like that. He used to come by my grandparents' little ranch a couple of times a year, riding an old horse, drifting across the country to visit kinfolks.

Folks said he had been a cowboy in his time, but his time was long since past. I vividly remember watching him ride up and ask my granddad if he had any tobacco. Granddad didn't use it, but he invited the old man to stay for supper. He always did, and Granddad found a place for him to roll out his blankets and stay the night.

At the time, being just a kid, I thought the old man was a romantic figure out of the colorful Old West. I marveled at his freedom, being able to roam wherever he wanted, when he wanted. It was a good many years before I was old enough to realize the tragedy of his situation.

One day he got down from his horse to open a wire gate a few miles up the lane from my grandparents' ranch. He suffered a heart attack and died there in the gate. There was irony in the fact that he had spent his younger years an open-range cowboy, and he died in the middle of a barbed-wire fence. He died the same way he had lived: all alone.

I used him in the story as a metaphor for Hewey, twenty-five or thirty years down the line, if he did not change his ways and settle down. In the book I had him die just as he died in real life. The only big liberty I took with him was that I moved him back thirty years in time, and changed his name. The Hewey Calloway of my book could have *been* the old man I saw when I was a boy.

That is a side of the cowboy story that not many people write about, or talk about. Most cowboy stories have a strong tinge of romanticism. It spoils the mood to tell about cowboys getting old and lonely and sick, to tell of them spending their final years stove up, living on social security in some poor little house in town, or in a nursing home, bored, broke and hurting.

But I have seen it happen too many times, to too many of the best. That is why you can laugh at the surface humor in *The Good Old Boys*. But you can cry a little too, at the sadness beneath. I used the same theme in a little different way in *The Man Who Rode Midnight*.

I have probably caught more flack from critics about *Stand Proud* than about any of my other books. Many of them disliked the main character, old cowman Frank Claymore, because he is so hard and unyielding, proud and stubborn and at times a little mean.

I didn't intend him to be any plaster saint. I meant him to be stubborn and difficult, because he had lived through a life that had made him that way. I tried to show that in the story. Some of his life was based on real history.

We fiction writers often borrow from real historic personages, though we may not call them by their true names, and we weave a certain amount of fiction around them. For instance, in *Stand Proud* you'll find a good bit of Charles Goodnight, under the guise of Frank Claymore. I am not the only one who has borrowed liberally from Goodnight. Ben Capps did it with his *Sam Chance*. Larry McMurtry did it in *Lonesome Dove*. I guess a lot of us owe some royalties to the Goodnight estate.

One of the points J. Evetts Haley made in his biography of Goodnight was that Goodnight had no particular allegiance to the Confederacy, and he joined the frontier Rangers as a means of avoiding service in the Confederate army. Deep down, he remained sympathetic to the Union.

My Frank Claymore shared that feeling with Goodnight. Scouting the frontier for Indians was preferable to fighting against the Union. In that service, however, he was bound under the orders of other men, and their folly got him into the disastrous battle of Dove Creek, which happened in real life just west of present San Angelo.

In the story, Claymore takes an arrow in his stomach. The arrowhead stays in him the rest of his life, a constant reminder that following other men's orders can get you killed. He makes up his mind that from now on, nobody will ever again be in a position to tell him what to do. He will do what he damn well pleases, whether right or wrong. Sometimes he is woefully wrong, and he suffers for it.

There is a scene in the book where Claymore, out scouting, rides up on a hill and looks down into the most beautiful valley he has ever seen. He has a hard time tearing himself away, and the valley stays in his dreams until some years later when he is able to return to it and make it his home, which he holds—or tries to hold—against all odds.

I based that incident on a story a Coke County old-timer, Ira Bird, told me about his father, who found such a valley and was haunted by the memory until he returned to it years later. Like that valley, the story haunted me for years. I kept hoping for the right circumstances to come along so I could use it in a book. I finally did.

Some of you have heard me tell about the part an elderly ranchwoman named Rachel Bingham played in my writing *The Day The Cowboys Quit*.

The book was loosely based on the cowboy strike at Tascosa in 1883. In real life the cowboys lost the strike. Many of them stayed around, taking up land, running cattle of their own. The big ranchers regarded some of them as thieves. They hired Pat Garrett to ride around over the country, be seen and perhaps scare some of the undesirables into leaving. Garrett was by that time famous for having killed Billy the Kid.

I had a character roughly based on Garrett, but I could not bring him to full life. He seemed just a flat, two-dimensional villain, like Jack Palance in the movie *Shane*. The story had a hole in it where that character was concerned. One day I interviewed an elderly ranchwoman named Rachel Bingham at Spur, and she told me a story about an old-time gunfighter named Pink Higgins. Higgins had been a good friend of her father's. He was well up in years by the time Mrs. Bingham was grown and married Al Bingham.

The ranchers there had been suffering some rustler problems and hired Pink Higgins to stop it. One day he met one of the main suspects, a cowboy, on horseback in the middle of the road. They both drew six-shooters, and the cowboy came out second. He was buried where he fell.

A headboard was put up to mark the grave, but cattle kept rubbing against it and knocking it over. Al Bingham decided finally to put a little fence around the grave and protect it from the cattle. He put some posts and wire and lumber in his wagon and started off.

As he worked on the fence, who should ride up but Pink Higgins? Higgins asked him what he was doing. Bingham couldn't lie to him. He told him he was putting a fence around that grave to protect it. He waited nervously then, wondering what Higgins' reaction would be.

Higgins thought about it a minute, then said, "That's a good idea. I'll help you." He helped Bingham put a fence around the grave of the man he himself had killed.

I interpolated that into my story. Suddenly the gunfighter, called Lafey Dodge in the book, came alive as a real human being with more than one side to his character. I think that one scene helped make the book. And I owe it to Mrs. Bingham's story.

Several years ago John Graves said you should never tell a fiction writer a story you want to use yourself, because he will pre-empt it, give it a few twists and make it his own. I have always tried to be honest in most ways, but when it comes to good stories, I am as shameless a thief as you'll meet. And you thought I came here just for the fellowship.

Index

Baylor County, Texas, 4, 273
Beardsley, Charlie, 179
Beatty's Cabin, 271
beaver, 271
Beefmaster cattle, 92
Belle Plain, Texas, 161, 163
Ben Ficklin (town), 151–52
Benge, Arch, 8
Berger, Joe, 80
Best, Texas, 204, 210, 276
Beulah, New Mexico., 254
Bexar County, Texas, 263
Beyond Beef, 22
Bible smuggling, 182–86
"Big Dry, The," 7–16
Big Lake, 58
"Big Lesson For Would-Be Cowboys: Learn How To Stay Out Of The Way," 146–50
Big Spring, Texas, 191, 237, 240, 249
Bighorn Basin, Wyoming, 259
bighorn sheep, 271
Billy the Kid, 291
Bingham, Al, 131–35, 291–92
Bingham, Newt, 135
Bingham, Rachel, 131–35, 291–92
Bird, George, 139
Bird, Ira A., 189–92, 291
Bird, Miller, 190
Bird, Mrs., 190
Bird & Mertz ranch, 153
Bird Trap, 139
black historic heritage, xi, 217–21, 264, 279
black soldiers, xi, 217–21
blackface sheep, 168
blacklands, 20
Blackwell, Texas, 192
Blocker, Ab, 56, 161
Blocker, John, 279
bluestem: big, 27; King Ranch, 19; little, 18, 27
bluetongue disease, 114
Boatright, Mody C., 222–24
Boatright family, 145
bobcats, 70, 269
bobwhites, 28
boll weevils, 80
bollworm, pink, 80
Bolt, Richard, 74–78

Bolt, Mrs., 77
Bolt, W.J. "Bo," 75
Boog–Scott, J.E., 265
"Boom In Midkiff Farming Area Caused By Younger Generation," 84–87
Boone, Bob, 273–75
Boone, Daniel, 273
Boone, Ed, 275
Boone, Inda, 275–76
Boone, J.C., 273
Boone, Pate, 246, 272–76
Boone, Tom, 275
Boston, Massachusetts, 68, 280, 284
Boston Garden Rodeo, 247
Bowman, Ronnie, 235
Box, Thad, 22–25
Boyd, Bill, 93, 94, 95
Boyd, Bob, 93, 94, 95
Boyer, Si, 165
Boys' Life, 259
Brady, Texas, 136, 137, 138, 139, 156, 157, 158
Brahman-cross cattle, 19, 92, 233, 236, 241
Branch, W.E., 214, 215
Brandenberger, Jim, 139
brands: Anchor B, 274; Lazy SB, 256; Lazy SOB, 256; Spade, 141; See also ranches
Brangus cattle, 73
Brazos River, 48, 160, 199, 227
Brazos Valley, 224
Breckenridge, Texas, 45, 46, 198
Brem, Linton, 93
Bremerhaven, Germany, 82
Brightman, Tex, 205
Brooklyn, New York, 109
Brookston, Texas, 28
broomweed, 45, 48
Brown, Freckles, 233–36
Brown County, Texas, 130, 227
Brownfield, Texas, 219, 221
Brownsville, Texas, 114
Brownwood, Texas, 88, 90, 111
brush control, 12, 20, 24, 25, 43, 46, 73, 140, 163, 192, 228; by fire, 56, 153; for water conservation, 35–37; See also mesquite
Bryan, Texas, 224

Rutherford, Bellcord, 287
Ryan, Tom, 146, 147

western ranges, 22–25, 268–69;
guarded by dogs, mules, donkeys,
88–91; Hampshire, 109; herding
with dogs, 72; industry leaders, 63,
69, 264, 277, 286; losses to
predators, 88, 204, 270, 284;
manadas, 67; Merino, 167; mutton
lambs, 113, 124, 154, 165, 167;
nose mark, 68; packer market,
107–16, 123–25; prices, 9, 10, 154,
280; raisers association, xv, 278–79;
Rambouillet, 69–73, 168, 277;
rustlers, 63–68, 72; theft, 120;
wool, 42, 58, 68, 73, 110, 124,
154, 165–66, 280, 283–85
Sheep and Goat Raiser Magazine, ix,
xv
sheep raisers vs. cattle raisers, 57,
63–68
Sheffield, Texas, 125
Sherwood, Texas, 152, 213–16
"Sherwood Land Rush Depended
More Upon Muscle Than Legs,"
213–16
"Shooting of Karnes Sheriff Started
Biggest Manhunt In Texas History,"
193–97
Shoulders, Jim, 233
Siegmund, Ray, 85
Sieker, Bob, 174
Sierra Blanca, Texas, 167
Silver Lake, 219, 220
Sims, Bill, 35, 36
Sims, Paul, 48
6 (Six) Ranch, 119–20, 121, 214–26
6666 (Sixes) Ranch, 75, 76, 133,
146–50, 250
Sixty Years in the Saddle, 147
Skeete, George, 36
Slaughter, ix
Slaughter, C.C., 191, 192
Slaughter, Sid, 167
Slaughter Camp, 134
Slaughter pasture, 143
Smeins, Fred, 29
Smiley Meadows, 28
Smith, Cal, 178
Smith, Erwin E., 131
Smith, H.W. "Happy," 176–81, 285
Smith, John, 88–91

Smith, Mrs., 89
Smith, Phil, 163
Smith, R.W., 178
Smith, Ray, 112, 115
Smokey (horse), 240
Smyer railroad siding, 143
"Snoring Mules, Muddy Roads,
Bothered Old-time Freighters,"
136–40
Snyder, Texas, 133
Socks (horse), 247
Soil and Water Conservation Society,
50
soil conservation, 16, 17–20, 36, 79
Soil Conservation Service (SCS), 17,
18, 20, 37
Sonnichsen, C.L., 282
Sonora, Texas, 70, 73, 156, 157, 284
Soper, Oklahoma, 233, 234
sourdough biscuit recipe, 76–77
South Carolina, 109, 110
South Dakota, 5, 129, 160, 173–75
South Laguna, California, 266
South Spur Camp, Spur Ranch, 133
Southeastern Oklahoma State
University, 243
Southern Baptist minister, 182
Southern Pacific Railroad, 167
Spade Ranch, 141–45
Spanish-American War, 122
Spanish horses, 122
Spanish interpreter, 193–94
Spanish ranchers, 52
Spearfish, S.D., 129, 160
Spence, Liter E., 20
Spring Creek, 152, 213
Spur, Texas, 131–33, 291
Spur Awards, ix
Spur Ranch, 132–35
spurs, "gal leg," 272
Stacy, Texas, 262
Stamford, Texas, 74, 134, 148
Stand Proud, ix, 198, 213, 226, 290
Standard-Times (San Angelo, Texas),
ix, xiv, xv, 7, 8, 12, 79
Stanton, Texas, 127, 273
Steiner, T.C. "Buck," 246–48
Stephens County, Texas, 199
Stephenville, Texas, 21
Sterling, William Warren, 193

ELMER KELTON has worked for the *San Angelo Standard Times*, *Sheep and Goat Raiser Magazine* and *Livestock Weekly*, from which he retired in 1990. He has won five Spur Awards from Western Writers of America and four Western Heritage (Wrangler) Awards from the National Cowboy Hall of Fame and has been honored for lifetime achievement in literature by the Texas Institute of Letters, the Western Literature Association, and Western Writers of America. His latest novel, *Slaughter*, won a Spur Award as the Best Novel of the West of 1992.